FOURTH EDITION

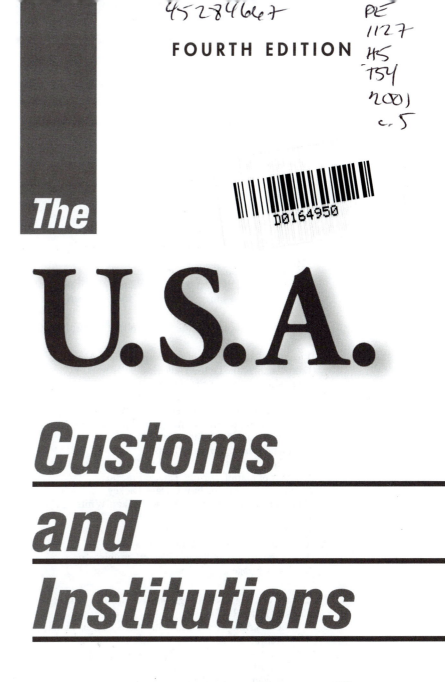

The
U.S.A.
Customs
and
Institutions

Ethel Tiersky

Martin Tiersky

Longman

The U.S.A. Customs and Institutions
Fourth edition

Pearson Education, 10 Bank Street, White Plains, NY 10606

Vice president, director of publishing: Allen Ascher
Editorial director: Louisa Hellegers
Acquisitions editor: Laura Le Dréan
Senior development manager: Penny Laporte
Development editors: Andrea Bryant, Michael Ryall
Vice president, director of design and production: Rhea Banker
Executive managing editor: Linda Moser
Production manager: Liza Pleva
Associate production editor: Sylvia Dare
Director of manufacturing: Patrice Fraccio
Senior manufacturing buyer: Dave Dickey
Photo research: Marianne Carello, Mykan White
Cover design: Patricia Wosczyk
Cover photo: © Photri–Microstock
Text design: Martin Yu, Ann France
Text composition and maps: ElectraGraphics, Inc.
Credits: see page x.

Library of Congress Cataloging-in-Publication Data
Tiersky, Ethel, 1937-
    The U.S.A.: customs and institutions / Ethel Tiersky, Martin
    Tiersky.—4th ed.
        p. cm.
    ISBN 0-13-026360-5 (alk.paper)
    1. Readers—United States. 2. English language—Textbooks for
    foreign speakers. 3. United States—Civilization—Problems, exer-
    cises, etc. I. Title: USA. II. Title: United States of America. III.
    Tiersky, Martin, 1935- IV. Title.

PE1127.H5 T5 2001
428.2'4—dc21   00-052159

ISBN: 0—13—026360-5

3 4 5 6 7 8 9 10—VHG—06 05 04 03

Dedication

In memory of our loving parents, three of whom went through the transition from immigrant to citizen.

With gratitude to our wonderful children—Howard and his wife, Lana, Arthur, and Marcia—who have kept us in touch with the customs of young America.

With admiration for ESL and EFL teachers everywhere, who juggle instruction in language, culture, and history to help their students gain a rich understanding of the American experience.

CONTENTS

PREFACE

To the Teacher

The U.S.A.: Customs and Institutions was first published in 1972. It has been called "a classic in its field," a description that thrilled its authors. With each new edition, the book has been updated and expanded. We firmly believe that it has also improved with age.

Over the decades, the primary goals of our text have remained the same: to provide newcomers to the United States an overview of American culture and traditions and to improve the reading comprehension of nonnative speakers of English. The content strives to create a general portrait of the United States, both its virtues and its short-comings. *The U.S.A.: Customs and Institutions* answers many questions that foreigners and immigrants ask about this nation and helps them understand Americans better.

Teachers familiar with the third edition will find the fourth edition similar in terms of topics covered but different in many other ways. One new chapter has been added—Chapter 18, "High-Tech Communications." All of the other chapters have been revised extensively, however, to update statistics, include new research, and explain new attitudes and customs. Although the book remains a high-intermediate to advanced reader, we have tried to deal with sophisticated ideas in the easiest language possible. In this edition, the vocabulary has been simplified and the sentences shortened to make the content accessible to a greater number of students. The readings remain long enough and difficult enough to challenge advanced students. However, with sufficient in-class assistance, students in the intermediate range will also be able to understand and enjoy them.

Here are some salient new features that make the fourth edition an even more effective teaching tool:

- **Prereading discussion questions** strengthen the background brought by students to each reading and introduce some of the vocabulary used in the chapter.

- **Prereading "Guess" questions** arouse curiosity and give students some specific information to look for as they read.

- **Completely new illustrations**—including many photographs and cartoons—stimulate discussion and make American culture come alive through visual images and humor.

- **"Check Your Comprehension" questions** now follow each section of the readings. These questions encourage students to reflect upon what they've learned, and teachers can use them as a starting point for general discussion, paired conversation, or writing assignments.

- **Exercises** have been greatly revised and are now longer and more varied in format. They are also more interactive, often involving paired or small-group work and sometimes even games. In addition to being more fun, the exercises are now broader in scope. As before, they emphasize comprehension, vocabulary, idioms, and reading skills. But now there is more work with punctuation, phonics, word parts, word endings, writing style, and dictionary skills.

- **Vocabulary lists** in the "Building Your Vocabulary" exercises contain brief notes that clarify confusing word forms, such as irregular plurals and words used only in the plural.

- The **reading-writing connection** has been strengthened in three ways:

  1. Every chapter includes one or two exercises that practice an important sentence pattern found in the reading.

  2. In the **"Issues"** section (Part A of "Sharing Ideas"), students are asked to discuss major controversies related to the chapter's topic. After exchanging ideas with classmates, they write about one of the issues.

  3. In **"On a Personal Note"** (Part B of "Sharing Ideas"), students are encouraged to write about their reactions by making cultural comparisons, expressing personal opinions, and discussing their unique experiences. The length of these writing assignments is left for the teacher to decide. For advanced students, some writing topics involve library research.

The U.S.A.: Customs and Institutions, fourth edition, like its predecessors, is designed to give teachers maximum freedom of choice. Chapters can be studied in any order, depending upon student interest and timeliness.

Accompanying this edition of the book is a new *Teacher's Manual,* which includes general teaching tips and a chapter-by-chapter guide that contains background information about the reading and the illustrations, suggestions for additional classroom activities, and answers to the book's exercises. In addition, it contains a reading comprehension quiz for each chapter.

To the Student

This fourth edition of *The U.S.A.: Customs and Institutions* has two main goals. The first is to introduce you to the lifestyles, attitudes, customs, and traditions of Americans. The second is to increase your knowledge of the most widespread American custom of all—the custom of communicating in English. To accomplish the first goal, the readings have been updated to give you a twenty-first century snapshot of life in the United States. To accomplish the second goal, this new edition contains greatly expanded exercises. They will help you to read with greater understanding, discuss your reactions to the ideas presented, learn a specific set of vocabulary words and idioms, and note some important conventions of written English.

The U.S.A.: Customs and Institutions discusses both strengths and weaknesses of American culture. However, its primary intent is to describe and analyze rather than evaluate. It is left to you, the reader, to compare American ways with those of other cultures and to form opinions about American lifestyles.

If your past instruction in English has been in British English, don't worry. The switch to American English will not present major problems. In terms of sentence structure, these two versions of English are almost the same. British English has more irregular verbs than American English (*learnt* versus *learned,* for example). There are some minor spelling differences (such as *colour* versus *color*) and some differences in vocabulary. (The British *lift* is the American *elevator;* a British *vest* is an American *undershirt.*) Still, you will find that British and American English are very much the same language.

As you probably know, English is rapidly becoming the global language of our shrinking world. It is spoken by about 1.5 billion people and is the language of international communication in business, diplomacy, technology, sports, travel, and entertainment. Wherever you go and whatever you do, your knowledge of English will come in handy.

We hope that *The U.S.A.: Customs and Institutions,* fourth edition, will help you improve your understanding of American English and American people. Whether you're living in the United States, visiting the country, working or studying with Americans who live in your country, or perhaps meeting Americans for the first time in the pages of this book, we want to extend you a warm welcome to the U.S.A.!

Ethel Tiersky
Associate Professor
Communications Dept. (English & ESL)
Harry S. Truman College
Chicago, Illinois

Martin Tiersky
Attorney-at-Law
Chicago, Illinois

Acknowledgments

With thanks to:

- our editors, Laura Le Dréan and Michael Ryall, for their expertise, encouragement, and dedication to this project;

- Marianne Carello and Mykan White for their photo research;

- Andrea Bryant, our development editor, and Sylvia Dare, our production editor;

- the hundreds of ESL students at Harry S. Truman College in Chicago who classroom-tested our book and whose questions told us what immigrants want to know.

Photo Credits

1 | The American Character

Faces of the U.S.A.: diversity as a way of life

BEFORE YOU READ

Discuss

1. Compare Americans to people in other countries. What differences have you noticed in behavior, attitudes, and values?

2. Look at the headings and subheadings in this chapter. Can you predict what each section might have to say about the U.S. and its residents?

3. Take a survey of the languages spoken by students in your class. Where in the world are these languages spoken?

Guess

Try to answer the questions. Then look for the answers in the reading.

1. What is the approximate population of the U.S.? Check (✓) one:

    _____ 125 million   _____ 275 million   _____ 425 million

2. Which is the largest ethnic minority in the U.S.? Check (✓) one:

    _____ Hispanics   _____ Asians   _____ African-Americans

The American Character

A Land of Diversity

1   What are Americans like? What do Americans like? These are very different questions. In answering them, this chapter will provide a sketch of the American character. "But wait," some readers say. "In this huge nation of people from everywhere, is there really a national **character**?" Let's tackle this third question first.

2   There is great **diversity** in the **ethnic** makeup of America. Nevertheless, many writers have **generalized** about typical American values, attitudes, and beliefs. For example, Mortimer B. Zuckerman, editor-in-chief of U.S. *News & World Report*, sees his country as "a unique culture of self-reliance, independence, resourcefulness, pragmatism, and novelty." He goes on to describe his fellow Americans in greater detail: "We are comfortable with change and with people who make things happen. In America, the new is better than the old; taking charge is valued over playing it safe; making money is superior to inheriting it; education and merit are favored over family ties."

3   The most important characteristic of the U.S.A. can be stated in one word: diversity. Most Americans take pride in the great **variety** found in the country's geography and population. Covering 3,700,000 square miles (9,590,000 square kilometers), the U.S. is the fourth-largest nation in the world (after Russia, China, and Canada). Within this vast nation are tall mountains and flat cornfields, deserts and tropical regions, prairies and forests, rugged coastlines and gentle, rolling hills. The climate, too, covers all extremes. In southern Florida, visitors come to swim and sunbathe in December. In northern Alaska, winter temperatures may drop to −75° Fahrenheit (−54° Celsius).

4   With roughly 275 million people, the U.S. is the third-largest nation in population after China and India. About 90% of the people now living in the U.S. were born there. Still, the U.S. has one of the world's most varied populations in terms of national ancestry. This diversity is often highlighted and celebrated at school and community festivals. Racially, the U.S. is about 82% white, 13% black, 4% Asian and Pacific Islander, and 1% Native American (including Eskimo and Aleut). Hispanics are roughly 12% of the entire American population, making Spanish-speaking people the nation's second largest ethnic **minority.** Some newcomers to the U.S. may be surprised by the varieties of skin color they see, but Americans take it for granted. Racism and prejudice are still serious

problems in the U.S.; however, most Americans believe in the ideals of equality and mutual respect.

5   Three significant population trends may change the American character to some extent. First, the U.S. Census Bureau estimates that, by the year 2050, the country's population will be 394 million. Will more crowded conditions lead to closer friendships or more disputes between neighbors? Second, in recent years, the average age of Americans has been increasing (from 28 in 1970 to about 35 today). This trend, often referred to as the "graying" of America, is expected to continue. By 2023, **demographers** say, about 18% of Americans will be 65 or older. By 2038, that figure will reach 34%. "America is a country of young men," wrote Ralph Waldo Emerson in the nineteenth century. Americans have often been accused of worshiping youth and undervaluing their elders. Now, the typical American is approaching middle age. Some 72,000 Americans are at least 100 years old! By 2050, there may be 800,000 centenarians. What will happen to the youth culture then? Third, the nation's ethnic and racial minority groups are growing much faster than the general population. Demographers predict that by 2050, this country's minority groups combined will make up the **majority** of the population. No doubt, this change will affect attitudes, values, and customs.

6   Regional variations also add diversity to the American character. Travel around the country and you'll notice differences in language, diet, recreation, and even regional character. Some Americans can tell what part of the country other Americans come from just by listening to their accents. Cooking styles also vary from place to place, influenced by the different immigrant groups that have settled in that area and by the edible plants, fish, seafood, and wildlife native to each region. Recreation also varies from place to place, influenced by climate, geography, and ethnic traditions. In addition, attitudes and behavior may differ somewhat from one region of the country to another. For example, New Englanders are commonly described as serious and self-reliant, Southerners as gracious and leisurely, and Westerners as casual and friendly. Californians are said to be eager to try new fads. Midwesterners are considered more **conservative** than Californians and less sophisticated than New Yorkers. Of course, many residents of a particular region do not fit these generalizations.

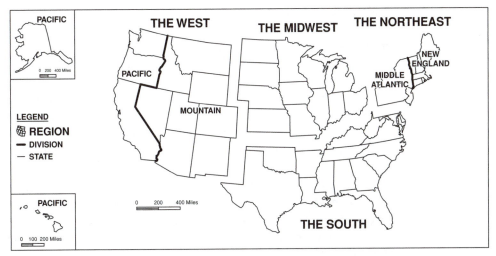

Regions of the United States

7   However, modern communication and mass production tend to decrease regional and ethnic differences. From the East Coast to the West Coast, travelers find similar shopping centers, supermarkets, department and discount stores, restaurants, hotels, motels, and apartment buildings. National advertising creates national tastes in clothing styles and other consumer goods. National news media influence Americans' reactions to world events. Television, movies, and schools help to create a body of American values and traditions. Despite the nation's great diversity, some generalizations can be made about what the typical American believes in, admires, values, and wants.

Check Your Comprehension

Why is the U.S. called "a land of diversity"?
What three population trends are predicted?

Democracy in Action

8   American **democracy** is based on the principle of majority rule. In a democratic legislative body, decisions are made by voting. In the U.S., voting is not just a tool for selecting political leaders and passing laws. It is also a way of making decisions in the business world, in social groups, in schools, and even within the family. Americans believe that people should take part in making the rules they must live by. American children are introduced to the ideas of majority rule and representative government at a very early age. Many families hold weekly meetings to determine household rules and activities. Most schools have student councils with elected representatives so that students can voice their opinions about school regulations and activities. In the adult world, all kinds of organizations (unions, religious groups, etc.) elect officers and make decisions by voting. In publicly owned companies, stockholders elect the directors.

9   "All men are created equal," says the Declaration of Independence. This statement does not mean that all human beings are equal in ability or ambition. It means that all people should be treated equally before the law and given equal privileges and opportunities. Equal opportunity means (among other things) an equal chance for a good education and a good job.

10   The American commitment to equality of opportunity inspires what is commonly called the American dream—the belief that anyone can achieve success through honesty and hard work. For many immigrant Americans, this dream became reality. Financial success has often been the result of taking a risk, of quitting a salaried position and starting one's own new business. Social mobility—movement from one social class to another—has always been characteristic of the U.S. It is usually achieved by improving one's educational level, occupation, and/or income.

11   A democratic, representative government gives citizens an opportunity (and a responsibility) to encourage positive social change. Ordinary citizens can improve conditions, especially if they unite in a common cause. "Grassroots" movements can bring about changes in laws and policies. In the past half-century, many such groups have forced change in local, state, and federal laws. Some groups have even influenced foreign policy—for example, those that opposed American participation in the Vietnam War of the 1960s. Other groups have persuaded lawmakers to pass stricter laws to pro-

tect Americans from drunk drivers, pollution, and the illegal use of handguns. Still other groups fight for the rights of minorities—African-Americans, Hispanics, gays and lesbians, people with disabilities, senior citizens, and so on. Americans know that, in the battle for human rights, there is strength in numbers.

✔ **Check Your Comprehension**

What American attitudes are related to democratic ideals?
What does majority rule *mean?*

"Try It—You'll Like It"

12   The great American novelist and humorist Mark Twain described the typical Englishman or -woman as a "person who does things because they have been done before" and the typical American as "a person who does things because they haven't been done before." Americans love to try something new out of curiosity and a belief that newer may be better.

13   As a nation of immigrants, the U.S. has had a continual influx of people with a pioneering spirit, with the courage to make major changes in their lives. In the mid-nineteenth century, this spirit led American settlers to make the long, difficult, and dangerous journey westward in search of gold or free land. The desire to make a fresh start in a new place is still noticeable throughout the nation. About 42 million Americans change residences every year. Some moves are due to changing jobs or going off to college. Other people move from big cities to suburbs (or vice versa). Some move to find adventure or a more pleasant climate. The pioneering spirit of Americans is evident in the working world, too. Employees change jobs and even careers as opportunities change.

14   Americans love science and technology because these fields involve new discoveries. The U.S. has embraced the age of communication with great enthusiasm. From preschoolers to senior citizens, Americans are learning to use computers—at school, at work, and at home. Robots, lasers, and other inventions of modern technology fascinate them. Americans subsidize all kinds of space exploration, from outside the Earth to inside the atom, in order to uncover the secrets of the universe.

15   Love of change is closely tied to faith in improvement. Americans have always been optimistic, believing in the perfectibility of people, the basic goodness of their country, and the ability of American ingenuity to improve the quality of life. But people have come to realize that, if life can become better, it can also become worse. The dangers of air and water pollution, nuclear power, and overpopulation have become clear.

✔ **Check Your Comprehension**

What are some examples of the American pioneering spirit?

Typical American Behavior and Values

16   Watching Americans in action, foreigners sometimes see behavior that seems rude, misguided, or just plain silly. The following traits are characteristically, but certainly not exclusively, American.

17   *Hurry, Hurry, Hurry.* Almost every American wears a watch, and, in nearly every room in an American home, there's a clock. "Be on time." "Don't waste time." "Time is money." "Time waits for no one." All these familiar sayings reflect the American obsession with promptness and efficiency. Students displease their teachers and employees displease their bosses when they arrive late. This desire to get the most out of every minute often makes Americans impatient when they have to wait. The pressure to make every moment count sometimes makes it difficult for Americans to relax.

18   The desire to save time and do work more quickly and easily leads Americans to buy many kinds of machines. These range from office equipment such as calculators, photocopy machines, and computers to dozens of home and personal appliances, such as microwave ovens.

19   *The Importance of Money.* After visiting the U.S. in the 1830s, the French historian Alexis de Tocqueville wrote, "I know of no country . . . where the love of money has taken stronger hold . . ." Americans are often accused of being **materialistic**, of valuing wealth and **possessions** above all else. Money is valued both as a symbol of success and also for a more obvious reason—its purchasing power. Many items that didn't even exist 50 years ago are now considered necessities in the American home. In addition, purchases are made in order to "keep up with the Joneses," to show friends that one can afford a bigger house or a fancier car. Also, advertising encourages people to keep buying things far beyond what they need. In the mid-nineteenth century, the American author Henry David Thoreau advised his countrymen, "Simplify your needs!" However, Americans have moved in the opposite direction. Now, just as Thoreau predicted, many find that their possessions own them. They must work hard to earn enough money to buy and maintain the many possessions they consider necessities.

20   Yes, Americans love to make a lot of money and spend it on themselves—to buy things that save time, give them pleasure, or serve as status symbols. However, Americans are also very generous and very willing to donate money to good causes. The American character includes a strong sense of obligation to help those in need.

21   *Say What You Mean, and Mean What You Say.* Americans believe that "honesty is the best policy." They are direct and **assertive**. They ask for what they want. In many cultures, respect for those in positions of authority keeps people from expressing their true feelings or intentions. In the U.S.A., however, children often argue with their parents and citizens express opposition to actions of the government. If the soup is cold or the meat is tough, the diner can complain to the waiter. If a teacher is wrong or confusing, a student may say so. If the boss makes a mistake, an employee may politely point it out. Assertive behavior sometimes seems improper and rude to foreigners, but it works well for Americans. In fact, assertiveness is almost a necessity in the business world.

22   *The Need to Win.* The extremely competitive nature of Americans is often criticized. Of course, **competition** isn't always bad. In fact, it promotes excellence by encouraging individuals (and businesses) to try to do their best. But the desire to get ahead of others sometimes causes people to do things that are unkind and even dishonest.

23   *The Practical Outlook.* Americans admire what is practical, fast, **efficient**, and new. Sometimes they fail to appreciate cultures that prefer more traditional, leisurely ways of doing things. Conversely, people from other cultures may dislike the practical, hectic American lifestyle.

24   Despite these traits, which many foreigners may view as faults, Americans are usually considered very likable. Most are friendly, kind-hearted, and eager to help visitors and immigrants. In this nation of immigrants, the foreigner does not remain an outsider for long.

AFTER YOU READ

I. Getting the Message

Work with a partner. Put a check (✔) in the correct column for each phrase listed below.

	Americans like or approve of this.	Americans don't like or approve of this.
1. forming groups to bring about change		
2. wasting time		
3. allowing citizens to influence lawmakers		
4. allowing social mobility		
5. protesting social evils non-violently		
6. doing things the way they've always been done in the past		
7. making decisions by voting		
8. buying as few possessions as possible		
9. being assertive		
10. competing to be the winner or the best		

II. Building Your Vocabulary

A. *These are the 15 key vocabulary words for this chapter. They are boldfaced in the reading. Pronounce these words after your teacher, and discuss their meanings.*

assertive	demographer	majority
character*	diversity	materialistic
competition	efficient	minority
conservative†	ethnic	possession
democracy	generalize	variety

Character is uncountable as it's used in this chapter.
†*Conservative* can be a noun or an adjective.

B. *With a partner, answer these questions with one word or a few words.*

1. Would a materialistic person have many possessions or few? _____

2. Do elections usually involve competition? _____

3. Does a conservative person like or dislike a lot of change? _____

4. If people work quickly but do poor work, are they efficient? _____

5. What does a demographer study? _____

6. What is the main characteristic of a democracy? _____

7. What are two expensive possessions that most Americans want to own? _____

_____

8. Do Americans think that it's good to be assertive? What do you think? _____

_____

III. Sharpening Reading Skills

Topic Sentences   A paragraph is a group of sentences that develops one idea. Most paragraphs contain a statement of the main idea. That statement is called the *topic sentence*. It is usually, but not always, the first sentence in the paragraph. It is the most important sentence in the paragraph. The other sentences develop the topic sentence, perhaps by giving reasons, causes, examples, facts, or descriptive details.

Reread the paragraphs listed and look for the topic sentence. Then write the first two words of the topic sentence on the line after the paragraph number.

Example

(3) _____The most_____

(5) _____   (8) _____   (17) _____

IV. Understanding Idioms and Expressions

Use the following 12 expressions to complete the sentences on page 9. Capitalize the first word at the beginning of a sentence. The numbers in parentheses give the paragraphs in which the expressions are used. Reread the paragraph if you have forgotten what the expression means.

"grassroots" movement (11)	point out (21)
keep up with the Joneses (19)	senior citizen (11,14)
majority rule (8)	status symbol (20)
make every moment count (17)	take it for granted (4)
mass production (7)	taking charge (2)
playing it safe (2)	vice versa (13)

1. My friend Joe rides his motorcycle 90 miles an hour. He doesn't believe in

   _____.

2. The twins expect their parents to give them a gift on their birthday. They

   _____.

3. Maria Johnson is very popular among the people in this state. In fact, there is

   a(n) _____ to elect her as the next governor.

4. They are a very happy couple. She loves him and _____.

5. Don't waste time. _____.

6. Teachers _____ mistakes so that students will

   learn the correct way to speak and write English.

7. An expensive car is a(n) _____. It makes the

   owner seem important.

8. My grandfather is 68 years old. Because he's a(n)

   _____, he gets a discount at many movie theaters.

9. _____ means that decisions are made by voting.

10. You don't have to buy a new car just because your friends did. You don't have to

    _____.

11. _____ helps to keep prices down.

12. John left the company, so Helen is _____ of the office now.

V. Taking Words Apart

Noun or Adjective Nouns serve as subjects of sentences and objects of verbs and prepositions. Adjectives are commonly used before nouns or after linking verbs (such as *be, seem,* and *feel*).

Underline the correct word form for each sentence.

1. The U.S. is a (*competition / competitive*) society.

2. Voting is an (*importance / important*) part of a democratic (*society / social*).

3. To have a successful democracy, it is (*necessity / necessary*) to have (*education / educated*) citizens.

4. To have a successful democracy, well-educated citizens are a (*necessity / necessary*).

5. Americans believe in (*equality / equal*) opportunity for all.

6. Most Americans understand the (*importance / important*) of participating in their (*democracy / democratic*) government.

(continued on the next page)

7. Americans are practical. In other words, they are (*pragmatism / pragmatic*).

8. Traveling from one (*region / regional*) of the country to another, American tourists see a great (*variety / varied*) of people and places.

9. There is a lot of (*ethnicity / ethnic*) (*diversity / diverse*) in the U.S.

10. Do Americans value money and possessions more than anything else? Are they (*materialism / materialistic*)?

What are four common endings on the nouns in this exercise? _____

What are four common endings on the adjectives in this exercise? _____

VI. Practicing Sentence Patterns

Dashes and Definitions

Reread the first and last sentences in paragraph 10. Note that dashes are used before definitions of the phrases American dream *and* social mobility. *On the lines below, write two sentences that include definitions of a phrase.*

1. *Write a sentence with the definition at the end. Use one dash.*

Example

I like cocoa—a hot drink with chocolate in it.

_____

2. *Write a sentence with the definition in the middle. Use two dashes.*

Example

I drink cocoa—a hot drink with chocolate in it—every morning for breakfast.

_____

VII. Sharing Ideas

A. Issues

Debate these issues in small groups. Then choose one and write about it.

1. Is there really equality of opportunity in the U.S.? If not, what can be done to create it?

2. What's good and what's bad about *majority rule*?

3. Americans are usually described as sociable, conventional people who join groups and try to behave like everyone else in the group. However, some American books and movies have made a hero of the person who fights the majority will and tries to accomplish something good independently. What's better—to be a *joiner* or a *loner*?

B. On a Personal Note

Write about one of these topics.

1. Do you think wealth and possessions make a person important? If not, what does?

2. In the 1980s, a Russian immigrant and popular entertainer named Yakov Smirnov became famous for his three-word reaction to the U.S. Whenever something surprised him, he said, "What a country!" What surprises you about the U.S.? Why?

3. Americans are often accused of admiring youthful beauty and energy over the experience and wisdom of older people. Who should be most respected—young adults, middle-aged people, or senior citizens? Why?

4. Would you like to live to be 100 years old? Why or why not?

2 Marriage: American Style

An American bride and groom cutting their wedding cake

BEFORE YOU READ

Discuss

1. Have you ever seen a wedding in the U.S.? What did you notice? What were the bride and groom wearing? Was anything confusing to you? What?

2. Think about the American couples you know. What have you noticed about American husband–wife relationships? What generalizations can you make about American marriages?

3. What does the first sentence of this reading mean?

Guess

Try to answer the questions. Then look for the answers in the reading.

1. What percentage of adult Americans (18 and older) are married? _____%
2. What does the American bride throw to her wedding guests? _____

Marriage: American Style

Before the Wedding

1   "Marriage halves our griefs, doubles our joys, and quadruples our expenses," says a well-known proverb. It also decreases both freedom and loneliness. Today's Americans seem willing to take the bad with the good because the institution of marriage continues to be popular in the U.S.A. By middle age, about 92% of Americans have been married at least once.

2   However, the country's single adult population is almost as large as the married population. Only 56% of American adults are married and living with their spouse. The number of unmarried adults, now around 77 million, has been growing much faster than the married population. One reason is that today's Americans are marrying at an older age. In 1970, the median age of a first-time **bride** was 20.6, and the median age of a **groom** was 22.5. Today, the median ages are about 25 for the bride and 27 for the groom. Among younger adults (ages 25 to 34), about 35% have never been married. Why are people staying single longer? Many young adults want to get their careers well established before marriage. Also, many couples live together without (or before) marrying.

3   Although Americans try to be practical in most matters, when they choose a spouse, the decision is usually based upon feelings of love rather than on practical considerations. In the U.S., parents do not arrange marriages for their children. Teenagers usually begin dating in high school and eventually find partners through their own social contacts. They want to "fall in love" before they think about marriage. Most parents encourage their children to marry someone of the same race and religion. Still, when young adults move away from their parents' home to attend college or to work in another city, they often date and then marry a person from a different ethnic background. Marriages between Americans of different religions or different national origins are common. However, marriages between blacks and whites continue to be rare, involving less than 0.3% of the nation's 58 million married couples.

4   When a man and woman become engaged (agree to marry each other), they enter a very exciting and busy period of their lives. At this time, it is traditional for the man to give his fiancée a gift she will (hopefully) wear and treasure for the rest of her life—a diamond **engagement** ring. During the engagement period, the bride-to-be and her fiancé meet each other's relatives, if they have not done so already. They also plan their

wedding and rent or buy an apartment or house. (In the U.S., very few newlyweds begin married life living with either set of parents.)

5   Engagement and wedding gifts help the couple to set up their new home. It is common for engaged couples to go to a department store bridal registry and fill out a list of the items they would like to receive, such as particular patterns of dishes, silverware, and glassware, plus cooking utensils, appliances, and linens. Wedding guests can choose gifts from this list before the wedding and have them mailed to the bride-to-be's home. In addition to wedding gifts, the couple also receives shower gifts. A *shower* is a party just for women at which each guest gives the bride-to-be something useful for her new home. Also, shortly before the wedding, the groom and his close friends and relatives celebrate at an all-male party called a *bachelor* or *stag* party. On this occasion, the groom often receives gifts, too.

✔ **Check Your Comprehension**   *What are three American engagement customs?*

The Big Day

6   Most wedding customs observed in the U.S. today began in other countries and past centuries. Some are based on old **superstitions** about ways to bring the couple good luck and many children. Others **symbolize** the marital promise of lifelong devotion.

7   The traditional American bride wears a long white gown and a **veil.** (In earlier times, people thought the veil would protect the bride from evil spirits. The white gown and veil also symbolize innocence.) Traditional brides also obey the well-known verse and wear "something old, something new, something borrowed, and something blue." The groom usually wears a tuxedo (a formal suit with a bow tie), which is commonly rented just for his wedding day. Tradition says that the groom should not see the bride's gown before the wedding. Also, on their wedding day, the bride and groom are not supposed to see each other until the **ceremony.**

8   The wedding ceremony may be held in a church, synagogue, home, hotel, or nice outdoor area. Guests are seated on either side of the center aisle, and the ceremony starts with a procession down the aisle. Traditional pieces of music played during the procession are the wedding march from Wagner's opera *Lohengrin* and orchestral music from Mendelssohn's *A Midsummer Night's Dream*, but today many couples select other music. The bridal party (the people participating in the ceremony) includes the bride and groom and their closest relatives and friends. There are usually bridesmaids and a maid of honor (all wearing matching dresses) and the groom's ushers and "best man" (usually his brother or best friend). Walking in front of the bride is a young "flower girl," who throws flower petals from a straw basket. The bride walks down the aisle with her father or both parents, who "give her away" to the groom. The bride and groom then face the cleric or judge conducting the service, and a traditional service is recited. The content of the service depends, to some extent, on the couple's religion.

9   During a typical ceremony, the bride and groom exchange **identical** wedding rings. The ring, a circle with no beginning and no end, symbolizes unending love and loyalty.

It is worn on the fourth finger of the left hand because of a very old (and incorrect) idea that a vein or nerve runs from this finger directly to the heart.

10   At the end of the wedding ceremony, the groom and bride are pronounced husband and wife and are invited to kiss each other. Then, the entire wedding procession walks back up the aisle. After a church wedding, guests may throw rose petals, confetti (small pieces of colored paper), or rice at the newlyweds as they leave the church. Rice, a common fertility symbol, is supposed to help the couple have children. Sometimes, the couple's car is decorated with tin cans, paper streamers, or old shoes, along with a "Just Married" sign. The tin cans and shoes reflect an old idea that noisemakers scare away evil spirits and bring good luck.

11   After the ceremony, there is a *reception*—a party with food, drinks, and dancing. During the reception, the wedding cake, which is usually tall with white frosting, is displayed. Most wedding cakes have a miniature bride and groom or miniature wedding bells on top. After the meal, the bride and groom cut the cake and it is served to the guests. Some guests take home a slice of cake in a little box. Some people believe that if a single woman sleeps with this piece of cake under her pillow she will dream of the man she is going to marry.

12   Just before the bride leaves the reception, she throws a bouquet of flowers backward over her head to a group of single women standing behind her. Supposedly, the one who catches the bouquet will be the next to marry. At some weddings, the groom throws his bride's garter to the single men. Catching the garter also means an approaching marriage.

13   There are, of course, endless variations on American weddings. Some weddings combine American customs with those of the couple's native countries. Many weddings blend customs from different cultures because the bride and groom are from different ethnic or religious backgrounds. Other couples discard tradition and "do their own thing." Some couples want their wedding to reflect their interests or display their talents. They may, for example, write their own wedding vows. They may get married on a mountaintop or a beach and wear blue jeans. Many couples have gotten married in front of the Statue of Liberty. One couple even held their wedding ceremony in an amusement park on a roller coaster!

14   Who pays for the wedding? In the past, the bride's parents were expected to pay for almost everything. But today the average American wedding costs about $19,000, and some large, lavish ones run as high as $80,000. Therefore, expenses are often shared by the parents on both sides. Of course, some couples (especially older ones) pay for their weddings themselves. To avoid the expense and trouble of planning a large wedding, some couples **elope.** Others go to City Hall, where a judge can "tie the knot." (These types of weddings may also be chosen when parents disapprove of the match.) People marrying for the second (or third, fourth, or fifth!) time may do so quietly with only a few guests present.

15   To be legally wed, a couple need only fulfill the requirements set by the state in which the ceremony is performed. State laws determine who may get a marriage **license.** In most states, teenagers 18 or older can marry without parental consent, but 16- and 17-year-olds must have parental permission. In most states, those under age 16 are not allowed to marry. Marriages between first cousins or people more closely related are for-

bidden in many states. Most states require medical examinations and certificates before issuing a marriage license, and some refuse licenses to people with certain physical or mental illnesses.

16   After the wedding, the newlyweds usually take a vacation called a **honeymoon.** This word means "month of honey" in French. It refers to a former custom—for newlyweds to share a drink made with honey every day during the first month of their marriage.

✔ **Check Your Comprehension**

List five American wedding customs.

The Contemporary American Marriage

17   Among married couples in the U.S., one finds a wide range of living patterns. Some older couples still have traditional marriages, with the man as breadwinner (money-earner) and the woman as homemaker. But most younger women today are not content to be full-time homemakers. The women's liberation movement, which swept the country in the 1960s, changed attitudes and behavior forever. Today's young American woman wants marriage, but she also wants to keep her own identity. She wants what men have always had—a marriage that is important but still allows time to pursue individual goals. The majority of American wives, even those with children, work outside the home. As a result, the older idea that housework, cooking, and child care are "women's work" is being discarded. In the contemporary American marriage, the husband and wife share both financial and domestic responsibilities. In most families, the working wife probably still handles the larger share of the housework, cooking, and child care, but she gets some help from her husband.

18   Sharing money-making and housekeeping responsibilities provides a better life for both parents. The typical American wife enjoys being out in the working world. Her husband discovers that cooking and child care can be fun and can bring him closer to his family. He may also find that it's nice to have his wife's help in supporting the family. Of course, problems can develop in the two-income family if the husband expects his working wife to be the perfect homemaker that his stay-at-home mother was. Also, there may be arguments if the wife expects her husband to help with household chores, but he is unwilling to do so.

"I'M GLAD WE'RE MARRIED, LORETTA . . . OTHERWISE WE'D BE FIGHTING WITH STRANGERS."

19   The contemporary American marriage is also characterized by a relationship of equality and shared decision making. Most American women today will not tolerate a husband who considers himself the boss. The American girl is given freedom and education equal to a boy's. After completing her education, she is able to get a job and support her-

self. She does not need to marry for financial security. She is self-sufficient and will not accept a submissive role in marriage. When husband and wife are able to share decision making and respect each other's viewpoints, their marriage is probably closer than those of past generations. When they battle for dominance, they're likely to end up in divorce court.

✔ **Check Your Comprehension** *How has women's liberation affected the American marriage?*

Divorce and Alternative Lifestyles

20   Americans believe that they are entitled to happiness, and they expect marriage to contribute to their enjoyment of life. But in one study in 1999, only 38% of the Americans questioned identified themselves as "very happy." (In 1970, the figure was 53%.) For every 100 marriages that take place today, there are about 50 divorces. The U.S. divorce rate is twice that of Europe and three times higher than Japan's.

21   What goes wrong? The fact that divorce is so common in the U.S. does not mean that Americans consider marriage a casual, unimportant relationship. Just the opposite is true. Americans expect a great deal from marriage. They seek physical, emotional, and intellectual compatibility. They want to be deeply loved and understood. It is because Americans expect so much from marriage that so many get divorced. They prefer no marriage at all to a marriage without love and understanding. With typical American **optimism,** they end one marriage hoping that the next will be happier. No-fault divorce laws in many states make it easier than ever to get a divorce.

22   When a couple gets divorced, the court may require the man to pay his former wife a monthly sum of money called **alimony.** The amount of alimony depends on the husband's income, the wife's needs, and the length of the marriage. If the woman is working and earns a good salary, she may receive no alimony at all. Occasionally, the court decides that a woman should pay her husband alimony. If the woman has supported her husband during the marriage, the court may decide that she must continue to support him after the divorce.

23   If a divorcing couple has children, the court must determine which parent the children will live with and who will provide for their support. In most cases, the children live with the mother and the father pays child support and has visitation rights. However, it is not uncommon for a father to get full custody or joint custody when this arrangement is in the children's best interest.

24   The high risk of divorce doesn't seem to make Americans afraid to marry again. Remarriage and the creation of new, blended families is extremely common in the U.S. One American joke tells of a wife calling to her second husband, "Quick, John! Come here and help me! Your children and my children are beating up our children!"

25   Although the majority of American adults marry, the number of people living alternative lifestyles is increasing, and their behavior is increasingly accepted by the general population. The number of unmarried couples living together rose from about half a million in 1970 to more than 4 million today. Many older people are upset by the grow-

ing number of unmarried couples living together. However, this is not just an American trend. It's quite common in Europe, too. The lifestyle of the gay population, which includes approximately 3.5% of American men and 2% of American women, is also considered alternative. Many gay people live with same-sex partners in relationships that last for many years, with the same loyalty, emotional attachment, and financial commitments as traditional marriages.

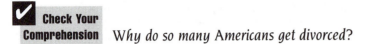

Check Your Comprehension *Why do so many Americans get divorced?*

Happy Anniversary!

26   Maintaining a good marriage has always been work as well as fun, so it's no wonder that Americans celebrate the completion of each successful year. Married couples celebrate most of their wedding **anniversaries** rather quietly, perhaps by going out for a romantic dinner for two or by sharing the occasion with family members or close friends. But certain anniversaries—especially the twenty-fifth and fiftieth—are considered more important and are commonly celebrated with big parties. A particular type of gift is traditional for each anniversary (clocks for the first, crystal or glass for the third, silverware for the fifth, and so on). This custom is often ignored except for the twenty-fifth anniversary, when silver is given, and the fiftieth, when a gift of gold is traditional. It is a joyous occasion when a couple celebrates a golden wedding anniversary with their children, grandchildren, and great-grandchildren around them. Reaching this moment is a goal of most young couples when they walk down the aisle as bride and groom.

AFTER YOU READ

I. Getting the Message

A. *Discuss or write answers to these questions on a separate piece of paper. Write complete sentences.*

1. What are three good things that paragraph 1 says about marriage?

2. What are two bad things that paragraph 1 says about marriage?

3. Compare American wedding customs to wedding customs in other countries. Which are the same or similar? Which are different?

4. What two alternative lifestyles are discussed in this chapter?

B. Chronological order *means "in order of time" or "in the order that events happened." Put the following events in chronological order by numbering them 1–6, starting with the earliest.*

_____ wedding day   _____ honeymoon

_____ silver anniversary   _____ engagement

_____ shower for the bride-to-be   _____ marriage proposal

II. Building Your Vocabulary

A. *These are the 15 key vocabulary words for this chapter. They are boldfaced in the reading. Pronounce these words after your teacher, and discuss their meanings.*

alimony	engagement	optimism
anniversary	groom	superstition
bride	honeymoon	symbolize
ceremony	identical	veil
elope	license	wedding

B. *Complete these sentences with some of the key vocabulary words. Make nouns plural if necessary, and put each verb into the correct tense and form.*

1. In order to get married, the engaged couple must get a marriage

   _____.

2. The traditional _____ walks down the aisle wearing a long white gown and a(n) _____ over her face.

3. During the ceremony, the bride and _____ exchange _____ wedding rings.

4. This exchange of rings _____ endless love.

5. Many contemporary wedding customs come from old _____ about protecting the bridal couple from bad luck.

6. Some couples _____. They get married secretly, with no family or friends at the ceremony.

7. Newlyweds usually take a vacation called a(n) _____.

8. The typical married American woman wears two rings: a(n) _____ ring and a(n) _____ ring.

9. When a married couple gets divorced, the man usually pays _____ to help support his ex-wife.

(continued on the next page)

10. A wedding _____ marks the beginning of a marriage.

11. With typical American _____, divorced people usually remarry.

12. A golden wedding _____ celebrates 50 years of marriage.

C. In academic writing, scientists and social scientists often present statistics, including the *median* and the *mean* (average). Look these words up in a dictionary. Note that paragraph 2 gives the median age of American brides and grooms. Since the median of a series of numbers is the middle number, it means that half of American brides today are older than 25, and half are younger.

Now answer the following questions:

1. What is the median in this series of numbers: 3, 4, 5, 11, 12? _____

2. What is the mean of this same series? _____

D. *Homonyms* are words that sound alike but have different meanings and spellings.

Pronounce and discuss the following two groups of homonyms. Then underline the correct words to complete the sentences below. Use a dictionary if you need help.

> I'll / aisle / isle   altar / alter

1. The bride walked down the (*aisle / isle*) to the (*altar / alter*).

2. If the bride wants to (*altar / alter*) her dress, (*isle / I'll*) help her.

E. Very few English words have accent marks. But some words that come into English from other languages keep the accent marks they had in the original language.

Look up the words fiancé *and* fiancée *in a dictionary. What is the difference in meaning?*

III. Sharpening Reading Skills

A. Scanning for Specific Information   Scanning is a useful reading skill. When you scan, you move your eyes quickly over a passage, looking for a particular fact (or facts) that you want.

Scan paragraph 8 to look for the people who are part of the wedding party. List six.

1. _____   3. _____   5. _____

2. _____   4. _____   6. _____

B. Context Clues   The word *just* is used in three different ways in this chapter. The three meanings are (1) only, (2) exactly, and (3) a very short time before.

1. Find *just* in each paragraph listed below. Then, on the blank lines, write the number that matches the meaning of *just* as it is used in each paragraph.

   a. paragraph 5 _____   c. paragraph 10 _____   e. paragraph 21 _____

   b. paragraph 7 _____   d. paragraph 12 _____   f. paragraph 25 _____

2. Now use context clues to determine the meanings of the italicized words in the paragraphs indicated. On each blank line, write the correct definition.

   In paragraph 5, *shower* means _____.
   - a. a party for a bride-to-be
   - b. a rainstorm
   - c. a way for a person to wash

   In paragraph 17, *domestic* means _____.
   - a. not foreign
   - b. a servant
   - c. household

IV. Understanding Idioms and Expressions

Choose the correct expression to answer each question and write it on the line. The numbers in parentheses give the paragraphs in which the expressions are used.

beat up (24)	maid of honor (8)
best man (8)	no wonder (26)
breadwinner (17)	set up (5)
do their own thing (13)	tie the knot (14)
fall in love (3)	walk down the aisle (26)

1. What two idioms mean "to get married"? _____

   _____

2. What do Americans call the person who earns the money for a family?

   _____

3. What expression means "to do things in their own way"?

   _____

4. What expression means "to hurt someone in a fight"?

   _____

5. What idiom means "to become romantically involved"?

   _____

6. Who is the person who helps the bride at a wedding?

   _____

(continued on the next page)

7. Who is the person who helps the groom at a wedding?

   _____

8. What expression means "to arrange things for a particular activity"?

   _____

9. What expression means that something is not surprising?

   _____

V. Taking Words Apart

Practice with Parts of Speech

A. *Look in a dictionary and find what part(s) of speech each of these words are used as. Write the part(s) of speech on the lines after the words.*

Example

marry: _____*verb*_____

marriage: _____   married: _____   marital: _____

B. *Write in the correct word—marry, marriage, married, or marital—to complete each statement.*

1. Joe and Sarah have been happily _____ for 35 years.
2. Their _____ has lasted a long time.
3. Did you know that _____ people live longer than single people?
4. _____ difficulties can lead to divorce.
5. I would like to get _____ next year.
6. Why did Janet _____ that strange man?

VI. Practicing Sentence Patterns

A. *Reread paragraphs 7, 10, and 11. Note the uses of the expression* be supposed to. *The meaning is similar to* should *or* be expected to. *Answer these questions using* supposed to.

1. What is something that young children are not supposed to do?

   _____

2. What is something that you are supposed to do often?

   _____

B. *Note the use of the word* supposedly *in paragraph 12. Discuss its meaning.*

C. *Discuss the different meanings of these two sentences:*

1. I suppose it will rain tonight.
2. Suppose it rains tonight.

VII. Sharing Ideas

A. Issues

Debate these issues in small groups. Then choose one and write about it.

1. Compare single life with married life. Which is better?

2. Is there any point in having a big wedding, or is it just a waste of money?

3. Is it necessary for a man to be the boss in a marriage for him to be happy?

B. On a Personal Note

Write about one of these topics.

1. Consider marital relationships in other countries. How are they similar to and how are they different from American marriages?

2. Pretend that you were a guest at an American wedding. Write a letter to a friend describing the ceremony and the reception.

3. In your opinion, should a person marry only after falling in love?

American Family Life

A birthday celebration

BEFORE YOU READ

Discuss

1. The term *nuclear family* refers to parents and their children; the *extended family* includes other relatives. Name as many of these relatives as you can, including those related by "blood" (genetically) and by marriage.

2. What major trends in American family life do you predict will be discussed in this chapter?

3. What is the age range for each of the following: *teenager, adult, middle age, senior citizen*?

Guess

Try to answer the questions. Then look for the answers in the reading.

1. What percentage of American mothers with children under age 18 are employed? Check (✓) one:

   _____ 31%   _____ 51%   _____ 71%

2. What's the most popular American pet? Check (✓) one:

   _____ dog   _____ cat   _____ bird

3. What is the approximate median family income in the U.S. today? Check (✓) one:

   _____ $22,000   _____ $42,000   _____ $62,000

American Family Life

Who's at Home?

1   The family—one of the oldest human institutions—has existed for about 300,000 years, continually changing with the times. In the U.S.A., as in all other nations, family life is the basis of individual security and cultural continuity. "We can choose our friends, but we can't choose our **relatives**," Americans sometimes complain. Yet there is also an American saying: "Blood is thicker than water." Our relatives may drive us crazy, but they are also the first people we call to report good news or to ask for help. Americans love, argue with, and live with their families. Of the 101 million households in the U.S., 70 million are families. Most other households consist of one person living alone. Less than 10% of households are made up of people not related to each other.

2   But today's typical American household is quite different from those of other times and places. The title of this section of the reading asks "Who's at home?" The answer reveals various aspects of the new lifestyles. Nowadays, 62% of American households have no children under age 18. About 71% of women with children under age 18 are employed. Why? Some work because the family needs the money, others because they find it more interesting than being full-time homemakers. Most women work for both of these reasons. The life of the working mother is stimulating but also very **hectic** and **stressful**. Working mothers who also try to handle all the homemaking tasks find that they are often tired and irritable. To avoid these problems, some women hire household help (but few have live-in servants). Others simply do less work around the house. A few nights a week, dinner comes from a carry-out restaurant (sometimes called a take-out restaurant) instead of the oven. Dust lies patiently on the furniture until the weekend.

3   When Mother is employed, the lives of her spouse and her children are affected. When Mother has less time for child care and housekeeping, her husband and older children usually become more involved in these tasks. In addition, older children must be more self-sufficient. Today's American mother may spend only a few hours a day with her children. Some people say this is okay if the time spent together is "**quality** time." Others feel that babies and young children need stay-at-home mothers and that this change in lifestyle weakens the family. In addition, the working mother has created another great social need—affordable, high-quality day-care facilities for preschool children.

4   There is also concern about the declining role of fathers in the lives of American children. About 40% of American children (24 million) do not live with their fathers. (Although about 75% of American families are headed by two parents, many children live with a mother and stepfather.) Two factors—the high divorce rate and the large number of children born to unmarried mothers (about 32% of American infants)—deprive millions of American children of daily contact with their father. Some see their fathers on a weekly basis, but, if the parents live in different parts of the country, Dad may become an infrequent companion.

5   On the other hand, about 2 million dads of children under 15 are primary caregivers. (That is, these dads are doing the mothering!) In some of these households, there is no mother. In others, the father is unemployed or a full-time student. But the occupation of *househusband* is usually a **temporary** career, not a permanent one. In homes where parents share childrearing responsibilities, children may spend about the same amount of time with each parent.

6   How else has family life changed for American children? In recent decades, the typical American family has been getting smaller. The statistical average is now 3.2 people. Because it is expensive to raise children and mothers need to work, most couples have only one or two children. Therefore, children don't have the kind of companionship they once did from a large group of siblings. Millions of preteens with two working parents come home from school to an empty house. To improve the situation, many schools and communities offer after-school programs that provide a place for children to go and interesting activities for them to get involved in.

7   If parents and children aren't home much in the American family, at least the pets are. Nearly 60 million Americans live with one or more animals. Dogs are most popular

(30 million of them!), and 27 million cats come next. Birds, fish, small rodents such as guinea pigs and gerbils, and even snakes add companionship and fun to the American family.

8   Most American children live with their parents at least until they finish high school at age 17 or 18. Then, many go away to college, leaving some parents sad and lonely in their "empty nest" and others happy to have fewer parental responsibilities. However, many young, single adults live with their parents during their college years or return home after college graduation. The high cost of housing keeps many young adults in their parents' home until they get married. Moreover, after a divorce, adults may return to the parental home temporarily or even on a long-term basis, especially if they are lonely, short of money, or in need of babysitting grandparents.

9   Although adult children sometimes come home to Mom and Dad, middle-aged and elderly people try to avoid moving in with their grown children. Older people take pride in their independence, enjoy their freedom, and do not want to be a burden to their children. The telephone, the car, the airplane, and e-mail keep families in close contact even when they live in different parts of the country.

10   In the U.S., it's common for a family to span four **generations**—from great-grandparents to infants. For babies born today, boys have a life expectancy of 73 and girls' life expectancy is 79. Some 35 million senior citizens (age 65 or older) make up almost 13% of the nation's population, and the nation's over-85 population is increasing rapidly. Senior citizens are often thought of as two different groups—the "young-old" (ages 65 to 80) and the "old-old" (over 80). Younger seniors tend to be quite active—working part time, traveling, enjoying leisure activities with friends, and crossing the country to visit their children and grandchildren. Americans proudly watched 77-year-old former senator and astronaut John Glenn riding through space and 75-year-old former president George Bush skydiving. They know that folks in their 70s are not stuck in rocking chairs.

11   But what about the "old-old"? Sometimes, newcomers to the U.S. mistakenly conclude that Americans simply leave their elderly parents in nursing homes and forget about them. Actually, only about 5% of today's senior citizens live in nursing homes. Millions of middle-aged Americans—members of the "sandwich generation"—take care of both their elderly parents and their children. However, for elderly people who are very ill or disabled, a nursing home may be the only alternative if their children are working and no one is home during the day to take care of them. Family members usually select a nursing home nearby so that they can visit often. Also, in many communities, retirement residences have been developed to provide living facilities for older people who don't need nursing care but who can no longer handle the burden of shopping and cooking for themselves. Americans are constantly seeking new ways of caring for increasing numbers of older people with physical limitations.

✔ **Check Your Comprehension**   *How has American family life changed as a result of American mothers working outside the home?*

Where Is Home?

12   The majority of Americans live in or near large cities, but small-town living is still **widespread.** A suburb (a smaller community near a big city) combines the advantages of safer, more intimate small-town life with the recreational and cultural facilities and job opportunities of the big city nearby.

13   About two-thirds of Americans live in homes or apartments that they own, but many people rent their residences. Apartment buildings range from walk-ups with two to six apartments to high-rise elevator buildings with more than a hundred units. Some apartments are very expensive and elegant; others are built for moderate- or low-income families. Many apartment buildings are condominiums (condos), which means that each family owns the unit it lives in. Some are co-ops, which means residents own shares of the whole building.

14   More than 7 million American households live in mobile homes—living quarters built on wheels. Mobile homes can be moved but are generally brought to a permanent site. After the wheels are removed, the home is attached to the ground. Because they cost less than conventional homes, mobile homes are especially popular with young couples and retired couples living on a limited income.

15   For the typical American family, home may be in a different place every five or six years. (Every year, about 16% of Americans change residences.) All this moving deprives the nuclear family of having many relatives and longtime friends living nearby. The nuclear family must now supply the companionship and help once provided in part by aunts, uncles, cousins, and close friends living in the neighborhood. Adult siblings may find jobs in different parts of the country. Retired grandparents may move to the Sun Belt (one of the southern or southwestern states), where the climate is warm. But family members hop into a car or onto a plane to come together for major turning points in one another's lives. Such events include birthdays, graduations, weddings, anniversaries, and funerals. Family parties may be all the more joyous when they bring together relatives who haven't seen each other for a while.

✓ **Check Your Comprehension**   *How does the mobility of Americans affect families?*

Who Pays the Bills?

16   The median family income in the U.S. is in the $42,000 range, but it may be significantly higher when both parents work full time. In 1940, only 15% of married women worked; today, about 54% do. Although men still tend to have more responsibility and earn higher wages in the American workplace, it is not uncommon for women to earn as much as or more than their husbands.

17   Mom's salary helps to buy the things the family wants—a computer, a second or third family car, and so on. The desire for nice and useful possessions makes the two-income family almost a necessity. However, a lot of money is needed not only for things but also for experiences: summer camp for the children, a vacation for the family, lessons in music or sports, religious instruction, and—most expensive of all—a college education.

18   While middle-class and wealthy families provide much to enrich their children's lives, about 19% of American children (13.5 million) grow up in poverty. Families with two

wage-earners are much less likely to be poor than those with only one. When there is only one wage-earner, and especially when it's the mother, the family's income may barely pay for the necessities of life.

19   What about children's earnings? In the past, children were a financial **asset.** They worked on the farm or elsewhere and contributed to the family's income. Today, state and federal laws limit the kinds of work children can do, how many hours a week they can work, and at what age they can begin to do certain types of work. Except for part-time jobs such as babysitting, shoveling snow, mowing lawns, or delivering newspapers, most American children do not work until they are 15 or 16 years old. Then, many work part time to save money for college or to have spending money for their personal needs. They aren't expected to contribute their earnings to the family.

✓ **Check Your Comprehension**   *Who pays for all the possessions of the American family?*

Who's in Charge?

20   No longer do American families say, "Father's word is law." Today's family tries to be democratic, to give all family members some voice in decisions that affect the house-hold. Of course, this approach is not always possible, but when parents must make the decisions, they are usually made by both parents.

21   The democratic approach to family life does not prevent all family **quarrels.** Ameri-cans have familiar phrases to describe various types of family arguments. First, there's the *battle of the sexes*, when husband and wife fight for control of the family. Then there's **sibling rivalry**—competition and jealousy between brothers and sisters. Americans also speak of the *generation gap*, the difficulty parents have understanding the attitudes and behavior of their children and vice versa. Married people often have in-law problems, especially when parents try to interfere in the lives of their married children.

22   The whole question of who's in charge becomes much more complicated when there is divorce and remarriage. Sometimes divorced parents don't agree on what's best for their children. Many American children have to adjust to a stepparent living in the home, supervising and disciplining them. When children are tossed back and forth be-tween different authority figures, they sometimes wonder who's in charge.

23   Problems between parent and child usually increase when children become teenagers and want greater freedom to make decisions for themselves. Teenagers are **ambivalent** about parental control and help, as Anthony Wolf's guidebook for parents of teenagers shows. Its title quotes a typical teenager's words: *Get out of my life, but first could you drive me and Cheryl to the mall?* Parents want to maintain a friendly relationship with their teenagers and also want to guide them toward proper behavior. However, par-ents and children often disagree about what is important and right. Arguments may concern such trivial matters as clothing or hair styles. More important quarrels may arise about schoolwork, after-school jobs, money, career decisions, use of the family car, dating, and sexual behavior.

24   Some parents have serious problems with teenagers who quit school, abuse alcohol, run away from home, get involved with gangs, have illegitimate children, or use illegal drugs. (In a recent study, 10% of 12- to 17-year-olds reported having used illegal drugs

within the preceding month.) Many of these problems are caused by influences outside the family. But the majority of teenagers are "good kids" and grow up into responsible adults.

25   A small percentage of troubled parents (especially those who were mistreated by their own parents) physically abuse their children. Child abuse has been much publicized in recent years, and the publicity creates an incorrect picture of the American family. In general, Americans are very loving, kind, generous, and permissive parents.

✔ Check Your Comprehension

What are some examples of battles for control within an American family?

Parenthood: A Choice

26   Having or not having children is mostly a matter of choice these days. Couples who don't want children have access to a wide range of birth control methods and, as a last resort, the option of **abortion**, which has been legal throughout the U.S. since 1973. For people who want children but have medical problems that interfere, modern science offers many new techniques to help them. If none of these work, there is always the possibility of **adoption**. Some Americans adopt babies or young children from other countries, especially those countries where wars and other tragedies have created a large population of **orphans**.

27   However parenting begins, it continues to be what it has always been—a wonderful (and difficult!) experience of giving, caring, and sharing. American children may spend less time with their family than children did in the past. Nevertheless, families still give children their most important experiences and values as well as their most enduring and significant relationships.

AFTER YOU READ

I. Getting the Message

Discuss or write answers to these questions on a separate piece of paper. Write complete sentences. Reread the paragraphs indicated if you need help.

1. What are two reasons that so many American children live with only one parent? (4)

2. For mothers, what are two advantages of working? What are two disadvantages? (2)

3. What changes have occurred in the American family now that so many American wives and mothers work? (3)

4. Why might some American children feel sad and lonely? (4, 6, 15)

5. What are two types of living facilities for seniors who can no longer live alone? (11)

6. What are some common reasons that parents argue with their teenage children? (23, 24)

II. Building Your Vocabulary

A. *These are the 15 key vocabulary words for this chapter. They are boldfaced in the reading. Pronounce these words after your teacher and discuss their meanings.*

abortion	hectic	rivalry
adoption	orphan	sibling
ambivalent	quality	stressful
asset	quarrel*	temporary
generation	relative	widespread

B. *Complete these sentences with some of the key vocabulary words.*

1. If your weekdays are very hectic, they are probably also _____.

2. The opposite of a liability (an expense, debt, or disadvantage) is a(n)

   _____.

3. The word *competition* has a meaning similar to the word _____.

4. The opposite of *permanent* is _____.

5. An argument is the same as a(n) _____.

6. Some mothers want to work, but they also want to stay home with their

   children. They have conflicting, or _____, feelings about working

   away from home.

7. The word _____ refers to how good or bad something is. But this

   word is also sometimes used to mean that something is good.

8. With five young children in the family, their parents have a(n)

   _____ life.

C. *Choose the right word to complete these statements about family members.*

1. Parents and their children are considered the _____ family. Aunts,

   uncles, and cousins are part of the _____ family. (*extended / nuclear*)

2. Your aunt's daughter and son are your _____. (*customers / cousins*)

3. Your mother's brother is your _____. (*uncle / aunt*)

4. If your father divorces your mother and remarries, his second wife is your

   _____. (*stepmother / second mother*)

---

*Quarrel can be a noun or a verb.

(continued on the next page)

5. If your father and his new wife have a daughter, she will be your
_____. (*sister / half-sister*)

6. Mr. Brown's sister has a son named Joe and a daughter named Jennifer. Joe is
Mr. Brown's _____, and Jennifer is Mr. Brown's _____.
(*nephew / niece*)

7. Joe and Jennifer are brother and sister. In other words, they are
_____. (*siblings / spouses*)

8. On an application, your husband or wife is referred to as your _____.
(*sibling / spouse*)

9. Your spouse's father is your _____. (*grandfather / father-in-law*)

10. The members of your family are your _____. (*orphans / relatives*)

11. Tom became a(n) _____ after his parents were killed. Then, through
_____, Tom found a new family. (*adoption / orphan*)

12. From grandparent to grandchild there are two _____. (*generals /
generations*)

III. Sharpening Reading Skills

A. Figures of Speech   *Figurative language* uses images that aren't taken literally.
Examples

"empty nest" (paragraph 8)   "sandwich generation" (paragraph 11)

*Look at these expressions. What is the mother whose children have gone off to college being
compared to? Who is in the middle of the "sandwich"? Write the meanings of these
expressions:*

1. "empty nest": _____

2. "sandwich generation": _____

B. Find the Meaning

*Read each quotation from the reading carefully. Then, on each blank line, write the letter of
the word or phrase that means the same thing. The paragraph number is in parentheses.*

1. ". . . dinner comes from a carry-out restaurant instead of the oven." (2)
   The dinner is eaten _____.
   a. at home
   b. at the restaurant

2. ". . . dinner comes from a carry-out restaurant instead of the oven." (2)
   The phrase *instead of* means _____.
   a. and
   b. not

3. "There is also concern about the declining role of fathers . . ." (4)
   This statement means that _____.
   a. people don't care about the situation
   b. people are worried about the situation

4. "There is also concern about the declining role of fathers . . ."
   Fathers are becoming _____.
   a. less important
   b. more important

5. ". . . a nursing home may be the only alternative . . ." (11)
   A nursing home is probably _____.
   a. the only choice
   b. where older people want to live

6. "In the past, children were a financial asset." (19)
   In the past, children _____.
   a. cost a lot of money
   b. earned money for the family

7. "No longer do American families say, 'Father's word is law.'" (20)
   No longer means _____.
   a. not anymore
   b. not very long

8. "However parenting begins . . ." (27)
   This phrase means _____.
   a. although parenting begins
   b. no matter how parenting begins

IV. Understanding Idioms and Expressions

A. *On each line, write the letter of the correct definition. The numbers in parentheses give the paragraphs in which the expressions are used. If necessary, use a dictionary for help.*

1. *Quality time* (3) means _____.
   a. enough time
   b. time spent together in a meaningful way

2. A *househusband* (5) is _____.
   a. a man who does most of the family's homemaking tasks
   b. a man who owns a house

3. The *Sun Belt* (15) refers to _____.
   a. the warmer states in the South and Southwest
   b. the diameter of the sun

4. A *turning point* (15) in a person's life refers to a _____.
   a. major change
   b. move to another city

(continued on the next page)

5. The *generation gap* (21) refers to _____.
   a. the number of years between parent and child
   b. the difficulty that parents and children have understanding each other

6. The person who is *in charge* (22) _____.
   a. makes the decisions
   b. uses the credit cards

B. *Which of the following statements can be completed with* vice versa? *Write in* vice versa *when it is correct.*

Example

Day follows night and ____vice versa____ .

1. Parents love their children and _____.
2. Cats eat mice and _____.
3. Children like to watch TV and _____.
4. Children enjoy playing with dogs and _____.

V. Taking Words Apart

Practice with Plurals

Review some rules about writing plurals in English. Then write the plurals of the following words. Use a dictionary for help if necessary. Be careful! Some of these words have irregular plural forms. One is an uncountable noun that has no plural. Write none *after that word.*

Example

activity: ____activities____

basis: _____   child: _____

life: _____   fish: _____, _____

poverty: _____   sister-in-law: _____

woman: _____

VI. Practicing Sentence Patterns

Question Word Order

The usual word order for questions in English is **helping verb, subject, main verb.**

	helping verb	subject	main verb
Why	**did**	**the American family**	**change?**

```
    helping              main
      verb    subject    verb
```
When **do** **you** **pay** the rent?

When the question word is the subject of the sentence, statement word order is used. With the simple present and simple past tenses, the helping verb is *not* used if the question word is the subject of the sentence.

```
          main
subject   verb
```
Who **pays** the rent for this office?

```
            main
subject     verb
```
What happened to your car?

Now write questions that the following paragraphs answer.

1. (paragraph 2) Why _____ ?

2. (paragraph 7) How many _____ ?

3. (paragraph 11) Where _____ ?

4. (paragraph 20) Who _____ ?

VII. Sharing Ideas

A. Issues

Debate these issues in small groups. Then choose one and write about it.

1. Social scientist Erich Fromm believed that mothers and fathers love their children in different ways. A mother's love is unconditional, he believed. She loves her child just because the child is hers, while a father's love has to be earned. Do you think this is true? How does a child "earn" love?

2. Some women decide to become pregnant by artificial insemination. Is this a good idea? If the father is an unidentified donor, the child will never know who he was. Is this fair to the child?

3. Some states and communities have parental-responsibility laws. If children commit crimes, their parents can be sued, fined, or even jailed. Is this a good idea? What if the parents contribute to the crime (for example, by carelessly leaving guns unlocked)?

B. On a Personal Note

Write about one of these topics.

1. Write about something you once had ambivalent feelings about doing. Tell whether you did it and whether you were glad or sorry about your decision.

2. Compare the problems of American families with the problems of families in other countries. Are there any similarities?

3. What is your idea of the perfect family?

American Etiquette

"We didn't have time to pick up a bottle of wine, but this is what we would have spent."

BEFORE YOU READ

Discuss

1. How do American manners compare to polite behavior in other countries?

2. On what occasions is it traditional to give gifts? Do you think this is the same everywhere?

3. Many workers who perform services for others expect to receive tips (extra money). Name the types of workers that you would tip.

Guess

Try to answer the questions. Then look for the answers in the reading.

1. What is the expected response to the formal greeting, "How do you do?"

   Check (✓) one:

   _____ "I'm fine."   _____ "I'm a student."   _____ "How do you do?"

2. What is the polite response when someone sneezes? Check (✓) one:

   _____ "My condolences."   _____ "Bless you."   _____ "Please cover your nose."

American Etiquette

American Attitudes and Good Manners

1   How do people know what is considered good **manners** in a particular culture? In the seventeenth-century court of King Louis XIV, it was easy. Visitors were given *une etiquette* (a ticket) listing rules of acceptable **behavior.** And that was the origin of today's English word **etiquette,** which refers to the proper way to behave in social situations.

2   "Etiquette?" some people laugh. "With Americans, anything goes." It's true that Americans are rather casual. Still, there are many social blunders that will offend them. Most American attitudes about good manners relate to showing respect and consideration for others.

3   Americans believe that all people are entitled to equal opportunity and respect. No one is privileged, and no one is worthless. A person who acts very humble and timid will make his or her American friends uncomfortable. On the other hand, a domineering person will have trouble keeping American friends. A **polite** but **assertive** manner is socially acceptable. No matter what your status is in relation to another person, feel free to look directly into his eyes and speak your true feelings. Occasionally, it is a social necessity to tell a "white lie" and **compliment** someone on something you don't really like. But, most of the time, you can express your true opinions. Americans won't mind if you disagree with them as long as you show respect for them and their ideas.

4   Here are some suggestions that may help you make friends, not enemies, in the U.S.:

- *Don't be "nosy."* Americans, like people everywhere, enjoy talking about themselves. Friendly interest is considered good manners as long as one doesn't ask for extremely personal information such as age, weight, income, or the cost of valuable possessions (home, car, jewelry, etc.). Asking these kinds of questions sounds "nosy," which is an **insult.** It's fine to ask a person's line of work. The question "What do you do?" means "What's your occupation?"

- *Don't smoke without permission.* Nonsmokers don't want the smell or the health risks of secondhand smoke. In the U.S., many offices, restaurants, and other public places are smoke-free environments. If you don't see ashtrays, that's probably the case. Also, nonsmokers usually don't like their homes polluted with cigarette smoke. Smokers who must have a cigarette or cigar should excuse themselves and go outside to smoke.

- *Don't get too close.* When conversing with casual **acquaintances,** Americans tend to stand closer than Asians do and farther apart than people from the Middle East, southern Europe, and Latin America. What difference does distance make? Standing too close may give the impression of forced intimacy or an attempt to dominate. Standing too far away seems formal, aloof, and cold. When in the U.S., notice the distances between people in public situations. Keep your distance from others similar to what you observe.
- *Don't touch.* Except for a brief, firm handshake as part of an introduction or a farewell, Americans don't usually touch people they don't know well, so hands off!
- *Don't make ethnic slurs.* The U.S. is a multi-ethnic, multi-racial culture, and there is considerable social interaction among different groups. Don't say anything negative about any ethnic group. Your new friend's spouse or brother-in-law may be a member of that group.

✔ Check Your Comprehension *How do American attitudes affect American manners?*

Introductions and Titles

5   Making introductions (presenting two strangers to each other) is one of the most common social duties. There are traditional rules for doing this properly. When introducing people of different sexes, it's polite to say the woman's name first; for example, "Mrs. Fox, this is my assistant, Mr. Wolf." But if the man is older or famous, then his name or title should come first: "Mr. President, I'd like you to meet my sister, Luisa Rivera." When two people of the same sex are introduced, the older person is named first: "Grandfather, this is my friend Narish Patel. Narish, this is my grandfather, Mr. Kim."

6   **Appropriate** responses to an introduction include "How do you do?" or "It's nice to meet you" or simply "Hello." When introduced to a stranger, Americans usually shake hands (each using the right hand). Handshaking is not reserved just for men. Women also shake hands—with men and with other women. According to tradition, the woman, the older person, or the more important person is expected to extend a hand first. Today, however, this formal rule of etiquette is not always followed. The custom of handshaking is not limited to introductions. In business or social situations, acquaintances and friends may also shake hands when they meet and when they conclude a conversation.

7   At the end of a conversation with a new acquaintance, it's polite to say, "Good-bye. It was nice meeting you." One might also add some appropriate remark that wishes the person a good time or good luck, such as "Enjoy your visit to our city" or "Good luck with your new job."

8   Proper forms of **address** are often a puzzle to foreigners. In the U.S., people in the same general age group tend to get on a first-name basis quickly. Coworkers, class-

mates, and neighbors often call each other by first names. But adults are likely to continue to call doctors, lawyers, teachers, religious leaders, and bosses by their titles and last names. Mr. is a title of respect for a man. It is pronounced *mister*. Miss is used for a single woman. Mrs. (pronounced *missus*) is the correct form of address for a woman who is married, divorced, or widowed. However, some women prefer to be addressed as Ms. (pronounced *miz*), a title which does not indicate marital status. Ms. is also useful when writing or speaking to a woman whose marital status is not known. In addressing a stranger, it's customary to use *sir* for a man and *miss* or *ma'am* for a woman. It's **rude** to call a man *mister* without the last name or a woman *lady*. The title *doctor* (Dr.) is used not only for medical doctors but also for dentists and people with academic doctoral degrees (a Ph.D.). Very few titles are used as forms of address without the last name (family name). Those that can be used alone include *Doctor*, *Professor*, *Officer*, *Captain*, and some titles for religious leaders (such as *Father* or *Rabbi*). It is *not* correct to call a teacher *Teacher*. In elementary and high schools, students address their teachers as Mr., Ms., Miss, or Mrs. plus the last name. In American colleges and universities, some instructors and professors are quite informal and encourage students to call them by their first names.

✔ **Check Your Comprehension**

When you introduce two people, what are some rules about whose name goes first?

Congratulations, Condolences, and Apologies

9   In general, it's polite to say **"Congratulations!"** (with a lot of enthusiasm) when a person has accomplished something. Examples of these kinds of occasions include graduation, job promotion, the birth of a child, and the purchase of a home. When congratulations are in order, it is sometimes also appropriate to give a gift, especially when invited to a birthday, graduation, wedding, or anniversary party.

10   An invitation may say RSVP on the bottom, an abbreviation that refers to a French expression meaning "respond, please" (write or phone to tell the host whether you can come). If the invitation says, "RSVP regrets only," it means "respond only if you cannot come."

11   Equal attention must be given to good manners on sad occasions. If a coworker, classmate, or neighbor experiences a death in the family, it is appropriate to express sympathy (**condolences**). In doing so, the words *die* or *death* should be avoided. It is best to simply say, "I was so sorry to hear about your loss" (or ". . . about your father"). It's also customary to send a sympathy card, but if you don't know the mourner's religion, be sure to select a card without religious symbols. Most customs regarding mourning relate to the family's religion and vary from one group to another, so don't send flowers or food unless you know it's appropriate.

12   The simple words "I'm sorry" display good manners in a great many difficult social situations. "I'm sorry" has two main uses: (1) to express sympathy to someone who has had a bad experience and (2) to express regret for bothering someone or causing a problem. Other expressions of apology are "Excuse me" and "Pardon me." Use one of these

expressions when you are trying to get out of a crowded elevator or stopping a stranger to ask directions.

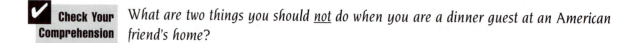

Check Your Comprehension *Name several occasions when it's appropriate to say "Congratulations!"*

Dining Etiquette

13   When invited to an American friend's home for dinner, try to arrive on time, but not early. It's okay to be 10 or 15 minutes late but not 45 minutes late. Dinner might be over-cooked and ruined by then. If you are going to be late, it is a good idea to call the host to tell him. When you go to someone's home for a meal, it's customary to bring a small gift, such as flowers or candy.

14   What do you do if you're served food you don't like or can't eat for religious or med-ical reasons? In situations like these, eat whatever you can and hope that no one no-tices what is left. If questioned, admit that you don't eat meat (or whatever), but say that you've enjoyed the other foods and have had "more than enough" to eat.

15   How long should you stay? Don't leave immediately after dinner, but don't overstay your welcome, either. When your host yawns or runs out of conversation, that's a good time to leave. The next day, phone or write to express your thanks again.

16   Dining out? It's a good idea to phone the restaurant and make a reservation to avoid waiting for a table. When you invite someone out to dinner, be prepared to pay the bill and reach for it when it arrives. However, if your companion insists on sharing the bill, don't get into an argument about it. In most American restaurants, a tip for the server (waiter or waitress) is not added to the bill. The word *tip* is an acronym for "to insure promptness." If the service was good, leave a tip equal to about 15% of the bill. In ex-pensive restaurants, leave a little more.

17   American table manners are easy to learn by observation. A few characteristics to note: The napkin should not be tucked into the collar or vest but should be placed across the lap; the **silverware** placement is quite different from the European style. In general, Americans use the pieces of silverware farthest from the plate first and work in toward the plate.

Check Your Comprehension *What are two things you should <u>not</u> do when you are a dinner guest at an American friend's home?*

Manners between Men and Women

18   In the 1960s and 1970s, the U.S. went through a social revolution commonly referred to as the women's liberation movement. The movement has benefited women in many ways, especially in terms of job opportunities and advancement. But it has also created

great confusion regarding manners. Formerly, men were considered the stronger and dominant sex, so etiquette required them to adopt a protective attitude toward the so-called weaker sex. That meant helping women on and off with their coats, opening doors for them, allowing them to exit from elevators first, and so on. Today, American women, who outlive (and often outearn) men, do not consider themselves weak and in need of male protection. Their self-sufficient attitude has led men to wonder whether traditional etiquette is still appropriate. Most men continue to perform many of the traditional courtesies, but both sexes are more casual about them. If a man does not help his date into and out of her chair in a restaurant, no one will think he's rude.

19   Traditionally, when a man invites a woman out on a date, he picks her up at home, pays the expenses for the evening, and takes her home at the end of the evening. Prior to women's liberation, the woman was expected to sit at home by the phone and wait for the man to call. Today, it is common for a woman to invite a man just about anywhere. If she does the inviting, she pays for the evening's expenses. When a man and woman who are just friends go out together it is usually *Dutch treat*, which means they share expenses.

20   Today, many men working in the U.S. have a female boss. Men who come from countries in which the woman's place is still in the home may find it difficult to take orders from a woman. But in the U.S., many women are judges, doctors, business executives, college presidents, and entrepreneurs. Men must show respect for a person who holds a position of responsibility and authority, whether that person is male or female.

21   On the job, it is important to treat others as coworkers, not as prospective romantic partners. Many sexual **harassment** lawsuits have been won in the U.S., so many companies mention this matter as part of their training for new employees.

✔ Check Your Comprehension *How has women's liberation affected manners between the sexes?*

Classroom Etiquette

22   The relationship between student and teacher is less formal in the U.S. than in many other countries, especially at the college level. American college students do not stand up when their teacher enters the room. Students are generally encouraged to ask questions during class, stop by the professor's office, phone, or e-mail if they want to discuss something. Most teachers let students enter class late or leave early when necessary.

23   Despite the lack of formality, students are still expected to be polite and considerate of their teacher and classmates. When students want to ask questions, they usually raise a hand and wait to be called on. But if a professor is giving a lecture, that is the wrong time to interrupt with a question. When the teacher or a student is speaking to the class, it's rude to begin whispering to another classmate. When a test is being given, talking to a classmate is not only rude but also risky. Most American teachers assume that students who are talking to each other during a test are cheating. The result may be a test grade of zero.

✔ Check Your Comprehension *Name some things students can do and shouldn't do in an American classroom.*

Language Etiquette

24   Americans are usually tolerant of nonnative speakers who have trouble understanding English. But they become a little annoyed when a person does something incorrectly because of misunderstanding what was said. No one wants *soap* when he asked for *soup*. So if you don't understand what is said to you, politely ask the person to repeat or explain.

25   For the confused nonnative English speaker, there are several ways to ask for help, for example, "Could you please repeat that?" or "Would you please speak more slowly?" If a definition is needed, ask "What does the word _____ mean?" To find out how to express a particular idea in English, ask "How do you say _____ in English?"

26   Here are a few more polite English expressions that must be part of your English vocabulary. The polite response to a compliment is "Thank you." (A smile and a nod are not enough.) The response to "Thank you" is, of course, "You're welcome." If someone asks "How are you?" don't start talking about your medical problems. Just say, "Fine, thanks. How are you?" What do Americans say when someone sneezes? Believe it or not, they say "God bless you" or simply "Bless you."

27   One final point: When in a group, it is quite rude to converse in a language that some of the people cannot understand. Those who don't speak the language will feel left out. If it becomes necessary to switch to a language that not everyone present understands, then it's polite to translate or summarize what was said.

28   This short review of good manners in the U.S.A. will help you be polite in English. And that will encourage American friends to be polite to you.

AFTER YOU READ

I. Getting the Message

A. *Discuss or write answers to these questions on a separate piece of paper. Write complete sentences. Reread the paragraphs indicated if you need help.*

1. What are three questions that a casual acquaintance should *not* ask an American? (4)

2. When should you send a sympathy card to a friend? (11)

3. What are two things you should *not* do in an American classroom? (8, 23)

4. What three things should you do when invited to an American friend's home for dinner? (13, 15)

5. Has women's liberation made life better or worse for women? What does the reading imply? (18–21)

B. *What are the polite responses in the following situations? Check (✓) the correct answer.*

1. Your friend says, "I missed class because my grandfather died." What do you say?
   a. _____ "I'm so sorry."
   b. _____ "How did he die?"

2. Your friend says, "I bought a new car a few weeks ago." What do you say?
   a. _____ "How much did it cost?"
   b. _____ "What kind of car?"

3. Your friend asks, "How are you?" What do you say?
   a. _____ "I have a headache, but I just took an aspirin, so I'm hoping to feel better soon."
   b. _____ "Fine, thanks. How are you?"

4. The elevator is crowded, and you're standing in the back when it arrives at your floor. What do you say?
   a. _____ "Move over. I have to get out."
   b. _____ "Excuse me, please. This is my floor."

5. Your friend tells you your sweater is very attractive. What do you say?
   a. _____ "Thank you."
   b. _____ "Do you really like this old thing?"

6. Your friend introduces you to his sister. What do you say?
   a. _____ "It's nice meeting you."
   b. _____ "It was nice meeting you."

II. Building Your Vocabulary

A. *These are the 15 key vocabulary words for this chapter. They are boldfaced in the reading. Pronounce these words after your teacher and discuss their meanings.*

acquaintance	compliment*	insult*
address*	condolences†	manners‡
appropriate	congratulations†	polite
assertive	etiquette	rude
behavior	harassment	silverware

---

*These words can be used as nouns or verbs.

†*Congratulations* and *condolences* are always plural.

‡*Manners* is plural when it refers to social behavior or etiquette.

B. *Complete these sentences with some of the key vocabulary words on page 43.*

1. Titles such as *Mr., Dr.,* or *Mrs.* are polite forms of _____.

2. When someone dies, you should express your _____ to the family.

3. When a couple gets engaged, it is polite to say "_____!"

4. Americans believe people should not be afraid to ask for the things they want. In other words, people should be _____.

5. Four uncountable nouns in this vocabulary list are _____, _____, _____, and _____.

6. The opposite of *polite* is _____. The opposite of an *insult* is a(n) _____.

7. Knives, forks, and spoons are pieces of _____.

8. A classmate or neighbor that you don't know well is a(n) _____.

III. Sharpening Reading Skills

Pronouns   Pronouns generally refer to a noun that appeared earlier in the sentence or in the preceding sentence. Remember that gerunds and infinitives are also nouns, so pronouns can refer back to them.

Examples

This cake is delicious. I love *it*. (*It* refers to the noun *cake*.)
We enjoy swimming, and we're good at *it*. (*It* refers to the gerund *swimming*.)

Write the noun that each of the following pronouns refers to. It may be an infinitive or a gerund.

1. In paragraph 3, the last sentence, what does *them* refer to? _____

2. In paragraph 5, sentence 2, what does *this* refer to? _____

3. In paragraph 18, sentence 4, what does *them* refer to? _____

4. In paragraph 19 sentence 1, what does *her* refer to? _____

IV. Understanding Idioms and Expressions

Match each expression in column 1 with the phrase in column 2 that means the same thing by writing the correct numbers on the lines. The numbers in parentheses give the paragraphs in which the expressions are used.

1. go Dutch treat (19)
2. go through something (18)
3. Hands off! (4)
4. keep your distance (4)
5. overstay your welcome (15)
6. run out of something (15)
7. a white lie (3)
8. What do you do? (4)
9. What if . . . ? (14)

_____ What's your occupation?

_____ Consider this possibility.

_____ stay too long

_____ a harmless untruth

_____ don't get too close

_____ Don't touch.

_____ share expenses

_____ use something all up

_____ experience something (often something difficult)

V. Taking Words Apart

A. Verb or Noun

Write in the correct word forms to complete the sentences. When the word is a verb, use the correct tense.

1. That child doesn't know how to ——————. His —————— is terrible. (*behave / behavior*)

2. Did you —————— him on his marriage? (*congratulate / congratulations*)

3. The boss —————— me on the good job I did. (*compliment / complimentary*)

4. It's difficult for me to —————— in English. But yesterday I had a long —————— with an American friend who speaks my language. (*converse / conversation*)

B. The Prefix *mis-*

The prefix mis- means wrong(ly) or bad(ly). Write the meanings of these words:

1. *misunderstand:* _____

2. *misspell:* _____

VI. Practicing Sentence Patterns

Imperative Sentences   Because this chapter gives advice to the reader, many sentences are written in the imperative. The subject (*you*) is not in the sentence; it is understood. Here are two examples of imperative statements:

Imperative, affirmative: Arrive on time.
Imperative, negative: Don't arrive late.

Now write imperative sentences giving advice to someone going to visit your country.

1. Affirmative: _____

2. Negative: _____

VII. Sharing Ideas

A. Issues

Debate these issues in small groups. Then choose one and write about it.

1. You have a new job in a nice office. However, an assistant at a nearby desk eats a sandwich with a lot of onion in it every day. The smell bothers you all afternoon. What is the best thing to do about this problem? Consider these possibilities: (a) complain to the boss and ask for a different desk; (b) ask the assistant to stop eating at his desk; (c) tell the other workers in the office and hope that your complaint will get back to the assistant; (d) buy an air-freshener spray and use it every day after lunch; (e) suffer in silence.

2. What differences have you noticed between American manners and European or Asian manners?

B. On a Personal Note

Write about one of these topics.

1. Tell about a time when you were embarrassed because you realized that you had done something socially improper.
2. Read a chapter in an American book on etiquette and summarize it. (Some famous authors in this field are Emily Post, Amy Vanderbilt, and Letitia Baldrige.)
3. What do you like about American manners? What do you dislike?

5 | What Americans Consume

Some fast food favorites: pizza, hot dogs, and subs

BEFORE YOU READ

Discuss

1. What do you consider typical American food? Do you like it?

2. Do you think the typical American diet is healthy? Why or why not?

3. What do people around the world eat for their first meal of the day? What do Americans eat for breakfast?

Guess

Try to answer the questions. Then look for the answers in the reading.

1. What percentage of the American food budget is spent on food eaten away from home? Check (✓) one:

   _____ 18%   _____ 40%   _____ 52%

2. What is pie à la mode? Check (✓) one:

   _____ hot pie   _____ pie with cheese   _____ pie with ice cream

What Americans Consume

American Meals and Snacks

1   Three square meals a day—that's a common description of American eating habits. But, in reality, most Americans add between-meal **snacks** and have either a "bite" or a meal about five times a day. The meal that breaks the overnight fast is, of course, breakfast. It's a meal that many adults skip, either because they're in a hurry or on a diet. Others have just orange juice or toast along with the traditional wake-up **beverage,** coffee. But some people add hot or cold cereal or eggs. Other popular breakfast items are pancakes, waffles, and French toast (bread soaked in a mixture of eggs and milk and fried), often served with maple syrup.

2   People who skip breakfast often snack a few hours after they get up. In the mid-morning, many office and factory workers are given a 10- to 15-minute "coffee break" from the job to relax and chat with coworkers. Not surprisingly, many have a cup of coffee and maybe a doughnut to dunk into it.

3   Most Americans eat lunch between noon and two o'clock. It's rare for workers to go home for lunch, and many schoolchildren eat at school. Some people *brown-bag it*—that is, they bring food from home, often in a brown paper bag. For this purpose, the sandwich is ideal. The sandwich chef needs only two pieces of bread, something moist to smear on the bread (such as butter, mayonnaise, mustard, or ketchup), and something to put in the middle. Some popular cold sandwiches are ham and cheese, peanut butter and jelly, sliced chicken, and tuna salad.

4   In restaurants, people often order hot sandwiches. The most popular are hamburgers and hot dogs. Hamburgers are patties of chopped beef, usually served in round buns. Hot dogs (also called red hots, frankfurters, or wieners) are 5- to 7-inch sausages served in long, thin buns. The term *hot dog* dates back to 1900 and was inspired by an American vendor who compared the frankfurter to the long-bodied German dog. His hot dachshund sausages eventually got shortened to *hot dogs*. To accompany the sandwich, a hungry diner might add a bowl of soup, a salad, french-fried potatoes or potato chips, and a sweet dessert or fruit.

5   In the U.S., people in a hurry can eat lunch quickly, but those who want a leisurely meal can find that, too. In a coffee shop, the diner who must "eat and run" can usually find an empty stool at a counter within 5 minutes. Fast-food restaurants (where customers stand in line, order food, and get it in about 2 minutes) also do a lot of business at lunchtime. Another timesaver is the **cafeteria,** where customers walk by displays of food, place what they want on their trays, and then pay a cashier at the end of the line. Large institutions such as factories, hospitals, and schools often have cafeterias. Some institutions also have food-dispensing machines from which customers can purchase soup, sandwiches, drinks, fruit, and sweets. Microwave ovens for heating the food are set up near these machines. On the other hand, at traditional restaurants, diners sometimes combine business and pleasure at a business luncheon, where work is discussed over cocktails and a nicely served, leisurely meal.

6   In the mid-afternoon, snack time comes again. Office and factory workers may take a second coffee break. Children coming home from school usually head for the refrigerator. In warm weather, ice cream is a popular snack. It's **consumed** in cones, bars, and sundaes (with a sweet sauce on top). It is also used in two popular drinks, milk shakes and ice cream sodas.

7   For Americans, the biggest meal of the day is dinner, usually served at about six o'clock on weekdays. Dinner may include several courses: an appetizer (such as fresh fruit, fruit juice, or a small portion of fish); soup; salad; an entrée (main course) of meat, poultry, or fish; and side dishes such as cooked vegetables, rice, or noodles. Coffee or tea and dessert finish off the meal. Most Americans prefer a sweet dessert such as cake, pie, or ice cream. Apple pie, served hot with a scoop of ice cream (à la mode) or with a **slice** of cheese, is a national favorite, hence the expression "as American as apple pie." Most Americans don't eat all these courses for dinner every evening. In fact, many restaurants offer the option of ordering these courses separately, or à la carte, for people who want to eat a little less.

8   With lunch and dinner, Americans drink water, fruit juice, coffee, tea, or a carbonated drink called *soda* or *pop*. (The term used depends on the region of the country.) Though children are urged to drink milk with every meal, many prefer soda or juice instead.

9   Since dinner is usually served early in the evening, an evening snack is customary. Children may have milk and cookies. Adults may nibble on fruit, sweets, or **leftovers.**

10   On weekends and holidays, the meal schedule may vary. On Saturday evenings, many people eat dinner at seven or even eight o'clock, especially when dining out. On Sundays, many families have brunch, a meal that combines breakfast and lunch. It is usually served between 11:00 A.M. and 2:00 P.M. and includes typical breakfast foods plus cheese, cake, and perhaps casserole dishes and cold fish. Families who go to church on Sunday morning may have breakfast before services and then eat their biggest meal of the day at about two o'clock. The main meal of the day is always called *dinner*, no matter what time it is served. When dinner is eaten in mid-afternoon, a smaller evening meal called *supper* is served around seven o'clock.

11   On Sundays and holidays when the weather is warm, Americans like to eat outdoors. They enjoy **picnics** in parks or backyard barbecues featuring charcoal-broiled steaks, hot dogs, or hamburgers. Another popular outdoor meal is the clambake, a picnic at the seashore, at which clams and other shellfish are baked on hot stones under seaweed.

12   In the U.S. as elsewhere, mealtime can be an important social event. In many homes, dinner may be the only time when everyone in the family gets together and shares the day's experiences. Dining out is also an important part of American social life. For single men and women, dates often begin with dinner at a nice restaurant. Married couples often get together with friends to eat out, especially on weekends. In their desire to use time efficiently, Americans may rush through breakfast and lunch, but dinner (especially on weekends) is usually a more leisurely meal at which enjoyment of food is enhanced by pleasant conversation.

✔ **Check Your Comprehension**   *Name five American meals, and tell at what time of day they're eaten.*

Easy Does It!

13   Being an American homemaker is easier now than ever before. Today's family shopper can go to just one store—the nearby supermarket—and find nearly everything the household needs. In addition to food and beverages, supermarkets sell paper goods, cleaning supplies, cooking utensils, cosmetics, over-the-counter medications, tobacco products, pet products, books and magazines, plants, and so on. Many are open until 10:00 P.M. or later. Some are even open 24 hours a day!

14   Not only is shopping quicker and easier than ever before; cooking is, too. Many foods can be bought partly or wholly prepared. A great variety of soups and sauces come in cans or in small packages. The cook just adds water, heats, and serves. Other timesavers include mixes for making mashed potatoes, pancakes, cookies, and cakes. To these, the cook adds just two or three **ingredients**—usually butter, milk, and eggs. There are also instant beverages—coffee, cocoa, lemonade, and many others—that can be made just by adding water. Many frozen foods are precooked and need only to be heated. A food processor instantly turns a bunch of apples into apple juice. A microwave oven can cook a turkey in a few hours. Cleanup is speedy, too, for those with an automatic dishwasher and a garbage disposal.

15   The ultimate in easy eating is, of course, eating out. Americans eat out quite a bit. About one-third of the food Americans consume is eaten away from home. Eating out is on the rise. In 1986, Americans spent about one-third of their food budget on eating out; today, the figure is 40%, and it's expected to go even higher. Nutritionists say that so much eating out has had a bad effect upon the American diet. People tend to eat more and to choose less healthy food when dining in a restaurant.

16   American restaurants range from inexpensive fast-food places to expensive, formal ones that serve attractively prepared food in an elegant setting. Most fast-food restaurants are **franchises**—individually owned businesses following strict guidelines from the company's central management. Fast-food franchises have been very successful in the U.S. Part of the appeal is the predictability. At the major hamburger or chicken franchises, people know what the food is going to taste like, wherever they buy it.

17   Carry-out meals are handy for working adults with no time to shop and cook. Some

restaurants prepare only carry-out food; many others serve diners in the restaurant but also pack up meals for carry-out customers and those who phone or fax in an order for delivery. Fast-food places and ethnic restaurants both do a big carry-out business.

18   Sometimes the American diner also carries home food after eating in a restaurant. In most restaurants, portions are generous. If a customer can't eat all that's served, especially in an informal restaurant, it's quite appropriate to ask the server to pack up the leftovers. Sometimes the server will offer to do this without even being asked. Years ago, a take-home package like this was put into a "doggie bag." Today, everyone openly admits that the food is for human consumption—probably for the next day's lunch.

✔ **Check Your Comprehension**   *Why is it easy for an American family to prepare dinner?*

Variety—The Spice of Life

19   For Americans seeking a dining adventure and for immigrants seeking their native **cuisine,** ethnic dining is the answer. The most widespread of the ethnic cuisines are probably Chinese, Italian, and Mexican. But that is just the tip of the iceberg. In New York, Chicago, and many other major American cities, the range of ethnic dining goes, if not from A to Z, at least from A to Y—Arabian, Armenian, Cuban, Ethiopian, Greek, Indian, Japanese, Korean, Persian, Peruvian, Russian, Thai, Turkish, Vietnamese, and Yugoslavian, among many other cooking styles.

20   Ethnic influences add variety to home-cooked meals, too. Ingredients for the more popular ethnic dishes are readily available in most supermarkets. Less well-known ingredients can be obtained at food stores in ethnic communities. The U.S. is commonly called a melting pot of people from everywhere. Therefore, it is not surprising that American cooking pots contain ingredients from all over the world.

21   Regional American food specialties add further variety to the American diet. From New England come wonderful seafood chowders (usually clams or lobsters stewed with vegetables and milk), baked beans, brown breads, and Boston cream pie. Southerners have created fried chicken, smoked ham, grits (a side dish made with corn meal and milk), and fritters (small fried cakes often containing fruit). New Orleans is famous for spicy Creole cooking, which combines French, Spanish, African-American, and Native American cuisine.

22   Because of the nation's varied climate and geography, a great variety of fruits and vegetables are grown in the U.S. and many more are imported. High-quality fruits and vegetables are available throughout the year, thanks to modern transportation and freezing techniques.

✔ **Check Your Comprehension**   *What are two reasons why American meals are so varied?*

Death by Consumption

23   Plenty of tasty, **nutritious** food is available in the U.S. Yet many Americans eat (or drink) themselves into an early grave. Nutritionists say that Americans eat too much unhealthy fat, salt, and sugar. In recent years, Americans have become aware of the fact that a person's diet affects appearance, performance, mental state, health, and longevity. As a result, many Americans try to eat more fruits, vegetables, and healthier sources of protein (such as fish, grains, and poultry). Many have cut down on products high in fat. Still, 33% of Americans are somewhat overweight and another 22% are **obese** (extremely overweight). In the U.S., cans, jars, and paper packages contain information regarding a food's ingredients as well as the calorie count and amounts of sodium (salt), fat, and important vitamins in each serving. This information helps consumers, especially those on special diets or those who need to lose weight.

24   "Everything enjoyable in life is either illegal, immoral, or fattening," complain those who are overweight. The American food industry has responded to this complaint. A wide assortment of American foods are made with **artificial** sweeteners instead of sugar. There are also low-fat and fat-free foods and some made with healthier types of fat or fat substitutes.

25   Health and social problems are also created by consumption of alcoholic beverages, cigarettes, and illegal drugs. About 5.4% of Americans are heavy drinkers. Those who engage in heavy drinking damage their own health, cause pain to their families, and are dangerous behind the wheel of an automobile. In recent years, many citizens' organizations have campaigned to keep the roads safer by increasing penalties for drunk driving.

26   Another way that Americans consume themselves to death is by smoking cigarettes. About 29% of American adults smoke. The medical expenses and human tragedy caused by this habit are immeasurable and well known. Unfortunately, the tobacco industry has a lot of political power. Therefore, although the government urges smokers to quit, it also pays farmers to grow tobacco. In recent years, the American tobacco industry has been sued for billions of dollars because of the illnesses its products cause.

27   One of the greatest concerns today is the large amount of illegal drugs consumed in the U.S., especially by teenagers and young adults. Marijuana usage, for example, is highest among the 18–25 age group, with about 12% of people in this group smoking "weed." The use of illegal drugs damages the body and also leads to an increase in crime. Many people who get hooked on (addicted to) cocaine or heroin are then forced to commit crimes in order to get enough money to buy these illegal (and therefore expensive) substances.

28   In dealing with these health problems—obesity, alcoholism, cigarette smoking, and drug **addiction**—Americans often turn to support groups of fellow sufferers. Groups such as Weight Watchers, Alcoholics Anonymous, and Narcotics Anonymous have helped people overcome destructive behavior. With the assistance of professional counselors and the support of a group, Americans work hard to rid themselves of dangerous habits.

29   At the other end of the health spectrum are people with great self-control. They **avoid** high-fat and high-salt foods. In addition, they worry about chemicals added to food. There are three common sources of these chemicals: (1) pesticides sprayed on plants to keep insects away, (2) additives used in some packaged foods to improve appearance

and lengthen shelf life, and (3) drugs fed to beef cattle to improve the quantity and taste of meat. Are these chemicals harmful to human beings? Those who believe they are read labels carefully, buy organic food, and shop in health food stores. Defenders of these chemicals say that the quantities used are too small to be harmful and that discontinuing their use would mean smaller harvests, less prime beef, faster food spoilage, and higher food prices. In the 1960s, people who were afraid of the typical American diet were called health food "nuts." Today, Americans realize that these people have had a good influence. As a result of the health food movement, many Americans consider the great variety of good things to eat and make wiser selections.

AFTER YOU READ

I. Getting the Message

A. *Answer these questions with a few words. You don't need to write complete sentences. Reread the paragraphs indicated in parentheses if you need help.*

1. What are two common breakfast beverages? (1) _____

   _____

2. What do Americans eat for lunch? (3–4) _____

3. What are two places where you can eat lunch quickly? (5) _____

   _____

4. Which meal is bigger—dinner or supper? (10) _____

5. What are two timesavers that Americans can use when preparing meals? (14)

   _____ _____

6. Would you go to an ethnic restaurant for a hot dog or hamburger? (19)

   _____

7. What two common food ingredients are unhealthy if eaten in large quantities?

   (23) _____ _____

B. *Discuss the difference between a* fact *and an* opinion. *Then, after considering the information in this chapter, mark each statement fact (F) or opinion (O).*

_____ 1. American food isn't healthy.

_____ 2. Many harmful chemicals are added to American foods.

_____ 3. The use of illegal drugs causes an increase in crime.

_____ 4. Addictive drugs should be legalized in the U.S.

_____ 5. Americans eat too many snacks.

_____ 6. Smoking cigarettes is bad for a person's health.

(continued on the next page)

_____ 7. Restaurant food is not as healthy as home-cooked food.

_____ 8. When Americans eat out, they tend to eat too much and choose less healthy food than they ordinarily have at home.

II. Building Your Vocabulary

A. *These are the 15 key vocabulary words for this chapter. They are boldfaced in the reading. Pronounce these words after your teacher, and discuss their meanings.*

addiction	consume	nutritious
artificial	cuisine	obese
avoid	franchise*	picnic
beverage	ingredient	slice*
cafeteria	leftovers	snack*

B. *Complete these sentences with some of the key vocabulary words. Make the nouns plural if necessary, and put each verb into the correct tense and form.*

1. A person who is overweight should _____ eating food with a lot of sugar and fat.

2. For breakfast, some people have two _____ of toast. For lunch, some have a piece (or _____) of pie. (Use the same word for both answers.)

3. A(n) _____ is a liquid that a person can drink.

4. In a(n) _____, customers don't tip because they serve themselves.

5. Ethnic _____ refers to the cooking style of a particular culture or group of people.

6. If shoppers want to know what's in a particular food, they can read the list of _____ on the box, package, jar, or can.

7. _____ people are more than a little overweight. They are extremely overweight.

8. *Consumers* are people who buy and use products. When people eat food, they _____ it.

9. People can develop a(n) _____ to cigarettes, coffee, alcohol, or cocaine.

10. _____ sweeteners don't have any calories, but sugar does.

---

*These words can be used as nouns or verbs.

C. Homonyms *are words that sound alike but have different meanings and spellings. Underline the words to complete the sentences below. Use a dictionary if you need help.*

Example

I want (<u>to</u> / too) have (<u>some</u> / sum) coffee.

1. Americans like to eat (*they're / their*) lunches quickly because (*they're / their*) often in a hurry.

2. Let's (*by / buy*) some (*meat / meet*) and then (*meat / meet*) (*by / buy*) the cashier.

3. Every (*Sunday / sundae*), I eat a chocolate (*Sunday / sundae*) for dessert.

4. Cooking styles (*vary / very*) a great deal in the U.S., so eating American food is (*vary / very*) interesting.

5. It's (*to / too*) late for breakfast and (*to / too*) early for lunch, but the (*too / two*) of us could go (*to / too*) a restaurant and have brunch.

III. Sharpening Reading Skills

A. Topic Sentences   Most paragraphs contain a *topic sentence* that states the main idea. The topic sentence is the most important sentence in the paragraph. It tells what the rest of the paragraph is about. The other sentences give details that support the main idea.

Reread the paragraphs listed, and look for the topic sentence. Then write the first two words of the topic sentence on the line after the paragraph number.

Example

(5) _____ In the _____

(10) _____   (15) _____

B. General and Specific

The underlined words are general categories. Three of the four words in the lines that follow refer to specific items of that category. Draw a line through the word that doesn't belong in that category.

Example

<u>Poultry</u>   chicken   duck   turkey   ~~fish~~

1. <u>Beverages</u>	juice	water	milk shake	apple
2. <u>Dairy products</u>	cheese	milk	fruit	butter
3. <u>Desserts</u>	eggs	cake	pie	ice cream
4. <u>Meals</u>	dinner	diner	brunch	supper
5. <u>Entrées</u>	chicken	cereal	salmon	steak
6. <u>Produce</u>	apples	lettuce	bread	carrots
7. <u>Bakery goods</u>	bread	candy	cake	cookies

IV. Understanding Idioms and Expressions

A. *Discuss the meanings of the following expressions. The numbers in parentheses give the paragraphs in which these expressions are used.*

> into an early grave (23)
> melting pot (20)
> the tip of the iceberg (19)
> three square meals a day (1)
> Variety is the spice of life. (heading above paragraph 19)

B. *Complete each sentence with one of the expressions listed. The numbers in parentheses give the paragraphs in which these expressions are used.*

> a bite (1)   coffee break (2)   over-the-counter (13)
> brown-bag it (3)   get hooked (27)   shelf life (29)
> carry-out (17)   nut (29)

1. After the movie, let's stop in this coffee shop for _____ to eat.

2. For lunch, do you _____, order _____ food, or go out to eat?

3. This is a(n) _____ medication. I can buy it without a prescription.

4. I can keep this medicine for 2 years. It has a long _____.

5. If you start smoking cigarettes, you might _____.

6. He calls me a health food _____ because I eat only organic food.

V. Taking Words Apart

A. Accent Marks in English

Sometimes words from another language become part of the English language, accent mark and all. Here are three examples. Pronounce them after your teacher. Then discuss and write their meanings.

1. entrée: _____

2. à la carte: _____

3. à la mode: _____

B. Adjectives to Nouns

1. *Write the noun form for each adjective listed. Use a dictionary if you need help. Then pronounce the word pairs after your teacher.*

Example

pleasant   ___pleasure___

1. crowded _____

2. healthy _____

3. important _____

4. nutritious _____

5. obese _____

6. spicy _____

7. traditional _____

8. varied _____

2. *Now choose one of these adjectives and its noun, and write a sentence with each.*

  a. adjective: _____

  b. noun: _____

VI. Practicing Sentence Patterns

Commas in a Series   The last two sentences in paragraph 3 and the last sentence in paragraph 4 illustrate the correct placement of commas in punctuating a series. When there are three or more items in the series, each item should be separated with a comma. The word *and* should be placed before the last item in the series.

1. *Add commas plus the word* and *where they are needed in this sentence:*

I put melted cheese on my baked potato my french fries most cooked vegetables.

2. *Now write a sentence listing three foods you had for dinner last night. Use commas where needed.*

_____

VII. Sharing Ideas

A. Issues

Debate these issues in small groups. Then choose one and write about it.

1. Some people argue that health-conscious Americans have taken all the fun out of eating. Has Americans' concern about calories and cholesterol turned food into an enemy to be feared and avoided? Does this attitude decrease the quality of their lives? Or are they better off because healthy eating probably increases their life span?

2. A common American expression is "You can never be too rich or too thin." This sentiment speaks especially to American women. Those who want to look glamorous must count calories carefully and often deny themselves the food they want. Do you agree with the saying "the thinner, the better"? Must a woman be thin to be beautiful?

3. Should cigarettes be made illegal? Or should people have the freedom to buy and use this product if they want to?

B. On a Personal Note

Write about one of these topics.

1. Do you have a healthy diet? Discuss why or why not.

2. Compare meals in other countries with American meals. (Think about when people eat, what they eat, and how much they eat at various times of the day.) Which eating habits do you prefer? Why?

3. Compare two similar packaged food products (for example, butter and margarine or two brands of vegetable soup). Check the ingredients, the number of calories, and the sodium (salt) and fat content. Which is healthier? Which one tastes better? Which one will you buy the next time you go shopping?

UNIT 2

The Salad

Bowl:

Cultural

Diversity

in the U.S.

A Nation of Immigrants

Mother and son, immigrants from Guatemala

BEFORE YOU READ

Discuss

1. What is an immigrant? What is a refugee? Are all immigrants refugees or vice versa?

2. What is an alien in the U.S.? What is an alien in a science fiction story? What is the difference between a legal alien and an illegal alien?

3. In your opinion, what are the main reasons why people immigrate?

Guess

Try to answer the questions. Then look for the answers in the reading.

1. Approximately what percentage of the U.S. population is foreign-born?
   Check (✓) one:

   _____ 5%   _____ 10%   _____ 20%

2. About how many illegal aliens currently live in the U.S.? Check (✓) one:

   _____ 1 million   _____ 3 million   _____ 6 million

3. More Americans say that their ancestors came from this country than from any
   other. Check (✓) one:

   _____ England   _____ Italy   _____ Germany

A Nation of Immigrants

1   Between 1821 and 1997, about 64 million **immigrants** came to the U.S.A. It was the largest migration the human race had ever known. What caused it? In his book A *Nation of Immigrants*, John F. Kennedy (later the nation's thirty-fifth president) explained: "Three strong forces—religious persecution, political **oppression**, and economic hardship—provided the chief **motives** for the mass migrations to our shores." Kennedy's great-grandfather had been one of those immigrants, a farmer who left Ireland during the potato famine in the 1840s.

Immigration before Independence

2   The earliest immigrants to the area now known as the U.S. were probably the Native Americans (or American Indians). They came to the Western Hemisphere from Asia about 15,000 years ago or perhaps even earlier. By the fifteenth century, there were 15 million to 20 million Native Americans in the Americas. Perhaps as many as 700,000 were living within the present limits of the U.S. when Christopher Columbus reached the Western Hemisphere in 1492.

3   During the 1500s, French, Spanish, Portuguese, and English explorers visited the New World. The Spanish founded the first European settlements in the area that is now the U.S. The first **permanent** British colony within present-day U.S. territory was established in Jamestown, Virginia, in 1607, by 104 British colonists. In 1620, a second British colony, consisting of 102 people, was founded in Plymouth, Massachusetts.

4   In 1790, the white population of the 13 original colonies totaled slightly more than 3 million. About 75% of these first Americans were of mostly British **ancestry**; the rest

man, Dutch, French, Swiss, and Spanish. The British gave the new nation its language, laws, and philosophy of government.

✔ **Check Your Comprehension**

Why is English, rather than French or Spanish, the major language of the U.S.?

Immigration from 1790 to 1920

5   American independence did not immediately stimulate immigration. Between 1790 and 1840, fewer than 1 million foreigners entered the country. But between 1841 and 1860, more than 4 million arrived. Potato crop failures in Ireland stimulated Irish immigration. Germans came to escape economic and political difficulties. During the last half of the nineteenth century, many Scandinavians came, attracted by good farmland. The Industrial Revolution and the westward movement gave new immigrants an important role in the nation's economic development. Employers needed factory workers. Landowners wanted tenants for western lands. They sent agents to Europe to "sell" America. Agents of steamship lines and railroad companies attracted thousands of immigrants with stories about a fabulous "land of opportunity."

6   Immigration took another great leap after 1880. Between 1881 and 1920, about 23.5 million **aliens** were admitted. Nearly 90% of these newcomers were from Europe. After 1882, the government kept Asian immigration to a minimum because American workers feared that new Asian immigrants would take their jobs or lower their wages.

7   In the 1890s, the sources of European immigration began to shift. Between 1881 and 1890, approximately 80% of American immigrants came from northern and western Europe. By 1911, about 77% were coming from southern, central, and eastern Europe—from Italy, Russia, Austria-Hungary, Romania, Bulgaria, Greece, and areas that later became Poland and Czechoslovakia. Many of those from Russia, Romania, and Poland were Jews **fleeing** religious **persecution.**

8   Most immigrants arriving between 1886 and 1924 came into New York Harbor, past the inspirational Statue of Liberty, which is 151 feet tall. She invited them to go through the "golden door." But first they were taken to nearby Ellis Island to be checked in. From 1901 to 1917, this facility processed 2,000 to 5,000 immigrants every day. Now, it is a museum.

The Statue of Liberty in New York Harbor

What historical developments in the U.S. stimulated immigration?
What problems in Europe stimulated emigration?

Immigration since 1920

9   During World War I, immigration declined due to traveling difficulties. After the war, Europeans once again began crowding aboard ships to the U.S. But American industry no longer needed them. During the 1920s, Congress passed the first quota law, limiting the total number of immigrants allowed and the number allowed from each country.

10   From 1930 to 1945, legal limits and World War II kept immigration to a minimum. When the war ended, immigration rose sharply because entrance was allowed to millions of people left homeless by the war. Special legislation admitted large numbers of displaced persons, **refugees,** orphans, and war brides.

11   During the last half of the twentieth century, the United States lifted immigration restrictions from time to time to take in refugees and ease suffering in other parts of the world. In the late 1950s, thousands of Hungarians were admitted. In the early 1960s, because of the Cuban revolution, more than 150,000 Cubans entered the U.S. To relieve crowded conditions in Hong Kong, several thousand nonquota Chinese were also permitted entry. In 1979, the U.S. admitted more than 20,000 Vietnamese refugees per month. In the late 1970s and 1980s, hundreds of thousands of Russians (mostly Jews) were also allowed to enter.

12   At the present time, immigration is permitted according to various categories. Immediate relatives of U.S. citizens may come in without numerical limit. The number of immigrants who are sponsored by family members living in the U.S. is limited to about 225,000 per year, and there are limits on how many visas can be issued per country. A significant number of people are allowed to immigrate because they have occupational skills needed in the U.S. The immigration laws are very complex. Someone wanting to immigrate should talk to an immigration lawyer or with the local office of the Immigration and Naturalization Service (INS).

13   Immigration **restrictions** may seem cruel to those who are living in difficult circumstances elsewhere, but they became necessary because, in the twentieth century, the U.S. population grew at a very rapid rate. By 1920, the population had reached 100 million. Fifty years later, it had **doubled.** A higher birthrate, lower infant mortality, and longer life expectancy all combined to cause this population explosion. Today, many Americans are having smaller families. However, the population is continuing to grow, so limits on immigration are likely to continue.

14   Looking back over some 200 years of immigration, which nations have sent the most people? The ten largest ancestry groups of today's Americans are (in decreasing order of size) German, Irish, English, African, Italian, Mexican, French, Polish, Native American, and Dutch.

✔ **Check Your Comprehension** *Why does the U.S. need immigration restrictions?*

Today's Foreign-Born Population

15   Here's a statistical snapshot of the **foreign**-born population in the U.S. today:
- About 10% of the U.S. population is foreign-born.
- Most foreign-born residents are Hispanics or Asian/Pacific Islanders.
- About 7 million (28%) of today's foreign-born residents come from Mexico. That's the largest foreign-born population from a single country in U.S. history.
- The five states with the largest foreign-born populations are California, New York, Florida, New Jersey, and Texas. California is home to about one-third of the nation's foreign-born residents, who make up about 28% of the state's population.
- How are immigrants doing in this "land of opportunity"? In 1996, the poverty rate for foreign-born citizens was 10%. That figure was *lower* than the poverty rate for American-born citizens, which was almost 13%. However, foreign-born noncitizens had a poverty rate of almost 27%.

Countries of Birth of U.S. Foreign-Born Population (1997)

Mexico: 7,017,000	Vietnam: 770,000	El Salvador: 607,000
Philippines: 1,132,000	India: 748,000	United Kingdom: 606,000
China: 1,107,000	Former Soviet Union: 734,000	Korea: 591,000
Cuba: 913,000	Dominican Republic: 632,000	Germany: 542,000

Source: U.S. Census Bureau

✔ **Check Your Comprehension** *Where have most of today's foreign-born U.S. residents come from?*

The Hispanic Population

16   About 35 million people living in the U.S. (about 2.5% of the population) belong to a Spanish-speaking ethnic group. More than half of them are foreign-born. Native speakers of Spanish are called H*ispanics* (or *Latinos*). Hispanics form the second-largest cultural minority in the U.S., after the nation's 36 million non-Hispanic African-Americans. The Hispanic population is younger than the national average, and its birthrate is higher. It is the most rapidly growing minority group in the country. Hispanics are expected to be the country's largest ethnic minority by the year 2005. For this large Spanish-speaking population, the U.S. now has Spanish radio and TV stations as well as Spanish newspapers, magazines, signs, and directions in many places.

17   Almost three-fourths of the nation's Hispanics live in five states: California, Texas,

New York, Florida, and Illinois. The three largest Hispanic groups in the U.S. are Mexicans, Puerto Ricans, and Cubans. Mexican immigrants and Mexican-Americans (those born in the U.S.) total about 13 million.

18   Mexicans have an important place in American history. They helped establish Los Angeles and many other settlements in the Southwest that later became major American cities. Also, they taught important methods of farming, mining, and ranching to Americans who settled in the West. When the Mexican–American War ended in 1848, the peace treaty gave the U.S. more than 525,000 square miles of territory in the Southwest. Mexicans living in this area were granted U.S. citizenship. Because of these Mexican-Americans, California, New Mexico, and Colorado were permitted to enter the union as **bilingual** states.

19   The island of Puerto Rico is located about 1,000 miles southeast of Florida. In 1878, during the brief Spanish–American War, the U.S. won Puerto Rico (along with Guam and the Philippine Islands) from Spain. Puerto Rico has remained part of the U.S. ever since. Puerto Ricans are American citizens, but, if they live in Puerto Rico, they don't vote in U.S. elections. They can travel to and from the nation's mainland without immigration restrictions. About 3 million Puerto Ricans live on the mainland, the majority in or near New York City.

20   Puerto Rico has what is called commonwealth status with the U.S. government. It receives protection and assistance from the federal government but has some local authority over its internal affairs. Among Puerto Ricans, there is disagreement about political goals for the island. Some are satisfied with the commonwealth status, some advocate statehood, and others want the island to become independent.

21   Cuban immigrants and their children make up the third largest group of Hispanics. About 1 million Cubans now live in the U.S. Most came as exiles during or after 1959, when Fidel Castro took over and the country became communist. Most Cubans in the U.S. live in southern Florida, Puerto Rico, New York City, and New Jersey. Many of these immigrants are well-educated with backgrounds in professions or business. As a result, they have a higher standard of living in the U.S. than many other Hispanics.

22   The influence of the Hispanic culture is felt and enjoyed by the rest of American society. Hispanic food is eagerly consumed everywhere. Nachos (corn chips with hot cheese on top) are about as popular as hot dogs in American ballparks. In supermarkets, salsa (a spicy sauce) sells almost as well as ketchup. Hispanic singers are very popular among younger Americans, as are Spanish dances such as the merengue, tango, samba, and—of course—salsa.

✔ **Check Your Comprehension**   *What historical events caused the U.S. to acquire a large Spanish-speaking population? Name at least three.*

Illegal Aliens

23   Illegal aliens are people living in the U.S. without proper authorization. Many enter the country by sneaking across the border. Others come on temporary student or visitor **visas** and do not leave when their visas **expire.** Most illegal aliens want to stay in the

U.S. because employment opportunities are so much greater than in their native countries. Since illegal aliens try hard not to be discovered by the government, it's impossible to get an accurate count of them. Census Bureau estimates set the number at about 6 million.

24 In 1986, the U.S. government adopted a new law affecting illegal aliens. It was designed to accomplish two main goals: (1) to allow illegal aliens who had been living in the country since January 1982 to gain legal status if they applied by May 4, 1988, and (2) to discourage others from coming into or staying in the country illegally by making it difficult for them to find employment. The law prohibits American employers from hiring illegals and provides for severe penalties—fines and even imprisonment—if they do so. Under the 1996 law, more than 1 million illegal aliens applied to become legal residents. But this law has also forced employers to check on all prospective employees to be sure that they are allowed to work in the U.S.

✔ Check Your Comprehension *Why has it become more difficult for an illegal alien to get a job?*

The Many Contributions of Immigrants

25 The wide variety of immigrant groups in the U.S. has given the nation great diversity in its industrial development. Germans, Scandinavians, and Poles share the credit for turning millions of acres of wilderness into farmland. Scandinavians and Canadians helped to develop the lumber industry. The Swedes built the first log cabins. The Swiss brought clock-making and cheese-making skills. The English were experienced in the handling of horses, cattle, and sheep. The Greeks, Italians, Portuguese, and Spanish grew citrus fruits and grapes. Italians started the wine industry. Chinese and Irish laborers built the first railroad that spanned the nation.

26 In addition to their skills, immigrants brought their political and social theories, religions, academic traditions, holidays, festivals, sports, arts, hobbies, and foods. The Germans introduced the Christmas tree, kindergarten, and the symphony orchestra. The Dutch brought ice-skating, bowling, golf, and the art of growing tulips. The French taught Americans elegant European cooking and dancing. Italians brought their talents in painting, sculpture, and architecture. The Irish established the Catholic Church as an English-speaking institution, introduced parochial schools, and built many Catholic colleges.

27 The American diet has also been delightfully affected by various immigrant groups. The Dutch taught Americans to make waffles and doughnuts. The Germans brought hamburgers and sausages. Italians introduced pizza, spaghetti, minestrone, and ravioli. Americans also enjoy Swiss cheeses and fondue, Irish stew, Chinese chow mein, Indian curries, Russian caviar, Middle Eastern shish kebab, Danish pastry, French chocolate mousse, and Turkish coffee.

28 The U.S. has often been called a melting pot because immigrants from all over have become part of this one nation and have shared a common culture and a common loyalty. But this doesn't mean that immigrants forget their past. On the contrary, immi-

grants from the same country tend to create their own neighborhoods and establish their native religious and cultural institutions. Most immigrant parents try to teach their children the language, traditions, religious customs, and moral outlook that is their heritage. Many cities and communities have ethnic festivals (featuring ethnic food, songs, dances, stories, and arts and crafts) to bring together people who share a common heritage. Some festivals are sponsored by one group (for example, people of Greek, Irish, or Polish descent). Others include people from dozens of different cultures. These events remind Americans that the nation is not really a melting pot at all. In fact, people now prefer to call it a salad bowl. Why? In a salad, many different elements are combined into a whole, but each ingredient also retains its individual identity. That is what happens to immigrants when they become American citizens.

29   In spite of the nation's immigrant tradition, it still isn't easy being a newcomer to the U.S. Often, there is family conflict because parents hold onto "old-country" ways while their children become Americanized. For many adult immigrants, learning English is a very difficult task. Finding a good job in this highly technological nation is another challenge. Nevertheless, most immigrants love their adopted land and live happily in it. The U.S. has given many people a sense of hope and safety that they never had before. In return, immigrants have enriched their adopted land with their skills, talents, ideas, and hard work. The U.S.A. is a strong and prosperous country largely because it is a nation of immigrants.

AFTER YOU READ

I. Getting the Message

A. *On each blank line, write the letter of the phrase that correctly completes each sentence.*

1. According to paragraph 1, John F. Kennedy wrote *A Nation of Immigrants* _____.
   a. after he became president
   b. before he became president

2. Paragraphs 3 and 4 suggest that Americans speak English because _____.
   a. the first Europeans to explore the area were English
   b. the majority of the American colonists were English

3. According to paragraph 16, the U.S. today has _____.
   a. more Hispanics than African-Americans
   b. more African-Americans than Hispanics

4. According to paragraph 20, Puerto Rico is _____.
   a. an American state
   b. a U.S. commonwealth

5. Paragraph 28 compares the U.S. to a salad bowl because _____.
   a. immigrants tend to forget their past
   b. immigrants tend to keep many traditions from their native country

B. *Answer these questions in small groups and then on a separate piece of paper. Write complete sentences.*

1. What did British immigrants give to the U.S.?

2. What three main situations have brought immigrants to the U.S.?

3. What are two main points that this chapter makes about American immigration?

II. Building Your Vocabulary

A. *These are the 15 key vocabulary words for this chapter. They are boldfaced in the reading. Pronounce these words after your teacher and discuss their meanings.*

alien	flee	permanent
ancestry	foreign	persecution
bilingual	immigrant	refugee
double	motive	restriction
expire	oppression	visa

B. *Complete these sentences with some of the key vocabulary words. Make the nouns plural if necessary, and put each verb into the correct tense and form.*

1. Refugees come to the U.S. after they _____ from their native country because of religious or political persecution.

2. People who leave their native land and come to live in the U.S. are called _____ or resident _____.

3. A passport is issued by a traveler's native country. A(n) _____ is issued by the country the traveler wishes to enter.

4. Travelers should leave the country before their visa _____.

5. _____ are people who come to the U.S. for protection and safety. If they returned to their native country, their lives might be in danger.

6. Two words that refer to cruel treatment of a group of people are _____ and _____.

7. From 1920 to 1970, the population of the U.S. increased from 100 million to 200 million. In other words, the population _____.

(continued on the next page)

8. One common reason or _____ for coming to the U.S. is to earn more money.

9. At some ethnic festivals, food and handmade items representing many _____ countries are sold.

10. A person who can speak two languages is _____.

III. Sharpening Reading Skills

Context Clues   Many words in English have more than one meaning. To understand what you read, you need to study the *context* (general situation) in which a particular word appears. This means that you should study the words and sentences that surround a word you don't know.

Read the paragraphs that contain the following words. On each line, write the letter of meaning as it is used in each paragraph.

1. The word *present* sometimes means "a gift." But what does it mean in paragraph 2? _____
   a. now, at the current time
   b. in the near future

2. In a science fiction movie, the word *aliens* means "creatures from another planet." But what does it mean in paragraph 6? _____
   a. foreign-born noncitizens living in the country
   b. illegal residents of the U.S.

3. The word *declined* sometimes means "refused." But what does it mean in the first sentence of paragraph 9? _____
   a. increased
   b. decreased

4. The word *admit* sometimes means "acknowledge or confess." But what does *admitted* mean in paragraph 11? _____
   a. allowed in
   b. refused admission to

IV. Understanding Idioms and Expressions

Use the following expressions to complete the sentences on page 69. The numbers in parentheses give the paragraphs in which the expressions are used.

from time to time (11)	old country (29)
great leap (6)	population explosion (13)
land of opportunity (5)	salad bowl (28)
melting pot (28)	standard of living (21)

1. An immigrant's homeland is sometimes referred to as the

   _____.

2. Because the U.S. is a nation made up of people from many different countries, it has been called a(n) _____ or a(n)

   _____.

3. The number of people living in the U.S. increased a great deal in a short time. This was called a(n) _____.

4. To attract Europeans to the U.S., the country was advertised as a(n)

   _____, where workers could find good jobs.

5. Many immigrants come to the U.S. to get higher-paying jobs so that they and their families can have a higher _____.

6. _____ means something happens occasionally and repeatedly.

7. When conditions were bad in some European countries, many people moved to the U.S. American immigration took a(n) _____.

V. Taking Words Apart

A. Names of Languages

In English, most names of languages end with -ese, -an, -ish, or -ch. In most cases, the same word is used to refer to the people or products of that country. Next to each country, write the name of the language or languages spoken there. Work in small groups. Use a dictionary, almanac, or encyclopedia if necessary.

Examples

France _____French_____
the Philippines _____Pilipino, English, Tagalog_____

1. Canada _____
2. China _____
3. Germany _____
4. Greece _____
5. Holland _____
6. India _____

7. Italy _____
8. Korea _____
9. Poland _____
10. Puerto Rico _____
11. Russia _____
12. Vietnam _____

B. Word Parts

In a dictionary, find the meanings of these word parts and write them on the blank lines.

Example

refuge in the word *refugee*: _____protection_____

1. *migrate* in the word *migration:* _____
2. *bi-* and *lingua-* in the word *bilingual:* _____ _____
3. *ex-* in the words *exile* and *explosion:* _____

VI. Practicing Sentence Patterns

In English, many different words and expressions can be used to contrast ideas. Some of them are but, however, nevertheless, in spite of, and on the contrary. Reread paragraphs 13, 28, and 29 and find examples of these words in sentences. With a partner, discuss the ideas that are being contrasted in the sentences. Then write your own sentences with contrasting thoughts.

1. _____, but _____.
2. In spite of the bad weather, I want _____.
3. I like _____.
   However, _____.
4. Your friend isn't _____.
   On the contrary, _____.
5. Being an immigrant is difficult. Nevertheless, _____
   _____.

VII. Sharing Ideas

A. Issues

Debate these issues in small groups. Then choose one and write about it.

1. Should immigrants live in neighborhoods with people from their native country? Or is it better to "mainstream" and mingle more with Americans and immigrants from other countries?
2. Should states provide free services—such as education and health care—to illegal aliens and their children?
3. Should states that have a small immigrant population contribute money to states with large numbers of immigrants to help provide funds for their needs?

B. On a Personal Note

Write about one of these topics.

1. People used to talk about immigrants "assimilating" (becoming similar to the people in their new country). Now, Americans talk about cultural diversity and about accepting and appreciating the customs of immigrants. In what areas of life do you think immigrants should assimilate? In what areas should they retain the customs and lifestyle of their native country? Consider moral outlook, attire, food, marriage customs, childrearing practices, language, and so on.

2. If you ever decide to move to another country, which country would you choose and why?

3. Are you an immigrant, student, or visitor in the U.S.? If so, write about why you came. Did you find what you wanted?

The African-American

An actress playing the role of
Congresswoman Barbara Jordan

BEFORE YOU READ

Discuss

1. What do you know about the history of African-Americans in the U.S.?

2. What famous African-Americans can you name? Why are they famous?

3. Name some difficulties that a person can overcome. Name some things that a person can be overcome by.

Guess

Try to answer the questions. Then look for the answers in the reading.

1. What percentage of the American population is African-American?

   Check (✓) one:

   _____ 4%   _____ 13%   _____ 21%

2. When did slavery end throughout the U.S.? Check (✓) one:

   _____ 1820   _____ 1865   _____ 1895

The African-American

1
    We shall **overcome,** we shall overcome
We shall overcome some day!
Oh deep in my heart, I do believe
We shall overcome some day!

These words are a variation of a song written in 1901. Portions of the melody go back even further. Yet, when Americans hear it, they think of the civil rights movement in the mid-twentieth century. Every year, Americans hear this beautiful song over and over on radio and TV, especially on Martin Luther King Jr.'s birthday (celebrated the third Monday in January) and during Black History Month (February).

2
    Most of today's black Americans are descendants of Africans brought to the U.S.A. by force and sold into slavery. After slavery was **abolished**, **segregation** in the South and **discrimination** in the North kept blacks second-class citizens for almost another century. Conditions have greatly improved for black Americans during the past 50 years. Among this nation's 35 million blacks are many successful, important, and famous people. However, as a group, African-Americans remain a disadvantaged minority. Their **struggle** for equal opportunity has been won in the courts of law, but they are still struggling for the respect and prosperity that most other Americans enjoy.

✔ Check Your Comprehension

What problems are African-Americans still trying to overcome?

Slavery—From Beginning to End

3
    In the fifteenth century, Europeans began to import **slaves** from the African continent. The discovery of the Americas increased the demand for cheap labor and therefore increased the slave trade. During the next 400 years, slave traders **kidnapped** about

15 million Africans and sold them into slavery. When the American Civil War began in 1860, there were about 4.5 million blacks in the United States, most of them slaves.

4   The vast majority of slaves lived in the South, where they worked in cotton, tobacco, and sugar-cane fields. Most were deprived of a formal education, although a few were taught to read and write. Their African religious practices were discouraged, and they were forced to convert to Christianity.

5   The slaves suffered greatly, both physically and emotionally. They worked long hours in the fields. They lived in crowded, primitive houses. Some were abused by cruel masters. Often, slave owners separated black families by selling a slave's husband, wife, or child. *Uncle Tom's Cabin*, a famous novel about southern slavery, emphasized all these evils. The book aroused so much antislavery feeling in the North that Abraham Lincoln said to its author, Harriet Beecher Stowe, "So you're the little woman who wrote the book that made this great war."

6   The "great war" that Lincoln was talking about was, of course, the American Civil War, also called (primarily in the South) the War between the States. Slavery was the **underlying** cause of this war. The agricultural South depended on slave labor to work the fields of its large **plantations.** The industrialized North had no use for slave labor, and slavery was against the law there. Northerners considered slavery a great evil, and, in fact, some white Northerners helped blacks escape to one of the free states. By the mid-nineteenth century, the nation was divided between slave states and free states. Whenever a new state wanted to enter the Union, the question of whether it would be slave or free was raised. Finally, the South decided to leave the Union and become a separate country—the Confederate States of America. President Lincoln would not allow this. In order to keep the U.S. united, Lincoln led his nation into a civil war. (For further information about Lincoln and the Civil War, see Chapter 23.) The war ended in 1865 with the North victorious, the country reunited, and slavery abolished.

7   In 1863, 2 years before the war ended, Lincoln's Emancipation Proclamation freed the slaves in the Confederate states. Shortly after the war ended in 1865, the Thirteenth Amendment to the Constitution freed all slaves. A few years later, the Fourteenth and Fifteenth Amendments gave the former slaves full civil rights, including giving African-American men the right to vote.

✔ **Check Your Comprehension**   *Why were there slaves in the South but not in the North?*

Freedom and Its Difficulties

8   By 1870, black Americans had been declared citizens with all the rights guaranteed to every citizen. But they were members of a **conspicuous** minority within a white society. Furthermore, most black Americans were uneducated, unskilled, and unprepared to provide for their own basic needs. With freedom, they found many new problems—legal, social, and economic.

9   After the Civil War, blacks began moving to the big cities in the North, and this trend continued in the twentieth century. In the North, blacks found greater freedom, but con-

ditions were still difficult and opportunities limited. Discrimination in the sale and rental of housing forced blacks into poor, crowded, mostly black communities.

10   Blacks who remained in the South endured even worse conditions. Southern blacks were forced to obey state laws (called Jim Crow laws) that kept them segregated from whites. Blacks and whites went to different schools, drank from different water fountains, used different public bathrooms, ate in different restaurants, and were buried in different cemeteries. Blacks were required to sit in the back of buses, even when there were plenty of seats in the front. For southern blacks, there was no justice in the courts of law. Once accused of a crime, blacks were almost certain to be found guilty by all-white juries.

11   Southern whites who wished to keep the power of the vote from the large black population of the South used the threat of violence to discourage blacks from registering to vote. When a black person did try to register, whites used many unfair ways to stop them—such as forcing blacks to pay a tax on the right to vote or to take a very difficult reading test.

✔ **Check Your Comprehension**   *In what ways were blacks kept separate from whites in the South?*

The Civil Rights Movement

12   The first change in the South's segregated way of life came in 1954 when the United States Supreme Court declared that no state could send students to different public schools based on race. After this historic decision, many other discriminatory practices were declared illegal.

13   The Supreme Court's school-desegregation decision stimulated the hopes of blacks for a better life in the U.S. During the mid-1950s, blacks throughout the nation began demanding equal rights and taking steps to accomplish this goal. There were **boycotts** (large numbers of people refusing to buy certain services or products). There were sit-ins (groups that included African-Americans sitting peacefully for hours at lunch counters or in restaurants that refused to serve them). There were freedom rides (busloads of northern liberals coming to the South to force integration of public **facilities**). And there were **protest** marches (large groups of people walking in the streets carrying signs that stated their goals). In many of these activities, African-Americans were joined by white Americans.

14   During the 1960s, the greatest black leader was Dr. Martin Luther King Jr. In 1955, King was a young Baptist minister in Montgomery, Alabama, when he formed an organization to boycott his city's buses. Because of regulations requiring blacks to sit in the back of the bus and to give their seats to whites if the bus got crowded, nearly all of Montgomery's 50,000 blacks refused to ride the city's buses for more than a year. Eventually, the U.S. Supreme Court declared that dividing buses into black and white sections was unconstitutional, and therefore, illegal.

15   The Montgomery bus boycott made Dr. King a famous man and the unofficial leader of the nation's growing civil rights movement. King's philosophy showed the influence

of his Christian beliefs and the example of Mohandas Gandhi, the great Indian leader whose nonviolent protests helped to free his country from British control. Like Gandhi, King urged people to refuse to obey evil laws and regulations, but to protest without fighting and without resisting arrest. For more than a decade, King led nonviolent protests and traveled around the country speaking to American audiences both in person and on television. His most famous speech was delivered in 1963 in front of the Lincoln Memorial in Washington, D.C., before a live audience of 200,000 and a TV audience that included almost the entire nation. His message included these memorable words: "I have a dream that one day this nation will rise up and live out the true meaning of its creed: 'We hold these truths to be self-evident; that all men are created equal.'"

16   In 1964, at the age of 35, Dr. King became the youngest person ever to win the Nobel Peace Prize. During the next few years, his concerns expanded from the problems of segregation in the South to discrimination in the North and, finally, to the suffering of poor people of all races. Dr. King was organizing a poor people's march at the time of his **assassination**, on April 4, 1968. He once said that the assassination of Gandhi only "shot him into the hearts of humanity." Surely the tragic killing of Dr. Martin Luther King Jr. led to the same result. Today, a great many buildings, streets, and schools are named after him, and his birthday is a national holiday.

17   During the 1960s, Americans of African descent rejected the term Negro and began referring to themselves as *black*. (Today, however, many prefer to be called *African-American*.) The popular slogan "Black is beautiful" expressed their newfound pride. Blacks also developed a greater sense of identification with their African heritage. African hair styles and clothing became fashionable. Courses in black history became common in college curricula as blacks became interested in studying about their African past and their role in the development of the United States.

✓ **Check Your Comprehension** *What were some of the activities that Martin Luther King Jr. led to help African-Americans fight for their civil rights?*

African-Americans Today

18   Since the 1960s, African-American leaders have worked hard to increase two kinds of black power—economic and political. Of course, there is a connection between these two. More political power can lead to increased state and federal spending to meet African-Americans' greatest needs—for education, financial assistance, job training, and better housing. Many urban blacks still live in poor neighborhoods, with deteriorating and abandoned buildings and empty lots. In these slum areas, the crime rate is high, drug dealers and addicts are common, and residents fear violent gangs.

19   Poverty continues to be a significant problem for blacks. African-Americans remain far behind white Americans in employment and income levels. The unemployment rate for blacks, about 8%, is about twice that of whites. The median household income for blacks is about $28,000, compared to about $44,000 for non-Hispanic whites. About 26% of blacks are poor, compared to 11% of whites. This high poverty rate is largely because many blacks do not have skills that are needed for better-paying jobs.

20   Realizing that more education will help them get better jobs, blacks are staying in school longer now than in past decades. In 1960, only about 20% of young black adults finished high school. Today, the figure is about 75%. In 1980, about 42% of black high schools graduates enrolled in college. Today, about 60% do (compared to 67% of whites).

21   Blacks are also trying to improve their financial position by going into professions or starting their own businesses. There are now more than 600,000 black-owned companies in the U.S. And blacks are more numerous than ever in the professions—as teachers, doctors, lawyers, judges, and ministers.

22   In politics, African-American gains have been impressive. Now that more blacks are voting, more are getting elected. For example, African-Americans hold positions as mayors of big cities and as members of Congress. However, blacks are still quite underrepresented in government. Although making up 13% of the population, they hold only 1.5% of the nation's elected offices. In the mid-1990s, they held about 8,000 of the 500,000 elective jobs in the U.S.

23   In 1952, Ralph Ellison, an African-American author, wrote a book about blacks in the U.S. called The **Invisible** Man. Since the 1960s, blacks have become more visible on TV and in movies and magazines. Networks, filmmakers, and advertisers now realize that black consumers want to see their race represented. Today, African-Americans in significant numbers work as newscasters, TV actors and actresses, and movie stars.

24   Despite progress in many areas, discrimination is still part of the African-American experience. Today, federal laws prohibit racial discrimination in housing and employment. However, fear and distrust still hamper race relations. Police officers and airport customs officials are more likely to search an African-American (or other minority group member) than a white person. And African-American comedians often joke about being invisible to taxi drivers.

✔ Check Your Comprehension

What are three different areas in which African-Americans have made great progress?

Contributions—Past and Present

25   An important influence of African-American culture—nationally and internationally—has been in the field of music. The familiar "Negro spirituals," the unusual rhythms and harmonies of jazz, the sad blues melodies—all these originated with the slaves. It is often said that what is best and most original in American popular music has its roots in black culture. Important black singers, composers, and instrumentalists are too numerous to list.

26   The contributions of individual African-Americans have extended into every field. Looking back, one of the most interesting of black American scientists was George Washington Carver, the famous botanist. Carver began his life (probably in 1859) as a slave. Later, he revolutionized the agriculture of the South. From the ordinary peanut, Carver developed more than 300 products, including soap and ink. And from the sweet potato, he developed 118 products, including flour, shoe polish, and candy.

27   In recent years, many blacks have become famous in a wide range of fields. Eddie Murphy and Bill Cosby are two of several well-known black comedians. Oprah Winfrey is one of the richest and most powerful people in the entertainment industry. Two superstars—singer Michael Jackson and former basketball player Michael Jordan—have become international idols of the young. In intellectual fields as well, blacks have made great contributions. Among the many outstanding black American authors of the twentieth century are poets Gwendolyn Brooks and Maya Angelou and novelists James Baldwin, Ralph Ellison, Richard Wright, Toni Morrison, and Alice Walker. Ben Carson, an African-American surgeon, is well known for developing new methods of separating co-joined twins. In 1972, Barbara Jordan became the first black congresswoman to come from the Deep South. Since 1991, Justice Clarence Thomas has been on the U.S. Supreme Court, the highest court in the land. The Reverend Jesse Jackson has run for president a few times and has been involved in resolving international crises concerning hostages. In 2000, General Colin Powell was the first African American chosen to be secretary of state.

28   Given equal opportunities, African-Americans will continue to enrich American life. The third verse of "We Shall Overcome" says, "We shall all be free some day." Americans of goodwill hope that someday soon African-Americans will live free of prejudice and share the prosperity of the country that is, after all, their home.

AFTER YOU READ

I. Getting the Message

A. *Reread the section entitled "Slavery—From Beginning to End." Then mark each statement true (T) or false (F).*

_____   1. The slave trade was begun by Americans.

_____   2. Before the Civil War, most blacks in the U.S. lived in the South.

_____   3. Before the Civil War, some states allowed slavery and some did not.

_____   4. Northerners didn't want more slave states to enter the Union.

_____   5. None of the slaves became free until after the Civil War ended.

B. *Reread paragraphs 15 and 16. Then compare the lives and deaths of Gandhi and King.*

1. What kind of protests did both men believe in?

_____

2. How did both men die? _____

C. *Discuss the difference between* a civil war *and* the Civil War.
(Both are used in paragraph 6.)

II. Building Your Vocabulary

A. *These are the 15 key vocabulary words for this chapter. They are boldfaced in the reading. Pronounce these words after your teacher, and discuss their meanings.*

abolish	facility	protest*
assassination	invisible	segregation
boycott*	kidnap	slave
conspicuous	overcome	struggle*
discrimination	plantation	underlying

B. *Complete these sentences with some of the key vocabulary words. Make the nouns plural where necessary, and put each verb into the correct tense and form.*

1. _____ means the killing of a person for political reasons.

2. The immediate cause of the Civil War was the secession of the South, but the _____ cause of the war was slavery.

3. Southern _____ were large farms on which cotton or tobacco were grown. The work was done by _____.

4. When slavery ended in the South, _____ became the way of life. State laws required blacks and whites to live, study, and play in different places.

5. In the 1960s, northern liberals and southern blacks participated in sit-ins and marches to _____ segregation.

6. When blacks in Montgomery, Alabama, _____ the buses, they didn't ride on them.

7. Because of _____, blacks sometimes did not get jobs that they were well qualified for.

8. African-Americans' _____ for equal opportunity is not yet over.

C. *Match each word or phrase in column 1 with the phrase in column 2 that means the same thing by writing the correct numbers on the lines.*

1. the North, the U.S.   _____ cannot be seen

2. the South   _____ the Union

3. abolish   _____ very noticeable; easy to see

4. conspicuous   _____ the Confederacy

5. invisible   _____ prohibit; no longer allow

6. protest   _____ express disagreement; strongly object

---

*These words can be used as nouns or verbs.

D. *The following words help readers understand the relationship between two ideas. Match each word in column 1 with its definition in column 2 by writing the correct numbers on the lines. The numbers in parentheses give the paragraphs in which the words are used.*

1. however (2, 17, 22, 24)   _____ after a long time

2. therefore (3)   _____ but, nevertheless

3. furthermore (8)   _____ in addition, also, and

4. eventually (14)   _____ as a result, so

III. Sharpening Reading Skills

Pronouns and possessive adjectives usually refer back to the nearest appropriate noun. Find the noun that each of the following words refers back to.

Example

The cat chased *its* tail. _____cat_____
(The possessive adjective *its* refers to the cat.)

1. *They* (paragraph 5, sentence 2): _____

2. *its* (paragraph 5, last sentence): _____

3. *its* (paragraph 6, sentence 3): _____

4. *it* (paragraph 6, sentence 7): _____

5. *they* (paragraph 8, sentence 2): _____

IV. Understanding Idioms and Expressions

On each blank line, write the letter of the correct phrase to complete the sentence. The numbers in parentheses give the paragraphs in which the expressions are used.

1. *Civil rights* (1, 7, 15) refers to _____.
   a. certain rights to liberty and equal opportunity guaranteed by law
   b. rights gained after a civil war
   c. rights given to some citizens but not to others

2. *Over and over* (1) means _____.
   a. upside down
   b. many times
   c. around and around

3. *Second-class* (2) means _____.
   a. not as good as first-class
   b. a military rank
   c. a grade in school

4. Before the Civil War, *free states* (6) were those that _____.
   a. didn't tax residents
   b. gave away land
   c. didn't allow residents to own slaves

5. In the 1960s, a *sit-in* (13) was _____.
   a. a game
   b. a way to protest segregation
   c. blacks having to sit at the back of the bus

V. Taking Words Apart

A. *L-i-v-e* spells two different words. One is a verb with a short *i* sound. The other is an adjective with a long *i* sound. The plural noun *lives* also has a long *i*. There is also an adjective *alive* (pronounced with a long *i* sound).

Complete these sentences with one of these words: the noun life *or* lives, *the adjective* live *or* alive, *or the verb* live *in the correct tense. Then read the following sentences aloud to practice the pronunciation of these words.*

1. Dr. King's speeches were heard by _____ audiences and by radio and TV audiences.

2. Black slaves _____ in primitive homes. Their _____ were very difficult.

3. Martin Luther King Jr. is no longer _____. His _____ was too short. He _____ a short time.

B. *Pronounce the following words with a silent* u.

1. building   2. guilty

VI. Practicing Sentence Patterns

Quotations within Quotations   In the last few sentences in paragraph 15, the authors of this book quoted Martin Luther King Jr., who was quoting from the Declaration of Independence. Note that the quotation within the quotation uses single quotation marks.

In small groups, practice writing sentences in which someone is telling what another person said. Use double quotation marks and single quotation marks. Remember, you must close both quotations, single and double.

(continued on the next page)

Example

Bob's mother said, "I will never forget the day my grandfather told me, 'You are the most wonderful child in the whole world.'"

VII. Sharing Ideas

A. Issues

Debate these issues in small groups. Then choose one and write about it.

1. *Affirmative action* is the name for a policy that was quite widespread in the latter part of the twentieth century. It gave members of certain groups greater consideration (for example, for jobs or admission to competitive colleges) to make up for past discrimination and to achieve greater diversity in the workplace and on college campuses. Is affirmative action a good idea?

2. Americans believe that people should have freedom of speech. However, they also believe that no one should say insulting things about another person's race, religion, or ethnic group. Sometimes these two beliefs conflict with each other. Which is more important to protect—the right to say whatever one thinks or the right to be protected from verbal abuse?

B. On a Personal Note

Write about one of these topics.

1. Have you ever experienced discrimination? What happened? Tell how you were treated, how it made you feel, and how you responded.

2. In any country you've lived in, have you noticed that some racial, religious, or ethnic minority group has been segregated or discriminated against? What group is it? How are they treated?

3. Do you believe that people should marry someone of their own race, or do you think that it doesn't matter?

8 | Religion in American Life

Norman Rockwell's painting, "The Golden Rule"

BEFORE YOU READ

Discuss

1. What do you think is the meaning of the painting above?

2. Do you think Americans are religious? What evidence supports your answer?

3. Do you think a total separation of government and religion is good or bad for a country?

Guess

Try to answer the questions. Then look for the answers in the reading.

1. What percentage of Americans are Christian? Check (✓) one:

   _____ 46%   _____ 66%   _____ 86%

2. About what percentage of Americans attend religious services regularly? Check (✓) one:

   _____ 25%   _____ 45%   _____ 65%

3. Are American high school students allowed to say prayers in school? Check (✓) one:

   _____ Yes   _____ No

Religion in American Life

Major American Religions

1   Christianity (belief in the teachings of Jesus Christ) has always been the dominant American faith. Today, about 86% of Americans are Christian (approximately 59% Protestant and 27% Catholic). However, this is a nation with great religious diversity. American Christians are divided into many different groups, including Roman Catholic, the various national **denominations** of the Eastern Orthodox churches, and hundreds of different Protestant denominations and sects. The largest Protestant groups are the Southern Baptist Convention, the United Methodist Church, and the National Baptist Convention. Among the non-Christian religions, Judaism is the largest, with roughly 2% of the population. In addition, the U.S.A. has a great variety of other religions, including about 5 million Muslims, nearly 2 million Buddhists, and about 800,000 Hindus. Americans are proud of their nation's religious diversity and of the religious freedom that all enjoy.

2   Perhaps the greatest influence that Protestantism has had on American life comes from its philosophy regarding a person's relationship to work. This philosophy—commonly called the Protestant work ethic—stresses the **moral** value of work, self-discipline, and personal responsibility. According to this ethic, people prove their worth to themselves and to God by working hard, being honest and thrifty, and avoiding luxury, excessive pleasure, and waste. The accumulation of wealth is not considered evil unless it leads to a life of idleness and **sin.** The Protestant work ethic has much in common with capitalism and with the American emphasis on financial success, practicality, efficiency, and self-sufficiency.

3   Two interesting Protestant groups founded in the U.S. are the Mormons and the Christian Scientists. The Mormons (officially known as the Church of Jesus Christ of

Latter-day Saints) were organized in New York in 1830. Because it was customary for Mormon men to have more than one wife, Mormons were forced out of several established communities. They traveled westward and settled in the unpopulated valley of the Great Salt Lake in Utah, where they built a successful community. Then the federal government passed laws against **polygamy** and refused to admit Utah as a state until 1896, after the Mormons discontinued this practice. Today, there are 4.8 million Mormon church members in the U.S. Most of them live in Utah and in eastern Idaho, where they are the major religious sect.

4   The Christian Science Church was founded by Mary Baker Eddy in 1879. Christian Scientists believe that healing of sickness results from **spiritual** understanding rather than standard medical treatment. The Christian Science movement now has about 3,000 **congregations** in 57 countries. About two-thirds of these are in the U.S.

5   Another interesting Protestant group is the Amish. Originally from Switzerland, this group (about 40,000 people) is now centered in the U.S. and Canada. Within the U.S., they have developed farming communities in 23 states, mostly in Pennsylvania and the midwestern states of Ohio, Indiana, Iowa, and Illinois. The Amish are easy to spot. Their clothing is old-fashioned and plain. The men have beards and wear wide-brimmed hats and the women wear long dresses and bonnets. Jewelry and buttons are not allowed. The Amish travel in horse-drawn wagons because their religion forbids them to use cars. They have no telephones or electricity in their homes. Amish children are educated through eighth grade only and are trained to be farmers.

6   The combined Protestant groups form the largest religious body in the United States. But Roman Catholicism is by far the largest unified religious group. Since many Catholics send their children to parochial (private religious) schools, Catholic funds have helped to build thousands of elementary and secondary schools, plus many fine colleges and universities. Catholics have also played a prominent role in American politics. However, not until 1960, when John F. Kennedy was elected president, did a Catholic hold the highest office in the land.

7   The largest non-Christian religion in the United States is Judaism. There are about 6 million Jews in the U.S. They belong to three major groups: Orthodox, Conservative, and Reform. During the Sabbath, observed from sundown Friday until sundown Saturday, Orthodox Jews do not work, and they travel only on foot. Jewish tradition imposes certain dietary **restrictions**, **prohibiting** pork, certain seafoods, and the serving of milk products at meals that include meat or poultry.

8   The Jewish people are relatively few in number in the U.S. and worldwide, but their intellectual and cultural contributions have been very great indeed. Among the great twentieth-century musicians, for example, were many Jewish violinists, pianists, and composers. American Jews have also been prominent lawyers, judges, authors, and doctors. Twentieth-century thought was greatly influenced by the original ideas of three European-born Jews: Karl Marx (the founder of communism), Albert Einstein (one of the founders of the Atomic Age), and Sigmund Freud (the founder of psychoanalysis).

9   Two other religions of significant size in the U.S. are Islam and Buddhism. Islam is the second-largest religion in the world (after Christianity). The word *Islam* means both "surrender" and "peace." The name refers to the peace that comes from surrendering to the will of God. Worldwide, Islam has about 1 billion followers in many different

countries. It is the religion preached by the prophet Muhammad, an Arab born in Mecca about A.D. 570. Believers in Islam are called *Muslims*. During the month of Ramadan, the ninth month in the Muslim lunar year, Muslims are required to fast (not eat or drink) from sunrise to sunset. At the end of this period, they celebrate a three-day festival, the Breaking of the Fast (*Bairam*). Buddhism is the religion founded by Siddhartha Gautama (who was given the title *Buddha*, which means "enlightened one"). Americans take great interest in ideas from Eastern religions such as Buddhism and Hinduism, which is the dominant religion in India. Many have found great benefits in meditation. Many are fascinated by the idea of reincarnation (the transference of a soul from one living being to another).

✔ Check Your Comprehension

In terms of numbers of members, what are the three main religions in the U.S.?

Religion and Government

10   Many immigrants came to the American colonies to escape religious persecution. Therefore, it was natural that the nation's founders demanded legal guarantees of religious freedom. The First Amendment to the Constitution forbids the establishment of an official national religion and prohibits governmental assistance to religious groups. It also prohibits state or federal interference with religious institutions or practices.

11   Separation of church and state has been interpreted to mean that any institution supported by the federal government or a state government must be free from the influence of religion. In many communities where Christian symbols (such as scenes depicting the birth of Christ) once decorated public buildings, citizens have filed lawsuits claiming that the presence of these symbols on public property is unconstitutional. There have been many other arguments about exactly what **violates** separation of church and state. Can a state government spend public funds to bus children to parochial schools? Can parents who send their children to parochial schools receive tax credits because they are not using the public schools? These matters are often hotly debated in legislative bodies, courtrooms, school districts, and election campaigns.

12   And what about **prayer** in the public schools? At one time, it was common for schools to begin the school day with a prayer. But **atheists** (people who don't believe in any God) objected, saying that required time for prayer violated separation of church and state. The government, they said, must not support any particular religion. But, in addition, it must avoid imposing upon people the idea of religion itself, the belief that a supernatural being influences human destiny. In 1963, the Supreme Court banned compulsory prayer in public schools. After that, it was assumed that any **worship** in public buildings was forbidden. However, in recent years, American high school students have been allowed to organize prayer clubs just as they are allowed to form other extracurricular special-interest groups. But these prayer sessions must be voluntary, student-run, and conducted outside of class time.

13   Of course, religious people want their government to behave in ways that their reli-

gion considers moral. When the laws of a religion and the laws of the state contradict each other, heated arguments develop. The best example is the issue of abortion. In 1973, the U.S. Supreme Court said that states could not make abortion illegal. Thus began the continuing struggle between those who are "pro-choice" (those who believe that a woman should have the legal right to end a pregnancy) and those who are "pro-life" (those who consider it murder to abort a human fetus). At present, abortion in the early months of pregnancy is legal in the U.S. But members of the "religious right" (more conservative religious people) continue to push for a change in this Supreme Court decision and often demonstrate outside medical clinics that perform abortions.

14   Although Americans strongly believe in separation of church and state, the vast majority have always been believers in God. Therefore, although it may seem inconsistent, many official American ceremonies and documents make reference to God. Sessions of Congress and state legislatures begin with prayers. The national motto (printed on U.S. money) is "In God We Trust." The Pledge of Allegiance to the flag calls the United States "one nation under God." These examples reflect the general American attitude—that there is a God, but that people are free to believe in God or not and to worship in whatever way they choose.

✔ **Check Your Comprehension**   *What does separation of church and state mean? Give some examples.*

Are Americans Religious?

15   History tells us that as societies become more industrial and more technological, they also tend to become more **secular** (less religious). This has happened to some extent in the U.S. but probably less so than in Europe. Roughly two-thirds of American adults are members of a church or synagogue. However, only about 40% to 45% say that they attend religious services on a weekly basis. What about the younger generation? Responses to a study of more than 1,000 children (ages 6 to 14) revealed that 95% believe in God, almost 50% go to religious services weekly, and about 80% pray. According to another poll, 90% of Americans believe in God, and 80% believe in life after death.

16   Generalizations about what religion really means to Americans are quite difficult to make. Religious participation varies immensely depending on many factors, including race, age, social class, economic condition, amount of education, and region of the country. For example, African-Americans attend church in greater numbers than any other race, with about 53% reporting attendance within the prior week. Older people, married people with children, and middle-income people are also more regular churchgoers than younger people, single people, the poor, and the rich. States such as Oklahoma, Arkansas, Tennessee, and Alabama report higher weekly church attendance than other areas of the country. These states are in the area of the country commonly called the *Bible Belt*. Many people in this area are religious fundamentalists—that is, they believe in the literal truth of the Bible. Also, they take their religion very seriously, so their religious views influence their attitudes toward many secular matters.

17   Clearly, many people who believe in God do not participate much in organized religion. Still, religion is important in several ways. It provides a personal identity, social contacts, and important rituals. Social groups, close friendships, and marriages are often formed with members of one's own religion. (However, intermarriage is increasingly more common.) In the U.S., religion provides the customs and ceremonies that mark life's most important events—the naming of a baby, coming-of-age ceremonies, weddings, and funerals. Perhaps most important, many religions promise the believer some form of **eternal** life, which is a great comfort, especially to the old and the sick.

18   The major American religions also provide the comfort of a personal God to turn to in times of trouble. However, Americans have never believed in simply waiting for God to solve their problems. In the U.S., religious faith lives side by side with a strong belief in free will and an admiration of self-reliance. Ben Franklin (the great eighteenth-century writer, inventor, and statesman) said, "God helps them that help themselves." During World War II, this same idea was expressed in the saying, "Praise the Lord, and pass the ammunition." Americans do not believe in accepting misfortune as God's will. They count on their own actions to improve the quality of life. Some turn to their religious leaders for advice in dealing with family problems or making important decisions in their lives. But secular advisers such as psychiatrists and psychologists have mostly taken over the counseling role.

19   If organized religion can fulfill so many human needs, why have so many people rejected it? Some feel that science now answers many questions that were once explained only by religion. (But many scientists are themselves religious and argue that the beauty and order of the universe are evidence of a divine creator.) Some point to all the pain and suffering in the world and say that if a personal, all-powerful God really **existed**, human life would be less painful. (Believers respond that God doesn't cause the cruelty that people show to one another.) Some people believe in God but dislike the rigid rules of organized religion. Many religions require followers to give up certain pleasures. Some people see no purpose in the willpower required. Finally, there is great competition for people's limited amount of leisure time, and many people prefer other activities to sitting in church.

20   Those who do make it to religious services regularly now have a new argument to make to their absent friends. Research has revealed that people who attend church services regularly live longer and enjoy better mental and physical health. Why? Two of many possible reasons are these: Churchgoing provides social support, and religious faith reduces stress. And less stress is something nearly all Americans seek and need.

AFTER YOU READ

I. Getting the Message

A. *Reread the paragraphs indicated in parentheses. Then mark each statement true* (T) *or false* (F).

_____ 1. Protestants and Christians are all Catholic. (1)

_____ 2. The national religion of the U.S. is Protestantism. (10)

_____ 3. In the U.S., all forms of prayer have been banned from public buildings. (12)

_____ 4. Abortion is legal in the U.S., but some religious people consider it immoral. (13)

_____ 5. The majority of Americans attend church services at least once a week. (15)

B. *Reread the paragraphs indicated in parentheses after each question. Discuss the questions in small groups. Then write answers using complete sentences.*

1. How does separation of church and state protect religious groups? Name two ways. (10)

   _____

   _____

2. How does separation of church and state protect the rights and freedom of individual citizens? Name two ways. (11–12)

   _____

   _____

3. What evidence supports the idea that most Americans believe in God? Name two points. (14–15)

   _____

   _____

II. Building Your Vocabulary

A. *These are the 15 key vocabulary words for this chapter. They are boldfaced in the reading. Pronounce these words after your teacher, and discuss their meanings.*

atheist	moral	secular
congregation	polygamy	sin*
denomination	prayer	spiritual
eternal	prohibit	violate
exist	restriction	worship*

---

*These words can be used as nouns or verbs. As a noun, *worship* is uncountable.

B. *Complete these sentences with some of the key vocabulary words on page 89. Make the nouns plural if necessary, and put each verb into the correct tense and form.*

1. A church is a place of _____.

2. In most religions, the idea of life after death refers to a(n) _____ life rather than a physical life. Life after death refers to _____ life, which continues forever.

3. _____ is illegal in the United States and is also generally considered a(n) _____.

4. Some people believe that God does not _____; these people are called _____.

5. A teacher cannot display a prayer in a public school classroom. That would be against the law because it would _____ laws about separation of church and state.

6. A religious _____ is a major division or branch of a particular religion. (Smaller groups are called *sects*.)

7. A(n) _____ is a group of people who attend the same individual church or synagogue. They often say _____ together.

8. _____ activities do not involve religion.

C. *Match each word or words in column 1 with the word or words in column 2 that mean the opposite (their antonyms) by writing the correct numbers on the lines.*

1. belief in God	_____ allow
2. forbid, prohibit, restrict	_____ monogamy
3. moral, ethical	_____ religious, sectarian
4. parochial	_____ public, secular
5. physical	_____ atheism
6. polygamy	_____ spiritual, mental
7. pro-choice	_____ sinful, evil
8. prominent	_____ unnoticed, unknown
9. secular	_____ mandatory, required
10. voluntary	_____ pro-life

III. Sharpening Reading Skills

Euphemisms   People sometimes use *euphemisms* when they want to talk about something unpleasant or improper in a nicer way. For example, a basement apartment is sometimes called a *garden apartment.* Readers need to be aware of euphemisms so that they are not fooled by them.

   This chapter mentions two common euphemisms used in the abortion debate: "I'm *pro-choice.*" That sounds better than saying, "I support abortions (killing unborn children)." "I'm *pro-life*" sounds better than saying, "I oppose abortions. I want to deny women the right to decide for themselves whether or not to have a baby." It usually sounds better to be *for* something than to be *against* something, so both sides of the abortion issue claim to be in favor of something good. (Choice is good; life is good.)

Here are some other widely used euphemisms. Can you translate them into simple, direct English? Work with a partner. Then share your answers with your classmates.

1. He's a senior citizen.

2. She passed away.

3. She was laid to rest yesterday.

4. That's an inner-city neighborhood.

5. That child is a slow learner.

6. He's living on a very limited income.

7. She's expecting.

8. He's terminally ill.

IV. Understanding Idioms and Expressions

On each blank line, write the letter of the correct phrase to complete the sentence. The numbers in parentheses give the paragraphs in which the expressions are used.

1. The *Protestant work ethic* (2) encourages people to _____.
   a. give a lot of money to the poor
   b. work hard and be successful

2. *Separation of church and state* (11) is good for Americans because it _____.
   a. limits religious freedom
   b. protects religious freedom

3. The *Bible Belt* (16) is _____.
   a. a ropelike belt worn by a religious person
   b. a section of the U.S. known for its conservative religious beliefs

4. *Free will* (18) refers to _____.
   a. God's control over human destiny
   b. personal control over human destiny

(continued on the next page)

5. *Willpower* (19) means _____.
   a. the ability to resist doing something pleasant that you shouldn't do
   b. a legal document telling what will happen to a person's money after his or her death

6. To *make it* (20) to religious services means to _____.
   a. attend
   b. perform

V. Taking Words Apart

A. *Underline the correct word to complete each sentence.*

1. He's an atheist. He doesn't believe in the (*exist / existence*) of God. Do you believe that a supernatural being (*exists / existence*)?

2. Does it (*violate / violation*) separation of church and state to say "under God" in the Pledge of Allegiance to the flag?

3. Many religions have (*restrict / restrictions*) about what its members can eat and wear.

4. He (*prayed / prayers*) for his little girl's recovery from her serious illness. When she got well, he said, "God answered my (*pray / prayers*)."

5. People (*congregate / congregation*) along a parade route to watch a parade. People who attend the same church are called a (*congregate / congregation*).

B. *Discuss the meanings of these two words beginning with self-. The numbers in parentheses give the paragraphs in which the words appear.*

self-discipline (2)   self-reliance (18)

C. *Study the meanings of these word parts. Then use them to complete the words defined below.*

con- = with, together	*inter-* = between	*poly-* = many
dis-, il-, un- = not	*mis-* = bad	

1. _____fere (try to stop an action between others)

2. _____marriage (marriage between people of different religions or races)

3. _____legal (not legal)

4. _____fortune (bad luck)

5. _____gregation (a group of people coming together for religious worship)

6. _____populated (nobody lives there)

7. _____continue (stop doing something)

8. _____gamy (multiple marriages at the same time)

VI. Practicing Sentence Patterns

Paragraphs 12 and 15 contain questions beginning with the words *What about . . . ?* This is an informal question phrase often used in conversation to ask for more information or to make a suggestion about doing something. There is no verb in this question. *What about* is usually followed by a gerund or other noun (perhaps with an adjective before it). Here are two more examples:

If you don't like the red sweater, what about buying the blue one? (a suggestion)

I know that Joe never goes to church, but what about his wife? (asking for information)

Now write a sentence of your own using the expression what about.

What about _____?

VII. Sharing Ideas

A. Issues

Debate these issues in small groups. Then choose one and write about it.

1. What if a person's religion requires an act that the government considers illegal? Which is more important—obeying the laws of one's country or one's religion?

2. Should a government have the right to force a citizen to go to war and kill an enemy? What if that person's religion forbids killing?

3. Most religions have rules about how a person must and must not behave. Does religion enrich a person's life enough to make up for this loss of personal freedom?

4. What's the difference between a crime and a sin? Can an act be a crime and not a sin and vice versa?

B. On a Personal Note

Write about one of these topics.

1. Do you believe in some sort of life after death? If so, describe it.

2. Over the last several millennia, has religion increased human misery or human happiness?

3. Write about a religious group that you think has some interesting or unusual beliefs or customs.

9 American Education: The First 12 Years

The 5th Wave   By Rich Tennant

©RICHTENNANT

"This afternoon I want everyone to go on line and find all you can about Native American culture, history of the old west and discount air fares to Hawaii for the two weeks I'll be on vacation."

BEFORE YOU READ

Discuss

1. In what ways are American schools different from those in other countries?

2. Do you think boys and girls should receive the same education and be in classes together?

3. Should school attendance be required? Why? Until what age?

Guess

Try to answer the questions. Then look for the answers in the reading.

1. What percentage of American adults are high school graduates? Check (✓) one:

   _____ 43%   _____ 63%   _____ 83%

2. Who sets guidelines for American public schools? Check (✓) one:

   _____ the federal government   _____ the 50 state governments

American Education: The First 12 Years

The Goals and Purpose of Public Education

1   American **elementary** and secondary education is a vast and complex enterprise. From **kindergarten** through high school, about 72 million students are enrolled in school. To educate this huge number of students, more than 3 million teachers are employed. They are by far the largest professional group in the country.

2   In the U.S.A., everyone has both the right and the obligation to become educated. Even children with physical or mental disabilities are entitled to be educated to whatever extent they can be. A lot of money is spent to provide special services and equipment for students who need extra help. For example, special assistance is provided to children who speak little or no English. In some schools, they attend English as a second language (ESL) classes for part of their schoolday and study other subjects in classes with English-speaking students. In schools where a sizable number of students speak a language other than English, a bilingual program may be offered. In transitional bilingual programs, students study English, but some **academic** subjects are taught in the native language. Students stay in these bilingual programs until they are fairly fluent in English (usually 1 to 3 years). Some bilingual programs continue to teach students at least one subject in the native language indefinitely to help them maintain fluency and literacy in their native language as well as English.

3   In order to develop an educated population (a necessity in a democracy), all states have **compulsory** school attendance laws. These laws vary from one state to another, but they generally require school attendance from ages 6 to 16. However, most students attend school at least until high school graduation, when they are 17 or 18 years old. About 83% of American adults are high school graduates.

✔ **Check Your Comprehension**   *What is the major goal of American public schools?*

Public and Private Schools

4   About 86% of American children receive their elementary and high school education in public schools. These schools have important characteristics in common:

- They are supported by state and local taxes and do not charge tuition.
- Most are neighborhood schools, open to students who live in the district.
- They are coeducational, which means that boys and girls attend the same schools and have nearly all their classes together. By providing girls with equal educational opportunity, public schools have helped to create self-sufficient American women.
- They are locally controlled. The individual states, not the federal government, are responsible for education. Public schools are required to follow some state guidelines regarding, for example, **curriculum** (what students study) and teacher qualifications. But most decisions about a school district are made by an elected board of education and the administrators that board hires. This system creates strong ties between the district's schools and its local community.
- Americans believe in separation of church and state. Therefore, American public schools are free from the influence of any religion. As a result, children of many different religions feel comfortable attending public schools. This secular public school system helps a diverse population share a common cultural heritage.

5   Private schools can be divided into two categories: **parochial** (supported by a particular religious group) and independent (not affiliated with any religious group). Private schools charge tuition and are not under direct public control, although many states set educational standards for them. To attend a private school, a student must apply and be accepted. Parochial (mostly Catholic) schools make up the largest group of private schools.

✔ **Check Your Comprehension**   *Summarize five important characteristics of public schools. What are some differences between public and private schools?*

Teaching Methods and Approaches

6   American education has been greatly influenced by John Dewey, a famous twentieth-century philosopher. Dewey believed that the only worthwhile knowledge was information that could be used. He considered it pointless to make students memorize useless facts that they would quickly forget. Rather, he felt, schools should teach thinking processes and skills. Dewey also influenced teaching techniques. Children learn best by doing, he said. Applying this idea today, science classes involve experimentation; the study of music involves making music; democratic principles are practiced in the student council; school projects encourage creativity and **teamwork**. Children don't spend the day working silently and alone. They often work in groups, share ideas, and complete projects together.

7   What do American schools see as their educational responsibility to students? The scope is very broad indeed. Schools teach a lot of skills and information once left

for parents to teach at home. For example, it's common for the curriculum to include driver's education, cooking and sewing classes, sex education, and a campaign against smoking and the use of illegal drugs. Also, some schools try to improve children's behavior by teaching them how to control anger and settle arguments in peaceful ways (a skill called *conflict resolution*). In some classrooms values and good character are discussed, as well.

"A lot of homework?"

Check Your Comprehension *What were John Dewey's ideas about what and how students should learn?*

Early Childhood Education

8   Free public education begins with kindergarten, usually half-day classes for 5-year-olds. At one time, the purpose of kindergarten was to teach children to get along with each other and to get used to classroom life. However, today at least half of the children who enter kindergarten have already had these experiences in nursery school or day-care settings. Therefore, kindergarten teachers have taken on the job of introducing some academics—for example, teaching letters, numbers, colors, and shapes. Still, there's a lot of time for play.

9   Most American parents want their children to attend school before the age of 5. They believe good preschools can be stimulating and valuable for children. Moreover, since most mothers have jobs, nursery school or day care is often a necessity. Nursery schools serve 3- to 5-year-olds, mostly in half-day programs. Many day-care centers take younger children also, and the children can stay for the whole day. Unlike many other countries, the U.S. has no national day-care system. Parents who place their children in preschool programs usually pay tuition, although some of these facilities are **subsidized**. Many places of business have day-care centers that serve the children of their employees. Many colleges and universities also have day-care facilities available for the children of their students and faculty.

Check Your Comprehension *What three types of preschool programs were discussed in the preceding section?*

Elementary Education

10   Formal academic work is divided into 12 levels called **grades**. One schoolyear (from late August or early September to mid-June) is required to complete each grade. Academic work—learning to read, write, and do arithmetic—begins when children enter first grade, at about age 6. Kindergarten, first grade, and second grade are commonly called the *primary grades*.

11   The first academic institution that a student attends is called *elementary school* or *grammar school*. In some school systems, elementary school goes through eighth grade. In others, there is a second division called *junior high school* or *middle school*. It usually includes grades 6–8, 5–8, or 7–9.

12   The typical schoolday is about 6 hours long and ends about 3:00 P.M. Classes are in session Monday through Friday. Traditional vacation periods include a 2-week winter vacation, a 1-week spring vacation, and a 2-month summer vacation. In addition, there are several 1-day holidays.

13   Academic subjects include language arts (reading, writing, spelling, and penmanship), mathematics, science, physical education (athletics and studying principles of good health), and social studies (mostly history and geography). Social studies emphasizes the multicultural nature of the U.S. by stressing the contributions of groups overlooked in the past: women, African-Americans, Hispanics, and non-Europeans. Elementary school programs also teach music and art if the school budget can cover these. Computer studies are also commonly a part of the elementary school curriculum.

14   In elementary school, students are grouped into classes that stay together for the schoolyear. In the primary grades, the class generally has the same teacher for most subjects, although art, music, and physical education are usually taught by **specialists** in these areas. In the upper elementary grades, students in some school systems have a different teacher for each major academic subject.

✔ **Check Your Comprehension**

How are the upper elementary grades different from the lower grades?

High School (Secondary Education)

15   American high schools have a **commitment** to offer both a general college preparatory program for those interested in higher education and **vocational** training for students who plan to enter the work force immediately after high school graduation. In American high schools, college-bound students find the courses they need for college entrance and, in addition, an opportunity to take Advanced Placement (AP) courses, for which they can earn college credit. But in the same building, other students may find work / study programs (to earn high school credit for on-the-job training).

16   Subjects are more specialized in high school than in elementary school. Social science is divided into American history, European history, and psychology. Math courses include algebra, geometry, and trigonometry. Science is divided into biology, chemistry, earth science, and physics. Most high school students study a foreign language, usually Spanish, French, or German. As in elementary school, health and physical education (gym) classes are generally required.

17   Students move from one classroom to another and study each subject with a different teacher and a different group of classmates. Many high schools group students according to academic ability and **motivation**. Some subjects are offered at two, three, or
even four different levels of difficulty.

18   The school day is very busy and very long for many high school students. Many take
five or six major academic subjects as well as physical education. During other periods,
students may be doing homework in a study hall, researching in the school library, or
participating in activities such as the school orchestra, student government, school
newspaper, or math club. Many extracurricular activities—such as team sports and dra-
matics—involve after-school practice. Students active in extracurricular activities may
be at school from early morning until dinner time. However, school activities are important. They help students find friends with similar interests, develop their talents,
gain self-confidence, and sometimes even discover their career goals.

✔ **Check Your**
Comprehension   *What two types of students must high schools serve?*
What are extracurricular activities?

School Problems and Possible Solutions

19   The quality of a child's education depends largely on where he or she goes to school.
Facilities and resources vary a lot from one school district to another. In education (as
in many other areas), money is both part of the problem and part of the solution. Most
of the money to operate American schools comes from local property taxes. As a result,
poorer communities have less money to spend on books, equipment, and teachers'
salaries. All these factors affect the quality of education. In areas where the community
is stable, the funding good, and the school environment orderly, a hardworking student
can get an excellent education. But schools in poor neighborhoods in the nation's large
cities are usually less successful. They do not always have the resources necessary to
support students with special needs. For example, some students may need help in
learning English. In some neighborhoods, the students in one classroom may have a
dozen different native languages! In poor neighborhoods, children move often and
therefore change schools often, which interferes with their education. In some inner-city
neighborhoods, some students miss school because they are afraid of violent gangs
that make walking to school dangerous.

20   Another problem is a serious **shortage** of qualified teachers. Teaching is a hard job,
and the rewards are not what they should be. Starting salaries for teachers are much
lower than for employees in many other occupations requiring a college degree. Teaching is a time-consuming job; lesson-planning and paper-grading are often done at
home. It is common for teachers to devote 60 hours a week to their job. Considering all
these factors, it's not surprising that many young adults choose other occupations.

21   Teachers and schools shouldn't be blamed for all the problems in American education. Students themselves are also responsible for how much they learn. Many students
do not study enough. Elementary schools are encouraging more studying nowadays by
retaining students (requiring them to repeat a grade) if they cannot pass tests on the
important material studied in that grade. In high school, some students are distracted

by part-time jobs, school activities, TV, and socializing. Others do not keep up with their schoolwork because of emotional problems, drinking or use of illegal drugs, or lack of motivation. About 11% drop out between the ages of 16 and 18.

22   Would public schools improve if they had more competition? Some people think so. Some parents, politicians, and educators support the idea of giving parents greater choice in selecting their children's schools. One such plan involves giving parents vouchers that can be used to pay part of the tuition at a private school. Tuition tax credits (deductions from state taxes) have also been provided to help parents afford private school tuition.

23   Parents who are dissatisfied with the regular public schools in their community may choose charter schools or even homeschooling. Charter schools have special agreements with their state board of education that free them from some of the restrictions placed upon regular public schools. Therefore, they are able to experiment with new teaching methods. There are about 1,700 charter schools in the U.S.A. today, and the numbers are growing. Homeschooling is a popular movement as well. About 1.5 million American children are taught at home.

24   American educators and policy makers have great confidence that computers are improving American education. About 90% of American schools have Internet access and, on average, one computer for every six students. Children as young as 3 years old are introduced to computers at home or at preschool.

25   Improving the school system is one of the nation's top priorities. In most states, teachers and school administrators are developing (or have developed) standards—statements of exactly what children are supposed to learn in each grade. They are also improving assessment—ways of finding out if students have met these standards. Tests that **evaluate** students also evaluate schools. Schools with low pass rates are expected to make changes that will lead to improvement. While Americans look for ways to make elementary and secondary education better, they are encouraged by the fact that 65% of the nation's high school graduates choose to continue their formal schooling at a college or university.

AFTER YOU READ

I. Getting the Message

A. True or False?

Reread the sections indicated. Then mark each statement true (T) or false (F).

"The Goals and Purpose of Public Education"

_____ 1. American children must go to school until they graduate from high school.

_____ 2. School attendance laws are the same in every state of the U.S.

_____ 3. Classes in English as a second language are called *bilingual instruction.*

_____ 4. In the U.S., parents can decide whether their children will receive an education or not.

"Elementary Education"

_____ 5. Poorer school districts are less likely to give students classes in music and art.

_____ 6. Most American children don't go to school in the summer.

"High School (Secondary Education)"

_____ 7. American secondary school students attend either a college preparatory high school or a vocational high school.

_____ 8. Most high schools offer courses in social science, arithmetic, and language arts.

_____ 9. Extracurricular activities always meet after school.

B. Which Comes Next?

Number the following academic levels in chronological order (1–6).

_____ first grade   _____ high school

_____ kindergarten   _____ grades 3–4

_____ junior high (middle school)   _____ nursery school

C. Why Preschool?

Reread paragraph 9. What are two main reasons that parents enroll young children in nursery schools and day-care centers? Write a sentence about each reason.

_____

_____

II. Building Your Vocabulary

A. _These are the 15 key vocabulary words for this chapter. They are boldfaced in the reading. Pronounce these words after your teacher and discuss their meanings._

academic*	evaluate	shortage
commitment	grade‡	specialist
compulsory	kindergarten	subsidize
curriculum†	motivation	teamwork
elementary	parochial	vocational

*Academic is an adjective. Academics is a noun.
†The plural of curriculum is irregular. It is curricula.
‡Grade can be a noun or verb.

B. *Complete these sentences with some of the key vocabulary words on page 101. Make the nouns plural if necessary, and put each verb into the correct tense and form.*

1. _____ involves cooperating and working together with other people.

2. Some day-care centers are _____ by the government, which means that the government contributes some of the money needed.

3. Information and skills taught in each grade of school are the _____ for that grade.

4. Children must attend school. School is _____.

5. _____ school is sometimes called grammar school.

6. In elementary school, a student usually passes or fails an entire grade, but in high school, a student's work in each course (subject) is _____ and _____ separately.

7. Some high school students study hard because they know that good grades will help them get into a good college or university. These students have a lot of _____ for trying to get good grades.

8. _____ schools are supported by a particular religious group. They teach its religious beliefs, celebrate its religious holidays, and encourage prayer.

9. Due to a teacher _____, some school districts hire teachers who have had little or no training in teaching methods.

10. Before first grade, children attend _____.

11. A music teacher is a(n) _____ in music.

12. _____ training is training to do a particular job.

C. *After each academic category, draw a line through the subject that doesn't belong in that category.*

Example

sciences:	biology	~~trigonometry~~	chemistry	physics
1. Mathematics:	algebra	geometry	chemistry	trigonometry
2. Social sciences:	history	psychology	geography	athletics
3. Language arts:	sociology	grammar	writing	spelling
4. Physical education (gym):	swimming	physics	team sports	health

III. Sharpening Reading Skills

Analyzing Paragraphs   Recognizing how the main idea of a paragraph is developed is a useful reading skill. Some paragraphs give reasons; some explain results; some list examples; some tell about one incident; some describe; some compare and contrast.

Reread each paragraph listed below. Then underline the sentence that best describes the paragraph.

1. paragraph 9:   a. Tells what children do in nursery schools.
                     b. Gives reasons why parents send children to nursery schools.

2. paragraph 18:   a. Describes a typical day in the life of a high school student.
                     b. Argues that high school students are too busy.

3. paragraph 19:   a. Tells what's wrong with bad schools in the U.S.
                     b. Contrasts American schools in poor communities and in wealthier ones.

4. paragraph 20:   a. Explains why there is a teacher shortage.
                     b. Talks about harmful effects of the teacher shortage.

IV. Understanding Idioms and Expressions

Match each expression in column 1 with the phrase in column 2 that means the same thing by writing the correct numbers on the lines. The numbers in parentheses give the paragraphs in which the expressions are used.

1. cover (13)   _____ become accustomed to; become familiar with

2. get along with (8)   _____ be able to pay for

3. get used to (8)   _____ connections to

4. ties between (4)   _____ not argue with; have a good relationship with

5. take on (8)   _____ agree to do; accept responsibility for

V. Taking Words Apart

Study the meanings of these word parts. Then use them to complete the words defined on page 104.

co- = together, with   dis-, un- = not
extra- = outside, beyond   -ful = full of, with
hetero- = different   ill- = badly
-less = without   pre- = before

(continued on the next page)

1. _____like (not similar to; not alike; different from)

2. point_____ (no good reason to do it)

3. _____curricular (activities in addition to academic work)

4. _____geneous (not all the same)

5. _____-prepared (not well-prepared)

6. _____school (before kindergarten)

7. un_____operative (doesn't work well with others)

8. use_____ (having no use)

9. _____educational (boys and girls in school together)

10. _____like (hate or not like)

11. _____prepared (not prepared at all)

12. harm_____ (it can hurt someone)

VI. Practicing Sentence Patterns

The Infinitive of Purpose   The reading contains these two infinitives of purpose. Paragraph 1 states: "To educate this huge number of students, more than 3 million teachers are employed." Paragraph 5 states: "To attend a private school, a student must apply and be accepted." The infinitive phrase in each sentence states a goal, and the main clause states a way of achieving that goal. Here's another example:

To earn extra money,   I plan to get a part-time job.

(my goal)   (the way I plan to achieve my goal)

Now complete these sentences that begin with infinitives of purpose.

1. To improve my English, I _____

   _____.

2. To get better grades, students _____

   _____.

3. To encourage more people to become teachers, school districts should

   _____.

VII. Sharing Ideas

A. Issues

Debate these issues in small groups. Then choose one and write about it.

1. Do bilingual education programs advance or slow down the academic development of immigrant students? Would all-day contact with American students help them more?

2. Should American public schools educate children who are in the U.S. illegally?

3. Should children who do very well in school be allowed to skip a grade? Should academically slow children be required to repeat a grade (be retained or failed)? Or is it better to keep children with their age group even if the schoolwork is too easy or too hard?

4. Should parents who send their children to parochial schools receive financial assistance from the government, or would that violate the constitutional requirement of separation of church and state?

B. On a Personal Note

Write about one of these topics.

1. What changes would you recommend to improve American schools?

2. If you had school-age children, would you educate them at home? Why or why not?

3. Compare American schools to schools in another country you're familiar with. Point out similarities and/or differences. In your opinion, which school system does a better job? Explain why.

10 | Higher Education in the U.S.

BEFORE YOU READ

Discuss

1. Why do people go to college?

2. Do you think everyone should go to college? Why or why not?

3. In the U.S., many colleges and universities are very expensive. What sources of money are available to help students?

Guess

Try to answer the questions. Then look for the answers in the reading.

1. How many institutions of higher learning are there in the U.S.? Check (✓) one:

   _____ about 1,700   _____ about 2,700   _____ about 3,700

2. What percentage of Americans over the age of 25 are college graduates?

   Check (✓) one:

   _____ about 15%   _____ about 25%   _____ about 45%

Higher Education in the U.S.

Why College?

1   "The more you learn, the more you earn," Americans often say. In the U.S.A., almost all jobs that pay well require some education or technical training beyond high school. In this high-tech society, college graduates outearn those without a college education, and people with advanced **degrees** are likely to earn even more. Though some college degrees are worth more than others in the job market, in general, education pays off.

2   A college education is not just preparation for a career, however. In addition to taking courses in their major field of study, students enroll in **elective** courses. They may take classes that help them understand more about people, nature, government, or the arts. Well-rounded people are likely to be better citizens, better parents, and more interesting and interested individuals.

3   Although two-thirds of American high school graduates enroll in college, recent high school graduates no longer dominate the college **campuses.** Adults of all ages return to the classroom, either for new vocational skills or for personal growth. In 1996, for example, almost 20% of American college students were over age 35. Some 500,000 college students are over 50.

4   American faith in the value of education is exemplified by the rising number of Americans who have at least a bachelor's degree. Almost one-quarter of Americans over age 25 are college graduates. College attendance is not reserved for the wealthy and the academically talented. It is available to anyone who wants to go. Right now, about 15 million students are taking advantage of the opportunity. For those not academically prepared to handle college-level work, about 80% of undergraduate schools offer remedial (sometimes called *developmental*) classes in reading, writing, and math.

✔ **Check Your Comprehension**   *Why do people go to college?*
List reasons mentioned in the preceding section and any others you can think of.

How to Find the Right College

5   The U.S. has about 3,700 institutions of higher learning. About 1,600 of these are 2-year schools. More than 2,000 are 4-year schools, many of which also have graduate programs. With so many colleges to choose from, how do prospective students find the right one for their needs? Information about schools is easy to obtain from school guidance counselors, college guidebooks, public libraries, the Internet, and the schools themselves. Students can write for brochures and applications. Some schools even mail out videos. Students can also use computer programs that allow them to specify particular interests (for a certain major, type of school, area of the country, etc.) and print out a list of schools that fit their description. Most institutions of higher learning also have Web sites. Many schools send college representatives to high schools and two-year colleges to recruit students. Finally, many students visit colleges, take tours of campuses, and talk to counselors.

6   Before selecting a school, students should consider these questions:
* Does the school have a major in your field of interest? Does this program have a good reputation?
* Are you likely to be accepted at this school, considering your grades and test scores?
* Do you like that area of the country, the climate, the topography?
* Which environment do you prefer—a big city, a small town, or a rural area?
* Is it a big or a small school? There are advantages to each. At a smaller school, you may feel less lonely and confused. At a bigger school, you'll have more choices of courses, programs, and extracurricular activities. What is most important to you?
* Can you afford the tuition and living expenses at this school? Could you get as good an education elsewhere for a lot less money?

✔ **Check Your Comprehension**   *What are some steps you can take to find the right American college?*

Undergraduate Education: Types of Schools

7   Two main categories of institutions of higher learning are *public* and *private*. All schools get money from tuition and from private contributors. However, public schools are also supported by the state in which they're located. Private schools do not receive state funding. As a result, tuition is generally lower at public schools, especially for permanent residents of that state. A third category is the proprietary (for-profit) school. These usually teach a particular workplace skill. Some of these schools are quite expensive.

8   Schools can also be grouped by the types of programs and degrees they offer. The three major groups are community colleges, 4-year colleges, and universities. Community colleges (sometimes called junior colleges) offer only the first 2 years of **undergraduate** studies (the **freshman** and **sophomore** years). They enroll about 5 million students a year. Most community colleges are public schools, supported by local and / or state funds. They serve two general types of students: those taking the first 2 years of college before they **transfer** to a 4-year school for their third and fourth (**junior**

and **senior**) years and those enrolled in 1- or 2-year job-training programs. Community colleges offer training in many areas, such as health occupations, office skills, computer science, police work, and automotive repair.

9   What is the difference between a college and a university? Size is only part of the answer. Some colleges have a student body of just a few hundred, while some state universities serve more than 100,000 students on several campuses. A university is usually bigger than a college because the scope of its programs is much greater. A university offers a wider range of undergraduate programs plus graduate studies. Part of the responsibility of a university is to encourage its **faculty** and graduate students to do research to advance human knowledge. Colleges, on the other hand, are primarily undergraduate schools. They have no obligation to conduct research.

10   Many excellent colleges are liberal arts schools, which means that they offer studies in the humanities, languages, mathematics, social sciences, and sciences. Liberal arts colleges generally do not offer degrees in engineering, business, journalism, education (teacher training), and many other specific vocations that a student can prepare for at a university.

11   Some colleges specialize in training students for one occupation (as agricultural colleges and teachers' colleges do). Many undergraduate institutions that are not called colleges also provide higher education in one specific occupation—for example, conservatories for music students, seminaries for students of religion, and fine arts schools for artists. For those wishing to prepare for military careers, the U.S. government maintains four military academies.

12   At colleges and universities, the academic year is about 9 months long (usually from September until early June or from late August until May). After completing 4 academic years with acceptable grades in an approved course of study, the student earns a bachelor's degree. Some students complete college in less than 4 years by attending summer sessions. At most colleges, the academic year is divided into either two semesters or three quarters, excluding the summer session. College grades, from highest to lowest, are usually A, B, C, D, and F (a failing grade). Generally, students must keep a C average to remain in school.

✔ **Check Your Comprehension**   *What are three differences between a college and a university?*

Graduate Education

13   American universities offer three kinds of graduate degrees: master's degrees, Ph.D. degrees, and professional degrees (for example, in medicine, law, or engineering). In most fields, a master's degree can be earned in 1 or 2 academic years of study beyond the B.S. or B.A. Earning a Ph.D. degree (doctor of philosophy) usually takes at least 3 years beyond the master's. To receive a Ph.D. in most fields, students must pass oral and written examinations and produce a long and comprehensive research paper that makes an original contribution to their field. In some fields, Ph.D. candidates must also

be able to read one or two foreign languages. Requirements are different for professional degrees.

14   In recent years, the graduate student population has become much more diverse than ever before. It now includes more women, foreign students, minority group members, older students, and part-time students. Also, the variety of degree programs offered has expanded greatly. Today's graduate students can choose from master's degrees in at least 1,000 fields and Ph.D.s in about 100 fields.

✔ **Check Your Comprehension**

What are four requirements most Ph.D. applicants must fulfill?

Life on an American Campus

15   A college community is an interesting and lively place. Students become involved in many different extracurricular activities. Among these are athletics, college newspapers, musical organizations, political groups, and religious groups. Many religious groups have their own meeting places, where services and social activities are held. Most colleges have a student union, where students can get together for lunch, study sessions, club meetings, and socializing.

16   On many campuses, social life revolves around fraternities (social and, in some cases, residential clubs for men) and sororities (similar clubs for women). Some are national groups with chapters at many schools. Their names are Greek letters, such as Alpha Delta Phi.

17   Sports are an important part of life on most campuses. Most coeducational and men's schools belong to various athletic leagues. Teams within these leagues compete against one another for the league championship. Football is the college sport that arouses the most national interest. Games, complete with student marching bands and cheerleaders, are major productions. Other sports—particularly basketball, swimming, and track—are also pursued with enthusiasm. Some schools also have competitive tennis, skiing, sailing, wrestling, soccer, baseball, and golf.

18   Is it fun to be a college student in the U.S.? For most students, the college years are exciting and rewarding, but they are certainly not easy or carefree. Just about all college students face the pressure of making important career decisions and **anxiety** about examinations and grades. Many students have additional problems—too little money, not enough sleep, and a feeling of loneliness because they're far from home. Some spend too much time at parties and get into trouble academically. Still, many Americans look back on their college years as the happiest time of their lives. Many **alumni** feel great loyalty to their former schools. Throughout their lives, they cheer for their school's athletic teams, donate money to help the institution grow, and go back to visit for homecoming festivities. Alumni refer to the school they attended as their *alma mater* (Latin for "fostering mother"). This expression indicates how much the college experience means to former students.

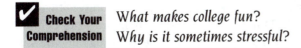**✔ Check Your Comprehension** *What makes college fun?*
Why is it sometimes stressful?

Financing Higher Education

19   College costs vary quite a bit, depending upon the type of school. At expensive private schools, annual costs (including **tuition,** room, board, books, travel to and from home, etc.) may exceed $30,000. Public universities are much cheaper. At these schools, tuition is significantly higher for out-of-state students than for permanent residents of that state. Tuition at community colleges averages about $1,500, approximately half the in-state tuition at public, 4-year schools.

20   During the 1990s, the cost of higher education rose about 7.5% a year. Difficulties making ends meet create serious problems for many students. Older students with a family to support may try to work full time while carrying a full academic courseload. They forget to leave themselves time to eat, sleep, and relax.

21   For those who need financial assistance, help is available. There are three main types of financial aid: (1) scholarships (grants), which are gifts that students do not repay; (2) loans to students and / or their parents; and (3) student employment (work / study), a part-time job that the school gives the student for the academic year. Most financial aid is need-based; that is, only students who need the money receive it. Financial assistance to excellent students who do not need the money (commonly called *merit-based aid*) is limited.

22   Funds for all this aid come from three main sources—the federal government, state governments, and private contributors. Every American college and university has a financial aid office to help students find out what kind of aid they might be eligible for and to assist them in completing the complicated application forms. Aliens who are permanent residents in the U.S. are eligible for government assistance, but foreign students are not.

✔ Check Your Comprehension *What are three kinds of financial aid?*
Which one do you think students like most?

Standardized Tests and Their Uses

23   Various standardized tests help students demonstrate their knowledge to college admissions personnel. Adults who have not finished high school can take the GED (Test of General Educational Development). The GED involves five exams—writing skills, social studies, science, literature and the arts, and mathematics. The tests are available in English, French, and Spanish. Students can study for the GED by taking a review course or using a review book on their own. Students who pass the test earn a high school equivalency certificate.

24   High school seniors wishing to apply to competitive colleges and universities take standardized tests commonly called ACTs and SATs. The tests help students demonstrate the ability to do college level work. Most colleges use these scores plus the students' high school grades to evaluate applicants. These tests are given several times a year throughout the U.S. and in other countries.

25   Students whose native language is not English will probably be required to take the TOEFL® (Test of English as a Foreign Language) when they apply for admission to a university. Students can study for the TOEFL® and many other standardized tests by taking a review course or by working independently with a review book or computer program.

26   When students come to the U.S. after completing some college work in another country, they should bring a **transcript** of previous college work and have those **credits** evaluated by an authorized organization. The transcript will probably need to be translated into English. Students who cannot prove that they have completed certain college courses can take some of the CLEP (College Level Examination Program) tests to demonstrate their knowledge.

27   Standardized tests are also required to apply for admission to graduate schools. The counseling office of a student's present or prospective school can answer questions about requirements for acceptance to graduate programs.

✔ **Check Your Comprehension**

What is the general purpose of standardized tests?

Lifelong Learning

28   In the U.S., the education of adults is a never-ending process going on in many different places for many different reasons. At least 76 million adults are enrolled in some type of classes, mostly as part-time students. The majority of these classes are taken not for credit but for knowledge that the student can use on the job, to pursue a hobby, or for personal growth. Many employees take classes at their workplace. Some companies pay the tuition when an employee goes back to school to learn a skill that the company needs. Noncredit programs, commonly called *adult education* or *continuing education*, are offered in many high schools, colleges, and museums. There are also private learning centers that offer inexpensive classes covering a wide variety of skills and activities. A typical catalog might have classes in how to cook a Chinese dinner, invest in the stock market, improve spelling, make friends, or even give your partner a massage.

29   Education, like everything else, takes advantage of technology. These days, students can be home with the family and go to school at the same time. They can take classes in their living rooms via TV. Many schools also offer distance learning—"attending" class and interacting with professors and classmates via the Internet. One 97-year-old man earned his Ph.D. that way!

30   In the U.S.A., technology rapidly makes some skills obsolete and new ones essential. Workers at all levels realize that lifelong learning is necessary. Even professional people—doctors, accountants, dentists, and engineers—continue to study to keep up

with changes in their fields. Education, on the college campus or elsewhere, is an important element in the life of an American adult. The American dream of becoming professionally and financially successful is most often achieved through higher education.

AFTER YOU READ

I. Getting the Message

A. Different Schools, Different Rules

Work with a partner. Put a check (✓) in the column if the statement accurately describes that type of school. Each statement may be true of one, two, all, or none of the schools.

Statements	2-year college	4-year college	University
1. You can earn a B.S.			
2. You can get financial aid to attend.			
3. You can major in liberal arts.			
4. There are both public and private schools of this type.			
5. This type of school doesn't charge tuition.			

B. Paragraphs That Make Contrasts

Answer these questions using complete sentences.

1. Reread paragraph 7. What two types of schools are contrasted here?

   _____

   Explain the main difference between them. _____

   _____

2. Reread paragraph 9. What two types of schools are contrasted here?

   _____

   What are two important differences between them? _____

   _____

II. Building Your Vocabulary

A. *These are the 15 key vocabulary words for this chapter. They are boldfaced in the reading. Pronounce these words after your teacher and discuss their meanings.*

alumni*	elective	sophomore
anxiety	faculty	transcript
campus	freshman	transfer†
credit	junior	tuition
degree	senior	undergraduate

B. *Complete these sentences with the key vocabulary words. Make the nouns plural if necessary, and put each verb into the correct tense and form.*

1. A school's buildings and the land around them are called the school's _____.

2. The first 4 years of college are called (in order) (first) _____, (second) _____, (third) _____, and (fourth) _____ years.

3. A student who has not yet earned a bachelor's degree is called a(n) _____.

4. Private schools generally charge higher _____ than public schools.

5. A student earns _____ for a course only if he or she gets a passing grade in it.

6. A student who wants to get a master's _____ must go to school for at least 1 or 2 years after getting a bachelor's degree.

7. The people who teach at a school are called its _____.

8. Students take courses in their major, and they also take _____ courses.

9. The graduates of a particular school are the school's _____.

10. A(n) _____ is a written record of a student's courses, grades, and credits.

11. Some students attend a community college for 2 years and then _____ to a university.

12. Some students have a lot of _____ about tests.

---

*Alumni is plural. The singular form is *alumnus.*
†*Transfer* can be a noun or a verb.

C. *Discuss the meanings of these abbreviations. Then write in the words.*

1. B.S. _____

2. B.A. _____

3. M.S. _____

4. M.A. _____

5. Ph.D. _____

6. TOEFL® _____

D. *Check (✓) the things that a person can earn.*

1. money _____

2. a job promotion _____

3. a good grade _____

4. a baby _____

5. talent _____

6. homework _____

7. college credits _____

8. praise _____

III. Sharpening Reading Skills

A. Topic Sentences

Reread the paragraphs listed and look for the topic sentence in each. (The topic sentence states the main idea of the paragraph.) Then write the first two words of the topic sentence on the line after the paragraph number.

(5) _____

(17) _____

(21) _____

(28) _____

B. Scanning

Scan the paragraphs indicated to find specific facts.

1. Approximately how many colleges and universities are there in the U.S.? (5)

   _____

2. How many years of college can a student complete at a community college? (8)

   _____

3. What is the highest (best) grade that a college student can get in a course? (12)

   _____

IV. Understanding Idioms and Expressions

Use context clues to determine the meanings of the italicized expressions in the title or paragraphs indicated. On each blank line, write the letter of the correct definition.

1. In the chapter title, *higher education* means _____.
   a. graduate school only
   b. undergraduate and graduate studies beyond high school

2. In paragraph 2, *well-rounded people* refers to people who are _____.
   a. knowledgeable about many different things
   b. overweight

3. In paragraph 4, *taking advantage of* means _____.
   a. using a good opportunity
   b. using another person for your benefit

4. In paragraph 9, *student body* means _____.
   a. a dead student
   b. all the students at a particular school

5. In paragraph 18, the Latin phrase *alma mater* refers to _____.
   a. the school that a person's mother attended
   b. the school that a person attended

6. In paragraph 20, *making ends meet* means _____.
   a. tying two strings together
   b. being able to pay for the things you need

V. Taking Words Apart

Countable and Uncountable Nouns   *Countable nouns* have a singular and a plural form. An article or a number word can be used before them. *Uncountable* nouns have no plural and cannot be preceded by a number or by *a / an*.

Write the plural of the four countable nouns listed below. Write a "u" after the four words that are always uncountable. For those that have both countable and uncountable meanings, put a check (✓) and write the plural. Use an ESL dictionary for help.

1. activity _____

2. alumnus _____

3. anxiety _____

4. campus _____

5. credit _____

6. education _____

7. faculty _____

8. fraternity _____

9. freshman _____

10. homework _____

11. knowledge _____

12. tuition _____

VI. Practicing Sentence Patterns

Notice the use of the phrases *too little money* and *too much time* in paragraph 18. In these phrases, the word *too* means more (or less) than is needed or wanted. Before uncountable nouns such as *money* and *time,* use *too much* or *too little.* Before plural nouns, use the phrases *too many* or *too few.*

Complete the following sentences with the correct phrase: too many, too much, too few, *or* too little.

1. I can't go to the movies with you tonight. I have _____ homework.

2. Joe has joined _____ school organizations. He doesn't have enough time to sleep.

3. John spends _____ money on clothes. Then he has _____ money for food.

4. Only four students enrolled in Advanced Statistics 543. That's _____ students for Professor Einstein to teach the course.

5. Friends are wonderful. A person can never have _____ friends.

6. A full-time student who also works full-time probably has _____ time to do homework.

VII. Sharing Ideas

A. Issues

Discuss these issues in small groups. Then choose one and write about it.

1. Many college students take out loans to pay tuition and living expenses. Students who attend expensive undergraduate and graduate schools may end up with $100,000–$200,000 of debt. Is it a good idea to borrow that much money for one's education? What are the pros and cons?

2. Should people who are paying for their own or their child's college education be given tax credits to offset some of the expense?

3. Is it better to go to college right after high school or to work or travel for a while first?

B. On a Personal Note

Write about one of these topics.

1. Still undecided about your college major? Consult the *Occupational Outlook Handbook,* a U.S. government publication. (Every American library has a copy.) Read about two careers that interest you. Then compare them. Which one seems the best choice in terms of job opportunities, wages, and benefits? Which one best matches your abilities and interests? Which one do you think you will pursue?

2. What are your academic and / or vocational goals? How do you expect to pursue them?

3. A survey of 260,000 college freshmen revealed that 30% of them had long, tiring daily schedules and lived under great stress. What can be done to make the college years less stressful, especially for people who are trying to handle school, work, and family obligations? What techniques do you use for handling stress and reducing anxiety?

11 Vacationing in the U.S.

Honolulu, Hawaii

St. Louis, Missouri

San Francisco, California

BEFORE YOU READ

Discuss

1. If you could vacation anyplace in the U.S., where would you go?

2. What is the most interesting place you've ever visited?

3. Have you ever been to a theme park? If so, tell what you did there.

Guess

Try to answer the questions. Then look for the answers in the reading.

1. What's the most popular vacation spot in the world? _____

2. What three American cities have the largest populations? List them in order:

   a. _____   b. _____   c. _____

3. Why has the island of Hawaii been getting bigger in recent years? _____

   _____

4. What is the English word for a very tall building? _____

Vacationing in the U.S.

Seeing the Sights

1   Most American workers receive an annual vacation of at least two weeks with pay, and it's traditional to use this time off for travel. Americans who have enough time and money are free to go almost anywhere. Getting a **passport** is a routine matter. Millions of Americans vacation abroad each year, but it's also possible to spend a lifetime of vacations in the U.S.A. and never run out of variety. This chapter will describe some of the most popular U.S. **tourist** spots.

2   Since vacations are usually family affairs, the most popular vacation periods are during the summer and during the 2-week school break **surrounding** the Christmas and New Year's holidays. These periods are also the most crowded and generally the most expensive times to travel, so people who can, usually vacation at other times.

3   The automobile is probably the least expensive way to travel, especially for families. It is also fairly fast and convenient. The excellent interstate highway system connects the nation's major cities and makes travel easy with its many motels and restaurants. Tourists in a hurry often fly to their **destination** and rent a car when they get there.

4   Cameras in hand, Americans sightsee with great enthusiasm. Then, they come home well equipped to bore their neighbors with snapshots, slides, and / or videos, showing off where they've been and what they've done.

✔ **Check Your Comprehension**   *When do most American families go away on vacation?*

Visiting Theme Parks

5   One important American contribution to vacation fun is the **theme** park. Theme parks are a variation on the outdoor entertainment complexes called **amusement** parks, which were so popular from the 1890s to the 1960s. Like amusement parks, theme parks

have carnival games, rides, shows, displays, shops that sell **souvenirs,** and restaurants and food stands. But theme parks tend to be much larger and more high-tech than the older amusement parks. Furthermore, they are not just assorted outdoor activities in one location. They are developed around a theme or idea, such as American or regional history, marine life, water sports, or African safaris. Many are quite educational as well as entertaining. Theme parks have great appeal to people of all ages and are often a family's primary vacation destination. As a result, American amusement and theme parks combined take in about $7 billion a year!

6   Walt Disney, the famous American cartoonist and filmmaker, started it all in 1955 when he opened the first theme park, Disneyland, near Los Angeles, California. Its theme is children's stories, specifically those that were made into Disney animated films. Disney cartoon characters such as Mickey Mouse and Donald Duck are also featured.

7   Disneyland's great success inspired the building of parks elsewhere in the U.S. and Europe. The largest is Walt Disney World, the most popular vacation spot in the world. This complex covers 43 square miles near Orlando, Florida. It includes four major theme parks plus several minor ones. First, there's the Magic Kingdom, which is similar to Disneyland. In addition to the wonderful rides, visitors love its amazing mechanical figures that appear in many exhibits—everything from dancing, singing bears to a life-sized, gesturing, speech-giving Abraham Lincoln. The second park, Epcot Center, contains two main sections: Future World highlights technologies of the future; World Showcase features the **architecture,** crafts, food, and entertainment of 11 nations. The third park, Disney–MGM Studios, has Hollywood movie-making as its theme. The newest park—Animal Kingdom—has about 1,000 animals, including some rare and endangered ones. The Walt Disney World complex includes four lakes and about 100 restaurants. It's impossible to see and do everything in Walt Disney World, even in several days. A visitor needs two important things—a pair of comfortable shoes and the patience to stand in long lines.

8   Disney is not the only American company in the theme park business. Six Flags has 14 theme parks and 3 water parks across the U.S. Six Flags Great America (near Chicago) has two themes—regions of the U.S. and comic strip characters. Six Flags over Texas (in Arlington, Texas) focuses on the history of Texas and the U.S. Many theme parks are combinations of amusement parks and zoos. In some (such as Great Adventure in Jackson, New Jersey, and Busch Gardens in Tampa, Florida), animals roam freely on huge areas of land and tourists drive or ride trains through the territory. Marine animal theme parks (such as Sea World in Orlando, Florida, and San Diego, California) have live dolphin shows. Around the country, there are many smaller theme parks built around water activities, where swimmers can cool off on water slides and in wave pools.

✔ **Check Your Comprehension**

What's a theme park?

What are some different types of theme parks?

Sightseeing in the Eastern Cities

9   The nation's major cities are among the most popular tourist attractions. New York City, with a population exceeding 7 million, is the largest city in the U.S. With a magnificent natural harbor and more than 500 miles of waterfront, it is also the largest port in

the world. The city has five sections, called *boroughs*. The best-known, and in many ways most important, borough is Manhattan, the commercial, cultural, and financial center of the city. Manhattan is an island connected to the other boroughs (Brooklyn, the Bronx, Queens, and Staten Island) by bridges, tunnels, and ferries.

10   All year, tourists crowd the streets and hotels of Manhattan. They visit the skyscrapers, particularly the Empire State Building, one of the tallest skyscrapers in the world. Its 102 floors reach a height of 1,250 feet (381 meters). Tourists visit museums and art galleries, shop in the city's department stores and specialty shops, and dine in elegant restaurants. Other attractions are the United Nations building, the New York Stock Exchange, Rockefeller Center, and the Metropolitan Opera. This world-famous opera company performs at Lincoln Center for the Performing Arts, a group of buildings that also houses concert halls, theaters, and the Juilliard School of Music, Drama, and Dance.

11   Live entertainment is plentiful in New York City. In addition to its many nightclubs for music and comedy, the city is the nation's most important area for theater. Plays performed "on Broadway" (in the larger midtown Manhattan theaters near the street called *Broadway*) often involve famous playwrights, producers, and performers. Smaller "off-Broadway" theaters feature less well known actors and sometimes more experimental productions.

12   New York City is also the home of a famous symbol—the **Statue** of Liberty. This enormous figure of a woman has been standing in New York Harbor since 1886. It was designed by two Frenchmen—the exterior by Frédéric-Auguste Bartholdi and the interior by Alexandre-Gustave Eiffel (creator of the Eiffel Tower in Paris)—and given to the United States by the French government. The Statue of Liberty is one of the largest statues in the world. Its height (from the tip of its torch to the base of the pedestal) is about 305 feet (93 meters), and its weight exceeds 200 tons (181,818 kg). The statue symbolizes American freedom and opportunity. Years ago, it welcomed nearly all American immigrants as they arrived in the United States by ship. Today, tourists take a 15-minute ferryboat ride to Liberty Island to get a closer look at the figure. Some even take the long climb up the stairs inside the statue to reach the viewing platform below its crown.

13   Vacationers interested in American history and government find the eastern part of the country fascinating. In Washington, D.C., the nation's capital, visitors can watch Congress in action in the Capitol, attend a session of the Supreme Court, and tour the White House, the home of the president. The Smithsonian Institution, with its many museums and art galleries, offers much of historical interest. Its exhibits include gowns of the First Ladies and the Wright brothers' first airplane. In Washington, there are also magnificent **monuments** to see. Most impressive are the memorials honoring Presidents Washington, Jefferson, Lincoln, and Franklin Delano Roosevelt.

14   One sad but beautiful monument is the Vietnam Veterans Memorial. It is a V-shaped black granite wall bearing the names of 58,000 Americans killed or missing in Vietnam. It was designed by a young Chinese-American architecture student named Maya Lin.

15   For American history buffs, the East has other interesting cities as well. Philadelphia, Pennsylvania, is the site of the building where the U.S. Constitution was signed in 1787. Boston, Massachusetts, has many colonial landmarks. In Virginia, there is colonial Williamsburg, with its 88 restored eighteenth- and early-nineteenth-century buildings

and hundreds of costumed "residents" dressed in clothing typical of the Revolutionary period.

✔ **Check Your Comprehension** *What are some structures of historical interest in the East?*

Visiting the Midwest

16   Chicago, long known as the "Second City," became the nation's third-largest city in terms of population in 1982, when Los Angeles surpassed it. With a population of almost 3 million, Chicago remains the largest city in the Midwest and the most interesting one as well. Tourists come to Chicago to visit its many fine theaters, restaurants, museums, and stores. The city's Outer Drive expressway along Lake Michigan gives visitors a scenic view of the beaches, harbors, parks, and skyscrapers. The city's most famous skyscraper is Sears Tower, the tallest building in the U.S.—1,454 feet (443 meters) high. Chicago is also famous for its modern architecture and impressive works of outdoor **sculpture** by internationally known artists, including Pablo Picasso and Alexander Calder. Other major attractions are the Museum of Science and Industry, with its exhibits showing applications of science to industry, and Buckingham Fountain, the world's largest lighted fountain, which is a beautiful multicolored sight on a summer evening.

17   St. Louis, the largest city in Missouri, is on the west bank of the Mississippi, the nation's longest river. During the 1800s, St. Louis was considered the gateway to the West. Today, tourists visiting the city cannot miss the beautiful Gateway Arch (the nation's tallest monument), designed by Eero Saarinen. Rising 630 feet (192 meters), it dominates the city's skyline. Inside the arch, there are small cars that carry visitors to the top.

18   On the western edge of the Midwest, in a section of the country often called the Great Plains, is South Dakota, home of Mount Rushmore. Here, carved into the rocks are enormous heads of four great American presidents: Washington, Jefferson, Lincoln, and Theodore Roosevelt. The heads are so big that they are visible from 62 miles away!

✔ **Check Your Comprehension** *Name three very large structures mentioned in this section.*

Visiting the South

19   One of the most popular American vacation states is Florida. Its tropical climate and beautiful sand beaches make it a year-round vacationland. Florida is ideal for water sports and for sightseeing as well. Besides Walt Disney World and other theme parks, tourists come to see the Everglades, one of the largest and most interesting swamp areas in the world, with its many unusual plants and birds; the John F. Kennedy Space Center on Cape Canaveral; and St. Augustine, the oldest permanent European settlement in the U.S.A.

20   New Orleans, Louisiana, a port city with exotic appeal, is located on the Mississippi River near the Gulf of Mexico. It contains many reminders of Old Europe and the Old South. The famous French Quarter, the Mardi Gras festival, and the Creoles (French-speaking descendants of early European settlers) all give the city an international flavor. New Orleans is the birthplace of jazz and also celebrates another form of uniquely American music—"Dixieland."

✔ **Check Your Comprehension**

What are four famous tourist sites in Florida?

Westward, Ho!

21   The West attracts tourists with vastly different tastes. The Rocky Mountains of Colorado draw skiers and snowmobilers. The casinos and nightclubs of Las Vegas, Nevada, attract vacationers who enjoy **gambling** and big-name entertainment. And the national parks in the West are a popular destination for vacationers interested in beautiful scenery, natural wonders, and wildlife. The Grand Canyon in Arizona attracts about 5 million visitors a year. Its huge, colorful rock formations are 277 miles long, 17 miles across, and more than a mile deep at the lowest point. The nation's largest national park—Yellowstone—covers about 3,500 square miles in Wyoming, Montana, and Idaho. Yellowstone contains the world's greatest geyser area, as well as **spectacular** waterfalls. Two other popular national parks in the West are Glacier National Park in Montana and Yosemite in California.

22   California offers a wealth of vacation experiences, especially for families. Because there is so much to see along California's Pacific Coast, travelers often fly there, then rent a car and drive up or down the mountain highway alongside the ocean, stopping at interesting cities and towns along the way, including, of course, Los Angeles and San Francisco.

23   Most California tourists want to see Los Angeles (L.A.), the nation's second-largest city. One section of L.A.—Hollywood—is the home of the American movie industry. People interested in films can spend a day at the Universal Movie Studios and get an idea of how movies are made. Driving around to see the fabulous homes of movie stars is another favorite L.A. pastime. So is shopping (or just looking) in the elegant shops on Rodeo Drive, where it's easy to find a $3,000 suit if you happen to need one.

24   San Francisco is one of the hilliest and most cosmopolitan of American cities. Situated between the Pacific Ocean and San Francisco Bay, San Francisco is the leading seaport of the Pacific Coast. Ships come and go beneath its beautiful Golden Gate Bridge. Cable cars clang loudly as they climb the city's steep hills. San Francisco is famous for its bridges, cable cars, breathtaking scenery, and fine dining—seafood on Fisherman's Wharf and Asian cuisine in Chinatown. And San Francisco visitors usually take a drive up to Muir Woods to see the giant sequoia (coastal redwood) trees. This type of tree is among the Earth's oldest and tallest living things. Some California sequoias are more than 2,000 years old and taller than a 30-story building!

25   For travelers with the time and money to go even farther west, the country's newest states—Alaska and Hawaii—offer many wonders. Northwest of the U.S. mainland is

Alaska, an amazing land of contrasts. To start with, it is the largest state in land area but one of the smallest in population. It is more than twice the size of Texas, but its population is only about 600,000. About 54,000 of its residents are of Asian descent—Inuits (Eskimos) and Aleuts. Alaska's climate and geography are also quite varied. Its sights include smoking **volcanoes,** grassy plains, rain forests, about 3 million lakes, 100,000 **glaciers,** and many high mountains including Mount McKinley, the highest mountain in North America. In some areas, the winter temperature can go down as low as –80° F (–62° C). In the northernmost part of Alaska, the sun doesn't set for 80 days in the summer; and for 50 days in the winter, it doesn't rise. Understandably, tourists tend to visit Alaska in the summer, when they can enjoy the milder weather and endless daylight.

An Alaskan glacier

26   Hawaii lies in the Pacific Ocean about 2,000 miles west of the U.S. mainland. It is made up of 20 tropical islands, including 8 major ones. The most densely populated island is Oahu, where the capital city of Honolulu is located. Oahu's Waikiki Beach, lined with hotels and apartment houses, is an international tourist attraction. The scenic island of Hawaii, almost twice the size of the others combined, has tall mountain peaks, forests, waterfalls, and the world's most active volcano (Kilauea). Since 1983, this island has grown more than 70 acres, thanks to the lava flow from Kilauea. The nation's fiftieth state has a diverse population, including many residents of Japanese, Filipino, and Chinese descent.

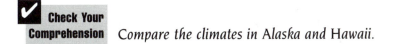

Check Your Comprehension   *Compare the climates in Alaska and Hawaii.*

Planning a Vacation

27   When planning a vacation, what do people want most? A change of scene. Folks who live in small towns or rural areas are eager to see big cities. On the other hand, for this

nation's urban population, the change of scene desired may be greater contact with nature, the great outdoors. There are many ways to enjoy nature besides visiting the vast (and usually crowded) national parks. Some families rent summer cottages near swimming and boating facilities. Some camp out (sleep outdoors) in tents. Some rent a houseboat and cruise down the Mississippi. Dude ranches in the West attract those who love horses or want to learn how to ride. Resorts cater to vacationers who want comfort and good meals, along with access to tennis, golf, swimming facilities, and wide open spaces.

28   How can one plan the perfect vacation? Guidebooks and travel magazines offer ideas. State tourist bureaus will gladly send information. Travel agencies are eager to assist with advice and reservations. But the best travel tips of all probably come from word of mouth, from people who have been there. So, if you're planning an American vacation, ask Americans about their favorite spot. You'll get an earful, along with a huge stack of photos to look at.

AFTER YOU READ

I. Getting the Message

A. *If you wanted to see these tourist attractions, where would you go? Write the name of the city or state. For some, there is more than one answer. Look back in the reading for help if necessary.*

1. the tallest building in the U.S.: _____

2. trees among the tallest on Earth: _____

3. a glacier: _____

4. the Statue of Liberty: _____

5. a Mardi Gras carnival: _____

6. the Gateway Arch: _____

7. the Kennedy Space Center: _____

8. the world's most active volcano: _____

9. a colonial city: _____

10. a dolphin show: _____

B. *Reread paragraph 25. Find three Alaskan contrasts mentioned. Write sentences about them.*

1. _____

2. _____

3. _____

C. According to paragraph 27, what is the most important benefit that most Americans look for when they go on vacation?

_____

II. Building Your Vocabulary

A. *These are the 15 key vocabulary words for this chapter. They are boldfaced in the reading. Pronounce these words after your teacher and discuss their meanings.*

amusement	monument	statue
architecture	passport	surrounding
destination	sculpture	theme
gambling	souvenir	tourist
glacier	spectacular	volcano

B. *Complete these sentences with some of the key vocabulary words. Make the nouns plural if necessary.*

1. The _____ of Liberty is a very large figure of a woman.

2. The Statue of Liberty is on Liberty Island, so there is water _____ it.

3. A statue is a(n) _____ of a human being or an animal.

4. A(n) _____ might be sculpture or architecture. It is built to remember and honor someone or some event.

5. This plane stops in Philadelphia, but its final _____ is Boston.

6. There are _____ in both Alaska and Hawaii.

7. Las Vegas, Nevada, is the place to go if you like _____.

8. Before the 1950s, the U.S. had _____ parks with rides and games, but the activities were not tied together by a common theme.

9. Disney World's Magic Kingdom is a(n) _____ park with children's storybook and film characters tying together most of the activities.

10. Did you bring home a lot of _____ from your trip to New York?

C. Two more homonyms are *capitol* and *capital*. Use *capitol* when writing about the building where state lawmakers meet. Use *Capitol* for the building in which the U.S. Congress meets in Washington, D.C. Use *capital* for all other meanings.

Now write the correct word in each sentence.

1. Every state in the U.S. has its own _____ city, which is the seat of its government.

(continued on the next page)

2. Washington, D.C., is the _____ of the U.S.

3. Congress meets there in the _____, a large white building with a domed top.

4. Note that the word *Capitol* begins with a _____ letter.

III. Sharpening Reading Skills

A. Making Inferences

What is suggested in each of these passages?

1. The last sentence in paragraph 7 tells the reader to wear comfortable shoes to Walt Disney World. What is implied (suggested, hinted at) by that advice? _____

   _____

2. In the last sentence in paragraph 23, the authors mention a $3,000 suit. What are they implying about Rodeo Drive? _____

   _____

3. In the last sentence of paragraph 28, what are the authors implying about the typical American tourist? _____

   _____

B. Map-Reading Practice

1. On a map of the U.S., point out California, Florida, the Atlantic and Pacific Coasts, the Mississippi River, the Great Lakes, the state of Washington, and Washington, D.C.

2. On a map of the world, locate Alaska and Hawaii. Where is Alaska in relation to Canada?

IV. Understanding Idioms and Expressions

Use the following expressions to complete the sentences below. The numbers in parentheses give the paragraphs in which the expressions are used. Put each verb into the correct tense and form.

as well as (5)	First Lady (13)	time off (1)
big-name (21)	get an earful (28)	word of mouth (28)
change of scene (27)	show off (4)	

1. Everyone enjoys going away on vacation because it provides a(n)

   _____.

2. My friend told me to visit Florida. I got the advice to go there by

   _____.

3. In New York City, I saw the Statue of Liberty

    _____ the Empire State Building.

4. I don't have to work tomorrow morning. My boss gave me some

    _____.

5. The wife of a U.S. president is called the _____.

6. A(n) _____ entertainer is someone famous and

    very well-known.

7. John drove to our house to _____ his new car.

8. When I visited Aunt Mary, I _____ about her

    recent trip.

V. Taking Words Apart

A. Compound Word Hunt

In this chapter, there are more than 30 compound words. A *compound word* is made up of two complete words.

Example   sidewalk (side + walk)   wildlife (wild + life)

Working with two classmates, scan the article (in 6 minutes) and see how many compound words you can find. Put each group's list on the board, and see which team found the most words. Then pronounce and discuss the meanings of the words. Compare the meaning of each compound word with the meanings of the words used separately. Note, for example, that wildlife (a compound word) has a quite different meaning from wild life (two words).

B. The Prefixes *inter-, intra-,* and *sub-*

Study the meanings of these word parts. Then discuss the answers to the questions below with a partner.

> *inter-* = between, among   *intra-* = within
> *sub-* = under, below, slightly

1. Would an *intercity* bus line travel within one city or between different cities?

2. Would a ship called a *submarine* travel under the water or only on top of it?

3. What kind of weather would you expect in a *subtropical* region?

4. What's the difference between an *intrastate* and an *interstate* highway?

VI. Practicing Sentence Patterns

Superlative statements tell about something that is the *most, best, least, worst, tallest,* and so on of a group of things, animals, or people. Many superlative patterns are used in this chapter, including examples in paragraphs 3, 7, 10, 12, 16, 17, 19, 21, 23, 24, 25, and 28.

1. *Write down five of these statements on a separate piece of paper. Put them into two groups: those using the short pattern (<u>the</u> tall<u>est</u>) and those using the long pattern (<u>the most</u> interesting or <u>the least</u> interesting).*

2. *Write your own superlative sentences, one in each pattern.*

short pattern: _____

long pattern: _____

VII. Sharing Ideas

A. Issues

Debate these issues in small groups. Then choose one and write about it.

1. What's the main purpose of a vacation? Should it provide rest, fun, new experiences, or something else?

2. Imagine this family argument: The Johnson family is trying to plan a winter vacation. Dad wants to go skiing in Colorado. Mom wants to lie on the beach in southern Florida. The teenage daughter wants the family to tour Mexico so she can practice her Spanish. The teenage son wants to stay home and spend the vacation "hanging out" with his friends. How can this family make a decision everyone will like?

B. On a Personal Note

Write about one of these topics.

1. Vacations can be divided into two main types: seeing or doing. Which do you prefer—sightseeing or going somewhere to enjoy some activity? Some vacations involve both. Describe a vacation you took or plan to take in terms of seeing and / or doing.

2. Tell about the best vacation you ever had.

3. Read about a place you'd like to visit in the U.S. Look in encyclopedias, guidebooks, and travel magazines. Write about what interests you the most about this place.

Leisure-Time Activities

Norman Rockwell's painting, "Be a Man"

BEFORE YOU READ

Discuss

1. What are your favorite leisure-time activities?

2. Compare baseball and tennis. In what ways are they similar? How are they different?

3. What are some noncompetitive sports?

Guess

Try to answer the questions. Then look for the answers in the reading.

1. What's the most popular form of exercise in the U.S. today? Check (✓) one:

   _____ swimming   _____ golf   _____ walking

2. Approximately how long is a standard marathon race? Check (✓) one:

   _____ 10 miles   _____ 26 miles   _____ 40 miles

3. What do all these have in common: cars, bicycles, horses, dogs, and pigs?

   _____

Leisure-Time Activities

1   At one time, **leisure** meant resting, relaxing, doing nothing, sitting on the front porch swing and watching the world go by. Today, however, most Americans crowd a lot of activities into their so-called leisure time. They may perform these activities to become physically fit, learn something new, do something creative, bring the family closer together, or have a great adventure. Having fun, of course, is another goal. But many Americans take their leisure pursuits quite seriously; they hope these activities will enrich their lives in some way.

The Big Three of American Team Sports

2   **Team** sports appeal to Americans' love of socializing and competing. The most popular team sports in the U.S.A.—baseball, football, and basketball—are both **spectator** sports and participatory sports. Boys and girls begin playing softball (a game similar to baseball but with a bigger, softer ball) when they are about 9 or 10 years old. In high school and college, football and baseball are played primarily by boys and men, and basketball is played by both sexes.

3   Baseball is often called the national pastime. People from other countries sometimes wonder why Americans enjoy this sport so much. "It's dull," they say. "Most of the time, the players are just standing still, waiting for someone to hit the ball." And that's true. But hitting that ball is quite a challenge. A pitch thrown by a professional pitcher usually travels more than 90 miles (145 kilometers) an hour. Hitting a ball thrown that fast is a difficult challenge for any athlete, so when a batter hits the ball out of the ball park (a home run!), the **fans** scream and cheer. The professional baseball season ends with the World Series, seven games played between the nation's top two teams. As with championship football, fans sometimes pay hundreds of dollars for a ticket to a World Series game. But those that watch the games at home on TV probably see them better.

4   Football involves knocking down a player who is trying to carry the ball down the field. Although players wear a lot of padding and other protective gear, injuries are fairly common. Versions of the game that involve less physical contact—flag football and touch football—are played by teams enjoying the sport just for fun and exercise.

5   As a spectator sport, football is extremely popular, especially among men. Women sometimes call themselves "football widows" because, during the football season, their boyfriends or husbands are either at the **stadium** or glued to the TV set. Both college football (played on Saturday afternoons) and professional football (played on Sunday afternoons and Monday nights) attract huge audiences. At the end of the college football season, the best teams **compete** in Bowl games. The day's festivities are colorful and exciting, involving parades with floats and marching bands. Bowl games attract huge crowds and big TV audiences. The professional football season ends with the Super Bowl, the game between the country's top two teams. More than 130 million people worldwide watch it on TV. It is the most watched TV show in the world. Because of this huge audience, advertisers pay about $2 million for a 30-second advertisement!

6   Note that the game Americans call *football* is not what Europeans call *football*. To Americans, that game is *soccer*. Soccer, the world's most popular sport, the national sport of most European and Latin American countries, has not been a great success in the U.S. as a professional sport. However, it is one of the fastest-growing team sports in U.S. elementary and high schools and is also a popular college sport.

7   While baseball and football are played outdoors (or in huge enclosed stadiums), basketball is the world's most popular indoor sport. Variations of the game are also played informally outdoors. Nearly every park in the U.S. has a basketball net and hard-surface playing area, and many American homes have a basketball net outdoors. In the U.S. there are 29 professional men's teams. In addition, women's professional basketball has been growing in popularity. Basketball is also played competitively by high school and college students.

8   Professional basketball players make almost impossible shots look easy and graceful. Michael Jordan, the former Chicago Bulls player, became famous worldwide because of his achievements on the basketball court. Jordan's 13-year career earnings (his salary for playing plus earnings for endorsing products in ads) exceeded $300 million! Is it any wonder that almost every tall American boy hopes to grow much taller and eventually play professional basketball?

✔ Check Your Comprehension   *What are the three most popular team sports in the U.S.?*
What's the difference between Bowl games and the Super Bowl?

Other Popular Sports

9   Americans know that **athletics** is good for the body and the mind. Those who are serious about exercising can find all kinds of activities to do, everything from winter sports to water sports. Some are safe, tame, and not very **strenuous.** Others require speed and great endurance. Some even require courage. Many Americans spend a lot of money on

equipment and instruction to participate in sports they enjoy. Others talk about exercising more but never get around to it.

10   One sport that can be played from about age 10 to 110 is golf. This popular sport is played all year except when the ground is covered with snow. Doctors highly recommend it for mild exercise, and they often practice what they preach. "Don't get sick on a Wednesday," people joke. That's doctors' traditional day off, and supposedly they're all on the golf course. The achievements of American golfer Tiger Woods have been an inspiration to golfers everywhere. He won the Masters Tournament in 1997, at the age of 21, and is still ranked the world's best golfer. He's also a one-man representative of American multiculturalism. His ethnic background is a blend of African-American, Native American, Chinese, European, and Thai!

11   Another sport that is not extremely strenuous and appeals to a wide age range is bowling. About 43 million people bowl in the U.S. Many bowling leagues (groups of teams that compete against each other) are formed by coworkers or members of community organizations.

12   Tennis, played by millions throughout the world, is also popular in the U.S. It is played all year, indoors or out, and provides a very vigorous workout. When two people are playing against each other, it's called *singles*; when four play (two teams of two players each), it's called *doubles*. As with other major sports, top professional tennis players win a lot of money and become famous.

13   Americans also enjoy winter sports on snow or ice. Skiing attracts both **individuals** and families. (It's not unusual to see 4-year-olds starting their skiing lessons.) In flatter areas of the country, "mountains" are artificially created and covered with artificial snow. Skiers also go to resorts with real mountains in places such as Aspen, Colorado. Ice-skating, indoors and outdoors, is also popular. Hockey (the national sport of Canada) is a popular team sport for boys in the U.S., too. Girls, however, are more likely to enjoy figure skating (doing various difficult maneuvers on ice).

14   The newest category of sports is called *extreme sports*. These are risky activities involving speed, high skill, and danger. They include daredevil tricks on snowboards, skateboards, and bicycles; parachute jumps off bridges or cliffs; bungee jumping; barefoot waterskiing; and skydiving. Most Americans consider extreme sports enthusiasts extremely foolish. However, others see them as carrying on the traditional pioneering, adventurous spirit that enabled Americans to conquer a wilderness.

✔ **Check Your Comprehension** *What are some important differences between golf and tennis?*

Exercise and the Great Outdoors

15   Some people get their exercise at health clubs, which have exercise equipment and exercise classes. Others equip their homes with treadmills and weights to work out in their bedroom or family room.

16   Can people exercise while sitting down? Of course! They can use stationary bicycles

or regular bicycles (nearly every American child has one). Other sit-down outdoor sports are motorcycling, snowmobiling, and riding a wave-runner (on water).

17   Can one exercise without expensive equipment? Yes, indeed. Walking, running, and jogging are also popular ways of keeping fit. In fact, walking is the most popular form of exercise in the U.S. Some shopping malls open early to allow members of walking clubs to exercise and window-shop at the same time. Before going to work, many Americans go jogging, using park trails or just running around the block. Runners with great endurance can enter marathon races (approximately 26 miles, or 42 kilometers, long).

18   Some Americans want to get away from urban life and get back to nature. They go hiking, camping, boating, or fishing. They enjoy waterskiing on a quiet lake or scuba diving in the ocean. And some, despite the disapproval of animal lovers, commune with nature by hunting small animals (such as ducks and rabbits) or large ones (such as deer and bear). About 16 million Americans get hunting licenses each year. Finally, many Americans enjoy the great outdoors at home by taking care of their lawns and gardens.

✔ **Check Your Comprehension**   *What are some activities to get exercise and enjoy the outdoors at the same time?*

Live Entertainment for Every Taste

19   In 1996, while Americans spent $6.4 billion to attend sporting events, they spent another $9.3 billion on theater, opera, and classical musical performances. Rock music concerts also attract millions of people, especially during the summer, when many concerts are held in huge outdoor areas. Many Americans are not satisfied to be merely spectators and listeners. **Amateur** performances, many of excellent quality, can be found all over the U.S. on any weekend. Theater groups, orchestras, and bands easily get enough volunteers to produce fine music and theater for the local community at very reasonable prices.

20   Entertainment involving animals is popular in many places. Most bigger cities have zoos and aquariums. Circuses travel around the country, bringing excitement when they come to town. And then there are rodeos, a form of entertainment popular in the American Southwest, Latin America, and Australia. Among other activities at rodeos, cowboys (and cowgirls) demonstrate their skills by climbing atop wild horses and bulls—for very short rides!

21   Animals also provide entertainment and an opportunity to lose money quickly at the racetrack. Americans race horses, dogs, pigeons, even pigs! Races are just one common form of gambling in a country with a great many other opportunities to do so. Fifty years ago, racetracks and Nevada casinos were almost the only forms of legal gambling in the U.S. Today, 37 states have lottery games, and 22 states have gambling casinos on Native American reservations. Many states have riverboat gambling casinos. There is also informal gambling among friends and coworkers, including bets on major sporting events or Friday evening poker games. Altogether, gambling in the U.S. is a multibillion-dollar industry.

Picture and Sound

22   By far, the most popular leisure-time activity is watching television. There is at least one TV set in 98% of American households, and many have two or three. About 82% of American homes have a videocassette recorder (VCR), which is capable of recording and playing back TV shows or movies.

23   What's on TV? Afternoon programming consists mostly of game shows, talk shows, and never-ending dramas commonly called *soap operas*. For children, daytime TV offers clever programs that educate while entertaining. There are also a lot of cartoons. At dinner time, news is broadcast. Evening entertainment consists mostly of situation comedies (sitcoms), which portray some aspect of life (families, singles, seniors, and so on) in a humorous way. There are also movies, adventure shows, dramas, and various weekly shows with the same cast of characters and general theme but a different story each week.

24   For those who want more TV than the free **stations** provide, cable TV is available in most parts of the country. To receive cable TV, one must pay a monthly **subscription** fee. Wires are attached to the TV set to enable the subscriber to receive the cable broadcasts. Cable channels tend to specialize in one type of program. There are stations for news, sports, movies, music videos, business, health, history, and the arts.

25   TV, at its best, is entertaining and educational. However, there are two problems: Most viewers watch too much, and the quality (especially on the free stations) is often poor. How much is too much? Studies indicate that the average American watches TV about 28 hours a week. (Children watch about 20 hours; older women are up to 42 hours.) According to one study in 1950, American 14-year-olds had a vocabulary of 25,000 words, but today's children the same age know only 10,000 words. The reason for the decrease may be that TV takes up a lot of leisure time kids once spent reading. Technology will continue to offer consumers bigger TV screens and clearer pictures at affordable prices. Moreover, TV of the future will be more interactive. (Viewers will have more control over the action.) Better technical quality may encourage viewers to watch even more—and, some say, become even less physically fit and more overweight.

26   And what about quality? On the commercial **networks** especially, many shows are silly, trite, in poor taste, or extremely violent. By the age of 18, the typical American has seen 40,000 killings on TV and in movies combined. Does all this fake bloodshed cause some teens to commit real violent crimes? Some people think there's a connection. American TV has earned the insulting nicknames "boob tube" and "idiot box." But for those who want to avoid either too much TV or bad TV, the solution is simple: Click the "off" button.

27   Movies are another common source of entertainment, viewed in theaters or at home. TV stations show movies, and there is a store that rents videotapes or DVDs in just about every neighborhood. Americans consume movies in great quantities, and movie

stars become public idols. Once a year, the movie industry gives out a whole series of honors to movie-makers. Nearly a billion people worldwide watch this televised awards presentation—the Academy Awards.

28   Other popular sources of entertainment are recordings and radio. Sales of recordings in all forms (compact discs and audiocassettes) exceed $12 billion annually, with compact discs by far the most popular medium. Radio, too, has its place in the American entertainment scene. It's a great companion in the car, on the treadmill, or on the jogging trail.

✔ **Check Your Comprehension**   *What are some problems with American TV? In your opinion, what's good about it?*

Leisure for Learning, Collecting, and Creating

29   No, radio and TV have not made reading obsolete. Nor is it true that Americans get all their news from radio or television. Reading is still an important leisure-time activity. The U.S.A. has about 1,800 daily newspapers with a total circulation of about 60 million. The country also produces thousands of magazines and journals—weeklies, monthlies, and quarterlies. Some are of general interest. Others are directed at people in a specific group based upon age, religion, occupation, or interests. Bookstores are thriving, too. The latest trend is toward the large bookstore that is much more than just a place to buy books. Customers come for lectures, workshops, and coffee. They bring the family, and everyone browses. They meet the author of a new mystery or how-to book. Libraries are also very busy because they offer a great deal to keep users coming back. Most libraries have computers equipped with the latest software and Internet access. And today's libraries also offer a wide variety of programs for all ages—from storytelling pajama parties for young children to travelogues for adults on the go. Americans visit libraries about three times as often as they go to movies.

30   Besides reading, there are endless numbers of **hobbies** that are not strenuous. Stamp collectors, coin collectors, Internet surfers, photographers, doll house furniture builders, painters, jewelry makers, orchid growers, and many others become skilled in a particular activity. Many hobbies have magazines and Internet groups devoted to their field.

✔ **Check Your Comprehension**   *What evidence is there that Americans still read a lot?*

31   Leisure-time activities probably define a person as much as his or her occupation does. Americans tend to begin and continue friendships with people who enjoy the same leisure pastimes. After all, mountain climbers don't have much in common with stamp collectors.

AFTER YOU READ

I. Getting the Message

A. *Underline the phrase that means the same as the one quoted from the reading. The numbers in parentheses give the paragraphs in which the phrases are used.*

1. "spectator sports and participatory sports" (2)
   a. sports to watch and sports to play
   b. team sports and individual sports

2. "professional baseball" (3)
   a. played by teams that get paid to play
   b. played for enjoyment

3. "physical contact" (4)
   a. running a lot
   b. touching each other

4. "endorsing products" (8)
   a. buying particular products
   b. saying in an ad that the particular products are good

5. "Is it any wonder?" (8)
   a. It shouldn't really be surprising.
   b. Do you ever want to know?

6. "despite the disapproval of animal lovers" (18)
   a. although people who love animals don't like this
   b. when animal lovers disapprove

7. "Amateur performances, many of excellent quality" (19)
   a. many good amateur performances
   b. a lot of amateur performances

8. "physically fit" (25)
   a. ready to go and exercise
   b. in good condition because of regular exercise

9. "No, radio and TV have not made reading obsolete." (29)
   a. People still read.
   b. Reading is no longer a popular activity.

10. "leisure-time activities" (31)
    a. things to do with one's free time
    b. activities that don't require much effort

B. *What activity would you perform to accomplish each goal? Write one activity on each line.*

1. become physically fit: _____

2. learn something new: _____

3. do something creative: _____

4. have a great adventure: _____

II. Building Your Vocabulary

A. *These are the 15 key vocabulary words for this chapter. They are boldfaced in the reading. Pronounce these words after your teacher and discuss their meanings.*

amateur*	hobby	stadium
athletics†	individual	station
compete	leisure*	strenuous
equipment	network	subscription
fan	spectator	team

B. *Complete these sentences with some of the key vocabulary words. Make the nouns plural if necessary, and put the verb into the correct tense and form.*

1. _____ is another word for sports.

2. Swimming and golf are usually _____ sports. Baseball and football are always _____ sports.

3. People often go to a(n) _____ to watch two teams _____ in a sporting event.

4. Spectators cheer for their favorite team. They are _____ of that team.

5. An athlete who doesn't get paid to play a sport is a(n) _____ athlete.

6. If you want a magazine delivered to your home regularly, you subscribe to it. You can also get a(n) _____ to cable TV channels you like.

7. Tennis is a(n) _____ sport. Players have to do a lot of running.

8. Most TV shows are produced by large companies called _____. Then, they are sold to various smaller TV _____.

Amateur and *leisure* can be adjectives or nouns.
†*Athletics* is sometimes singular and sometimes plural.

C. With a partner, write the correct word to make a phrase meaning the opposite of each phrase listed.

Example

a small audience / a _____huge_____ audience

1. an amateur team / a _____ team

2. real, natural snow / _____ snow

3. mental activity / _____ activity

4. participants in a game / _____ of a game (the people watching it)

III. Sharpening Reading Skills

Inferences

What is suggested in each of these paragraphs? Discuss your inferences with a partner.

1. paragraph 5: "The 'football widow' says her husband is 'glued to the TV set.'" Is this a literal or a figurative statement? Is he really glued? What does the wife mean?

2. paragraph 20: Why do you think the rides are short? What happens to the riders?

3. paragraph 21: Why do people who come to the racetrack lose money quickly?

4. paragraph 29: Guess what a "how-to" book is. Give some examples. Find the words *browse* and *thriving,* and try to determine their meanings from context. Then check your dictionary.

IV. Understanding Idioms and Expressions

On each blank line, write the letter of the correct phrase to complete the sentence. The numbers in parentheses give the paragraphs in which the expressions are used.

1. Baseball is called the *national pastime* (3) because it _____.
   a. is a very popular sport throughout the U.S.
   b. was very popular in the past

2. If doctors *practice what they preach* (10), they _____.
   a. do what they advise others to do
   b. give a lot of speeches

3. People who *work out* (15) a lot _____.
   a. have an outdoor job
   b. exercise often

4. If you are *window-shopping* (17), you are _____.
   a. not spending any money at that time
   b. buying new windows for your house

5. People who are trying to *get back to nature* (18) _____.
   a. play golf or tennis
   b. go hiking in the woods

6. A *soap opera* (23) is a _____.
   a. radio or TV story that continues day after day
   b. long, sad opera

7. The nicknames *boob tube* and *idiot box* (26) _____.
   a. are insulting references to TV
   b. are complimentary references to TV

V. Taking Words Apart

On the line next to each verb, write the word for the person who performs this activity. You need to add -r ,-or, or -er and sometimes also double the final consonant. Review the rules for doubling before doing the exercise. Then read the pairs of words aloud and discuss their meanings.

Examples

pitch: _____*pitcher*_____
shop: _____*shopper*_____
jog: _____*jogger*_____

1. advertise: _____
2. collect: _____
3. perform: _____
4. play: _____

5. run: _____
6. ski: _____
7. subscribe: _____
8. view: _____

VI. Practicing Sentence Patterns

A. Comparative Patterns with Adjectives   There are two comparative patterns for adjectives. For short adjectives: Bowling is easi<u>er</u> <u>than</u> baseball. For longer adjectives: Some TV shows are <u>more</u> interesting <u>than</u> others.

Work with a partner and take turns answering these questions with complete statements.

1. Which sport is more popular—walking or jogging?

2. Which sport is more strenuous—tennis or golf?

3. Which activity do you think children like better—reading a book or going to a circus?

4. Which is easier—shooting a ball into a basket or hitting a baseball?

B. Beginning Sentences with Gerunds   This chapter contains many examples of gerunds (verbals ending in *-ing*) used as subjects of sentences, objects of verbs, and objects of prepositions.

With a partner, scan paragraphs 1–3 looking for gerunds. Then complete the following sentences, using a gerund in each.

1. _____ is the most popular form of exercise in the U.S.

2. Let's go _____ this afternoon.

3. He is thinking about _____ next summer.

VII. Sharing Ideas

A. Issues

Debate these issues in small groups. Then choose one and write about it.

1. Is it beneficial or harmful for children to be involved in competitive athletics?

2. Is it wrong for people to train animals to perform for human amusement? Or is it acceptable if the animals are treated well?

3. According to a major study, the average American child spends a total of 38 hours a week using TV, radio, recordings, video games, and computers. Is this good or bad?

B. On a Personal Note

Write about one of these topics.

1. Do research in an encyclopedia or on the Internet to find information about a sport that interests you. Look up (a) when and where the game was first played or (b) how the game is played now. Write about what you learned. Don't copy from your source. Paraphrase the information, that is, use your own words.

2. What do you do with your leisure time? What do these activities contribute to your life?

3. Have you ever gone hunting or fishing? Would you? Why or why not?

4. Write a descriptive piece about how you feel when playing some sport. Describe your physical, mental, and emotional reactions.

13 | The Constitution and the Federal System

The U.S. Capitol, where Congress meets
(Washington, D.C.)

BEFORE YOU READ

Discuss

1. Why does a country need laws? List several reasons.

2. The U.S. Constitution is the "supreme law of the land." What do you know about the U.S. Constitution? What kind of government does it outline?

3. Do you think the U.S. Constitution is different from the constitutions of other countries? If so, in what ways?

Guess

Try to answer the questions. Then look for the answers in the reading.

1. Including the 10 amendments of the Bill of Rights, how many times has the U.S. Constitution been changed (amended)? Check (✓) one:

   _____ 15   _____ 27   _____ 42

2. How many people are employed by the executive branch of the U.S. government? Check (✓) one:

   _____ 300,000   _____ 1,500,000   _____ 3,000,000

The Constitution and the Federal System

The Constitution

1   Daniel Webster, the nineteenth-century American statesman, once said: "We may be tossed upon an ocean where we can see no land—nor perhaps the sun or stars. But there is a chart* and a compass for us to study, to consult, and to obey. That chart is the **Constitution**."

2   The Constitution of the United States was adopted on June 21, 1788. It is the oldest written constitution still in use. What is this Constitution? It is the basic law from which the U.S. government gets all its power. It is the law that protects those who live in the U.S.A. from unreasonable actions by the national government or any state government.

3   The Constitution defines three branches of government. They are the **legislative** branch, which enacts (makes) laws; the **executive** branch, which enforces those laws; and the **judicial** branch, which **interprets** them (decides what they mean).

4   The legislative branch is called **Congress.** It is made up of two groups of legislators— the Senate and the House of **Representatives.** A member of the Senate is addressed as *Senator.* Members of the House of Representatives are called *congressmen* or *congresswomen.* The Senate is often referred to as the upper house. It has 100 members—two **senators** from each state. Both senators represent the entire state. Senators are elected for six-year terms. Every two years, one-third of all senators face reelection.

5   The lower house, which is called the House of Representatives, has 435 members, all of whom are elected every two years. The number of representatives from each state is determined by that state's population. While the seven smallest states have only one representative each, California, the most populous state, had 52 representatives in the

---

*A map of a body of water.

106th Congress (1998 to 2000). For the purpose of electing representatives, each state is divided into congressional districts. The districts within a state are about equal in population. One representative is elected from each district. One of a representative's major duties is to protect the interests of the people in that district.

6   The job of Congress is to pass laws. Before a law is passed, it is called a *bill*. In order to become a law, a bill must be approved by a majority of each house of Congress and by the president. If the president **vetoes** (disapproves of) a bill, it can still become law if at least two-thirds of the members of each house of Congress override the veto by voting for it when it is voted on again.

7   The president is the nation's chief executive. As such, he must see that all national laws are carried out. The president also spends much of his time making decisions about foreign policy (the relationships between the U.S. and other nations). Of course, a very large staff of advisers and other employees assist the president. In fact, the executive branch employs almost 3 million people located all over the world. The most important group of advisers is called the **cabinet.** The cabinet consists of the heads of the 14 departments of the executive branch, such as the Secretaries of Education, Defense, and Agriculture. Cabinet members are chosen by the president with the approval of the Senate. The president also appoints ambassadors and other consular heads who represent the U.S. abroad. In addition, he appoints judges of the **federal** courts.

8   The vice president is the only other elected person in the executive branch. One important constitutional duty of the person holding this office is to serve as president of the Senate. The vice president's most important function is to become president upon the death, resignation, or disability of the president. Out of 37 presidents elected, eight have died in office, and one resigned. In each case, the vice president became president.

9   The judicial branch consists of the federal courts, including the highest court of the U.S., the Supreme Court. One of the unusual features of the American judicial system is the power of the courts to declare legislation **unconstitutional** and, therefore, **void**. The power of the federal government is limited by the Constitution. Federal laws cannot violate the terms of the Constitution. For example, Congress could not pass a law that members of the House of Representatives be elected for four-year terms because the Constitution says that they are to be elected for two-year terms.

10   Federal laws are in some way controlled or affected by all three branches of government—Congress makes them; the president approves and enforces them; and the courts determine what they mean and whether they are constitutional. This is one example of the government's system of checks and balances, by which each branch of government prevents improper actions by the other branches.

11   Checks and balances were put to an important test in 1974 when it was discovered that President Richard Nixon had been involved in obstruction of justice (hiding crimes) in connection with the Watergate scandal. Both Congress and the prosecutor appointed by Congress demanded that the president give them certain papers and tape recordings that he had. The president refused. He said that neither the judicial nor the legislative branch could tell the president, the head of the executive branch, what to do. He was relying on a doctrine known as the *separation of powers*. This means that one branch of the government cannot interfere with the others. During this conflict, two important questions were raised: (1) Could the president withhold information about possible crimes

from Congress and the courts? (2) Did the doctrine of separation of powers mean that the judicial branch (courts) could not order a member of the executive branch (the president) to give evidence to the prosecutor?

12   After considering these questions, the Supreme Court ordered the president to give the evidence to the prosecutor. After examining the evidence, Congress began the constitutional procedure to remove the president from office—**impeachment** (an official accusation of wrongdoing) and trial. However, before the process was completed, President Nixon resigned from office. The checks and balances prevented a major governmental crisis, and the presidency passed smoothly to the vice president, Gerald Ford. The "chart" had kept the country on course, even when the captain tried to stray.

> ✔ **Check Your Comprehension**
>
> *What is the job of each branch of government?*
> *What is the President's cabinet?*

The Amendments to the Constitution

13   Amendments to the Constitution are first proposed by a two-thirds vote of both houses of Congress. Then, they must be approved by the legislatures of three-quarters of the states or by a vote of conventions in three-quarters of the states.

14   Since the addition of the Bill of Rights (the first 10 amendments) in 1791, the Constitution has been changed (amended) only 17 times, and one of those **amendments** simply canceled another. (The Seventeenth Amendment prohibited the manufacture and sale of alcoholic beverages; the Twenty-first Amendment repealed the Seventeenth Amendment.)

15   Probably the most significant portion of the Constitution is the Bill of Rights, the first 10 amendments to the Constitution. The first of these assures freedom of religion, speech, and the press and the right to complain to and about the government. Speech is protected no matter how unpopular or repulsive, so long as it does not create an immediate and serious danger to life or property. Free speech means that the government cannot prevent people from saying or writing whatever they want, nor can it punish people for expressing ideas that criticize the government. Free speech is at the very heart of democracy. Former Supreme Court Justice Louis Brandeis said that, for a democracy to work, people must be allowed to express new, unusual, and unpopular ideas so that they can be debated and examined and then adopted or rejected. After all, democracy itself was a new and strange idea in the eighteenth century, and it still is in many parts of the world.

16   Freedom of religion means that each person can belong (or not belong) to any religious group. An individual can follow any religion's teachings as long as these do not seriously interfere with the rights of others. Religious freedom also means that neither the federal government nor any state government can encourage or prevent the practice of religion. This idea has been called the wall of separation between church and state.

17   The Fourth, Fifth, Sixth, and Eighth Amendments protect people suspected or accused of crimes. But these amendments also protect all U.S. residents. Government officials and police cannot arrest people or search them, their property, or their homes without some reason to believe that they have committed a crime.

18   Recently, the Second Amendment has created much discussion and controversy. This amendment deals with the right of people to keep and bear arms (guns). In view of the large number of guns in the U.S. and the increased use of them in committing crimes, especially murder, many people are recommending greater limitations on gun ownership and possession.

19   Certainly, the most important of the remaining amendments is the Fourteenth, which grew out of the Civil War. It was passed to protect former slaves from state laws that discriminated against them. But its effect has been much broader than that. It gives full federal and state citizenship to all people born in the U.S. or naturalized there (including former slaves). It prohibits states from violating the rights of American citizens. But the most significant provision is that no state may "deprive any person of life, liberty or property, without due process of law; nor deny to any person within its jurisdiction the equal protection of the laws." That means that all persons have equal legal rights and that their rights or possessions cannot be taken without a proper trial. These last provisions apply not only to U.S. citizens but to all persons in the country. Originally, the Bill of Rights did not protect people from state action, but only from federal action. The Fourteenth Amendment has been interpreted by the Supreme Court to apply almost all of the provisions in the Bill of Rights to the individual states. Thus, the Fourteenth Amendment is one of the most valuable protections that people living in the U.S. have.

✔ **Check Your Comprehension**   *Name some of the most important rights granted in the Bill of Rights. Why is the Fourteenth Amendment so important?*

The Federal System

20   The United States is organized as a federal system. This means that the power to govern is divided between the national (federal) government, located in Washington, D.C., and the state governments. Laws passed by Congress (federal laws) must be authorized by the U.S. Constitution. That is what is meant by the statement that the United States government gets all its powers from the Constitution. All matters over which the federal government does not have power can be regulated only by the individual states (such as ownership of property, divorce, and education).

21   The original purpose of a national central government was to perform those tasks that could not be performed efficiently by each state individually. For example, dealing with foreign nations, establishing a monetary system, and regulating commerce between states could be done better by a single national authority. Other governmental responsibilities, such as public school systems, local roads, and police and fire protection, were left to the states and their subdivisions.

22   While the federal government's power is limited by the Constitution, the individual states are given the power to pass any law that is not prohibited by the Constitution. In those areas where both the states and the federal government have the power to pass laws, state laws cannot conflict with those passed by the federal government.

23   Most state governments are quite similar in structure to the national government. Each is headed by an elected executive called a *governor*. The legislative branch may be called a *state legislature* or *general assembly*, or have some other name, but it generally func-

tions much as Congress does. Most of the state legislatures also have two houses. The state court systems generally follow the three-level federal court plan, which provides for a trial court, an appellate (appeals) court, and a supreme court.

24   States are divided into smaller governmental units, such as counties, cities, towns, and villages. These units can pass laws that are authorized by the state in which they are located, and they are responsible for making and enforcing these laws within their boundaries.

25   The U.S.A. and its Constitution have withstood many crises and criticisms. Since the Constitution was written, this nation has changed from a rural and agricultural society to a highly industrialized, urban society. The population has grown from less than 4 million to about 275 million. Still, the "chart" that Daniel Webster mentioned continues to keep the nation securely on course. The American experiment in democracy has proved conclusively that government "of the people, by the people, for the people" can function effectively for the good of its citizens.

AFTER YOU READ

I. Getting the Message

A. *On each blank line, write the letter of the correct word or phrase to complete the sentence.*

1. The Bill of Rights is _____.
   a. part of the U.S. Constitution
   b. a separate document

2. In this reading, the word cabinet refers to _____.
   a. a piece of furniture
   b. a group of people who advise the president

3. Amendments to the U.S. Constitution _____.
   a. were part of the original document
   b. must be approved by the states

4. The members of the Senate are _____.
   a. elected for a 6-year term
   b. appointed for life

5. A state legislative body _____ pass a law that violates the U.S. Constitution.
   a. can
   b. cannot

B. *Who's elected? Who's appointed? Discuss the meanings of these words. Then, put a check (✓) in the correct column for each job listed.*

Government employees	Elected	Appointed
1. the president		
2. the cabinet		
3. the vice president		
4. senators		
5. state governors		
6. federal judges		

C. *Reread paragraphs 11 and 12. Then discuss why President Nixon's argument made to the Supreme Court was important. What did the outcome prove?*

D. *Read these sentences with the word* nor. *Then answer the question that follows.*

1. paragraph 15, sentence 4: Can the government punish a person for saying something bad about the country or its leaders? Yes / No

2. paragraph 16, sentence 3: Can the federal government encourage the practice of one particular religion? Yes / No

II. Building Your Vocabulary

A. *These are the 15 key vocabulary words for this chapter. They are boldfaced in the reading. Pronounce these words after your teacher and discuss their meanings.*

amendment	federal	representative*
cabinet	impeachment	senator
Congress	interpret	unconstitutional
constitution†	judicial	veto‡
executive*	legislative	void§

---

*These words can be nouns or adjectives.

†The word *constitution* is capitalized when it refers to the U.S. Constitution.

‡This word can be a noun or a verb.

§This word can be a noun, a verb, or an adjective.

B. *Complete these sentences with some of the key vocabulary words on page 149. Make the nouns plural if necessary.*

1. The first 10 _____ to the U.S. Constitution are called the Bill of Rights.

2. One of the jobs of the Supreme Court is to _____ the Constitution.

3. In a(n) _____ system of government, the governing powers are divided between the state governments and the national government.

4. If Congress votes in favor of making a bill a law, the president can still stop that bill from becoming law by using the _____ power.

5. To avoid _____, President Nixon resigned from office.

6. Every state elects two _____ to the Senate, but in the House of Representatives, the number of _____ from each state varies, depending on the state's population.

7. The House of Representatives and the Senate together make up

   _____.

8. When a law violates the U.S. Constitution, the judicial branch of government will declare it _____.

III. Sharpening Reading Skills

A. Metaphors   *Metaphors* compare things that are not really alike. The comparison is figurative (imaginary), not literal (real). For example, in paragraph 1, the U.S. Constitution is compared to a chart (map) that guides someone sailing a ship. Note that metaphors compare two things without using the words *as* or *like*.

Answer the following questions by looking for metaphors in the paragraphs indicated.

1. What is President Nixon compared to? (12) _____

2. What is the amendment requiring separation of church and state compared to? (16) _____

B. Analogies   An analogy is another type of comparison. In *analogies,* the comparisons are between things that are similar.

Example

The president is to the national government as a _____ is to a state government. (senator, governor, representative)
Governor is the answer because both are heads of the executive branch of government.

Complete these analogies by writing the correct choices on the blank lines.

1. In paragraph 1, the chart and compass are to a ship as the _____ is/are to the U.S. (ocean, stars, Constitution)

2. Congressmen and congresswomen are to the House of Representatives as _____ are to the Senate. (senators, judges, cabinet members)

IV. Understanding Idioms and Expressions

On each blank line, write the letter of the correct phrase to complete the sentence. The numbers in parentheses give the paragraphs in which the expressions are used.

1. The *upper house* (4) of Congress _____.
   a. meets in a room above the lower house
   b. is called the Senate

2. Each member of the *lower house* (5) is _____.
   a. elected by one district of a state
   b. called a senator

3. *Such as* (7, 20, 21) means _____.
   a. of course
   b. for example

4. *Carried out* (7) means _____.
   a. followed, performed, done
   b. removed by force

5. The expression *checks and balances* (10) refers to _____.
   a. the relationship between the two houses of Congress
   b. the relationship between the three branches of the federal government

6. *Obstruction of justice* (11) means _____.
   a. committing a crime
   b. withholding evidence about a crime

7. *Free speech* (15) means _____.
   a. people have the right to express all kinds of ideas
   b. there is no charge to hear speeches

V. Taking Words Apart

In English, many verbs can be made into nouns by adding the suffix -tion or -ment. Change each of the following verbs into a noun that ends with one of these two suffixes. Be careful. Sometimes additional spelling changes are needed before adding the suffix. Use a dictionary for help. Read the word pairs aloud.

1. amend _____

2. apply _____

3. appoint _____

4. elect _____

5. govern _____

6. interpret _____

7. prohibit _____

8. protect _____

9. regulate _____

10. resign _____

11. separate _____

12. state (say) _____

13. violate _____

VI. Practicing Sentence Patterns

Notice the use of *neither* and *nor* in the fourth sentence of paragraph 11. These are negative words. When they are used, the verb is affirmative, but the meaning of the sentence is negative.

Example

I have neither a car nor a bicycle. (I don't have either one.)

Also notice that in *neither / nor* sentences, the verb must agree with the closest noun.

Examples

Neither my dad nor my <u>sisters</u> <u>have</u> a car.
Neither my sisters nor my <u>dad</u> <u>has</u> a car.

Write two sentences with neither / nor using the subjects given and information from the text.

1. president / vice president: _____

    _____

2. senators / congressmen: _____

    _____

VII. Sharing Ideas

A. Issues

Debate these issues in small groups. Then choose one and write about it.

1. In a federal system, should the individual states have the right to leave the federation (the national government) and become independent?

2. Should the national government protect children from pornographic material on TV, in movies, in popular songs, or in magazines? Or do laws making pornography illegal violate freedom of speech?

3. To what extent should the government regulate the sale and ownership of handguns?

B. On a Personal Note

Write about one of these topics.

1. Compare the job of the U.S. president with the job of the head of state in another country. Which person has more power? Who has the more difficult job?

2. Would you ever want to run for political office? Explain why or why not.

3. In other countries that you know about, is the government limited in what it can force citizens to do or prevent citizens from doing? Compare freedom and human rights in the U.S. and one other country.

14 Choosing the Nation's President

The White House, home of the President
(Washington, D.C.)

BEFORE YOU READ

Discuss

1. How do Americans choose their president? Tell what you know about the process.

2. How does a person become the leader in other countries you're familiar with?

3. Do you think the leader of a country should be elected by all the citizens?

Guess

Try to answer the questions. Then look for the answers in the reading.

1. In the 1996 presidential election, how much money was spent on all the campaigns? Check (✓) one:

   _____ $23 million   _____ $400 million   _____ $1.2 billion

2. Does the presidential candidate with the greatest number of votes always win the election? Check (✓) one:

   _____ Yes   _____ No

3. Which political party is called the GOP (Grand Old Party)? Check (✓) one:

   _____ the Democrats   _____ the Republicans

Choosing the Nation's President

Selecting the Candidates

1   Every four years, Americans participate in a unique and exciting ritual—selecting the nation's president and vice president. Beginning early in a presidential election year, people who would like to "run" for the office of president try to win **delegates** to their party's national political **convention.** Delegates are chosen from each state. Some are selected at state caucuses (local meetings of voters and **party** officials) and others by party conventions. But most are chosen by **primary** elections. Primaries give voters an opportunity to indicate whom they want to be their party's presidential **candidate.** In a primary election, a presidential candidate is running against other candidates in the same political party, competing for that state's delegate votes.

2   The summer before the election, each of the two major political parties—the Democrats and the Republicans—holds a national convention lasting about four days. At these conventions, delegates select the people who will be candidates for president and vice president. The number of delegates from each state is determined by its population and its support for that party in previous elections. The total number of delegates at a convention ranges from about 2,000 to about 4,000.

3   Convention business usually begins with the creation and acceptance of the party's **platform**. A platform is a general statement of the party's philosophy, positions, and goals on **issues** of national and international concern. A majority of the convention delegates must vote in favor of the various planks of the platform in order for them to be accepted. (A *plank* is a statement on one subject.)

4   The next order of business is the nomination of prospective presidential candidates. A speaker **nominates** each nominee, telling that person's strengths and accomplishments. Each nominating speech is followed by a long, noisy **demonstration.** Bands play, and thousands of delegates wave flags and signs, sing, yell, and clap. When the

convention quiets down, a seconding speech is given for each nominee. This is also followed by a noisy display of support.

5   After the nominations, the delegates get down to the serious work of choosing their party's presidential candidate. What qualities are delegates looking for in their candidate? The most important qualification is the ability to win the election. In addition, delegates consider a nominee's integrity, philosophy, and talent for leadership. Votes are taken alphabetically by state. At some conventions, one nominee gets the majority of delegate votes on the first roll call. At others, several roll calls may be necessary before one nominee wins the majority of votes. Sometimes, state delegations bargain with the major nominees. Delegates may agree to switch their votes in exchange for some political favor or governmental position. For example, an agreement might be made that, in exchange for a state's votes, the nominee will recommend a certain person to be the vice presidential candidate. Eventually, enough deals are made that one person receives a majority of the votes and becomes the party's presidential candidate.

The 2000 Republican National Convention

6   In recent years, more and more states have held primary elections. As a result, it has become common for one candidate to win a majority of the delegates' votes during the primaries. In that event, the party's presidential candidate has already been chosen before the convention even begins.

7   After the presidential candidate is selected, the vice presidential candidate must be chosen. Traditionally, the convention officially elects whomever the presidential candidate wants as his running mate. It is customary (and good politics) for a party's presidential and vice presidential candidates to come from different parts of the country and to have somewhat different political views. That way, the team appeals to voters with different viewpoints and concerns. At the convention, the two candidates are formally nominated, elected as the party's candidates, and cheered greatly before and after they give their acceptance speeches. Finally, the convention adjourns (ends).

The Campaign

8   Campaigning for the general election traditionally begins on Labor Day in early September. From that time until Election Day, in early November, voters are bombarded from all sides—by radio, television, newspapers, mail, and personal communications—with political material. Long-standing friendships and even marriages can become battlegrounds as Americans argue about issues and candidates. Ordinarily soft-spoken people become outspoken supporters of their candidate. Neighborhood political workers from each party knock on doors and give voters information about the candidates they support.

9   Each candidate tries to convince a majority of the American voters that he is best qualified to lead the country for the next 4 years. Since the candidate has only 2 months in which to do this, he must **campaign** very hard, day and night. All of the resources of modern communication are used to acquaint the voters with the candidates' views and personalities. Television has become a powerful influence. The candidate who lacks personal appeal on TV is at a great disadvantage. In 1960, a series of televised debates between Richard Nixon and John Kennedy probably influenced enough voters to change the election results. It has been said that if Abraham Lincoln were alive today, he probably wouldn't be elected president because he wasn't handsome.

10   Although modern communications have better acquainted voters with candidates and issues, the resulting costs of election campaigns have created a serious problem. The various candidates who participated in the 1996 presidential campaign spent a combined total of more than $400 million. About $152 million of this total was contributed by the federal government. To receive government campaign money, candidates must raise an equal amount from private donations. Accepting private donations means that the person elected has many "friends" who may expect political favors in return for their financial help. Also, sometimes very well-qualified people cannot raise enough money to campaign for the presidency.

11   Campaigning is extremely expensive, and a candidate must receive a majority of the electoral votes to be elected; therefore, only the candidates of the two major parties can expect to win. Still, third parties play an important role in American politics by focusing attention on particular issues and by influencing the policies of the major parties.

12   Critics often ask, "Does it matter who wins? Are there any real differences between the two political parties?" No candidate can hope to win by appealing to only one or two groups of voters, such as farmers or businesspeople. Because of the need for broad appeal, the philosophies of both parties usually take a middle course so as not to offend any large groups of voters. The government does change somewhat depending on which party is in power, but it doesn't change as much as political campaign speeches might lead one to believe.

13   During an election campaign, one hears a lot of political labels, such as reactionary, **conservative**, moderate (middle-of-the-road), **liberal**, and radical. Most Democrats are

moderates or liberals. Most Republicans are moderates or conservatives. People sometimes refer to liberals as being *to the left* and conservatives as being *to the right*. In terms of specific programs, Democrats (or liberals) tend to favor more spending for social programs to help poorer people and less spending for military programs. Republicans' (or conservatives') goals tend to be the opposite. Traditionally, Democrats have also favored a stronger federal government while Republicans have emphasized states' rights. The Democratic party is generally considered more supportive of the poor and the middle-class worker. Republican policies generally support big business and the rich.

14   Each party has a familiar symbol. For the Democrats, it is a donkey, known for its stubbornness. The Republican symbol is an elephant, an animal that is supposed to have a long memory. These symbols were created by Thomas Nast, a famous nineteenth-century political cartoonist. The Republican party is also called the GOP (Grand Old Party).

15   To preserve free democratic elections, candidates in all elections are allowed to express their opinions publicly. They may even severely criticize other candidates and their viewpoints, without fear of punishment. This is true even when an **opponent** is an **incumbent** president (one who is currently holding office).

Check Your Comprehension

What are the two major political parties in the U.S.?
What are some differences between them?

The Election

16   On the Tuesday following the first Monday in November, voters cast their ballots for president and vice president. A party's presidential and vice presidential candidates are voted for as a team, not individually. The entire House of Representatives, one-third of the Senate, and many state and local officials are also elected at this time. Thanks to voting machines and computers, Americans usually know most of the winners by late evening. In fact, the television networks often predict the results of an election as soon as the polls close. They do this by conducting exit polls—asking voters in scientifically selected precincts how they voted.

17   The president and vice president are not actually chosen by how many people vote for them (the popular vote); instead, they are chosen by *electoral votes*. Altogether, there are 538 electoral votes; it takes 270 (a majority) to win. When citizens cast votes for presidential and vice presidential candidates, they are selecting their state's electors (people chosen under state laws and procedures to cast each state's votes for president and vice president). Each elector is expected (although not legally required) to vote for the candidate who wins the majority of the popular votes in that state. These electors as a group are called the *Electoral College*.

18   The number of electors for each state is equal to the total number of representatives and senators who represent that state in Congress. (In addition, the District of Columbia has three electoral votes.) Thus, states with larger populations have more electoral votes. In all states except Maine and Nebraska, the candidate who receives the largest

number of popular votes receives *all* of a state's electoral votes. With this system, it is possible for a candidate to receive more popular votes than an opponent but fewer electoral votes and, therefore, lose the election. This can happen when a candidate loses by small margins in states with many electoral votes and wins by large margins in states with few electoral votes (as shown in the chart below). Only three American presidents have reached the White House by losing the popular vote but winning the majority of electoral votes. This happened in 2000, when George W. Bush was elected. When the Electoral College votes, it is also possible, in some states, for an elector *not* to cast his ballot for the candidate who won the popular vote in that state. However, since electors are important members of their political parties, this rarely happens.

Sample of Popular and Electoral Votes from the 2000 Presidential Election

States	Popular Vote		Electoral Vote
	Democrat (Al Gore)	Republican (George W. Bush)	
Iowa	634,475	629,521	7 Democrat
Kansas	391,026	614,419	6 Republican
Utah	201,732	512,161	5 Republican
Wisconsin	1,240,266	1,234,167	11 Democrat
Totals	2,467,499	2,990,268	18 Democrat 11 Republican

19   To be elected, candidates for president and vice president must receive a majority of the votes in the Electoral College. If no candidate receives a majority, the House of Representatives chooses the president from the top three candidates. Each state has one vote for president. The Senate chooses the vice president from the two top candidates. Each senator has a vote. This has only happened once, in 1824, when John Quincy Adams was elected.

20   This Electoral College method of choosing the president has been criticized as old-fashioned and undemocratic. However, states with small populations do not want to change it. They have a greater proportional vote in the Electoral College than they would have if the president were chosen by popular vote.

✔ **Check Your Comprehension**   *What's the difference between popular votes and electoral votes? Which type of vote elects a president?*

The Inauguration

21   The newly elected president and vice president are inaugurated (formally sworn in) on January 20 following the election. The **inauguration** is nationally televised and is followed by a parade and many parties. The president then moves into the White House and appoints members of the cabinet (the president's closest advisers, who are also the heads of the various departments of the executive branch). Between the election and the inauguration, the outgoing president meets with the newly elected president and his staff to plan for a smooth transition from one administration to the next. Because the outgoing president is only awaiting the end of his term, he is often referred to as a "lame duck." Sometimes the new president and the majority of the members of Congress belong to different parties. When this happens, it is more difficult for the president to keep promises made during the campaign.

22   Since the two major parties are not extremely different, there is seldom a sudden shift in national policy when a new president from a different party takes office. Change occurs only with the passage of time, as the new administration becomes accustomed to its powers.

AFTER YOU READ

I. Getting the Message

A. *Work with a partner. Number the events in chronological order from 1–10, starting with the earliest. The first one is done for you.*

_____ primary elections

_____ the inauguration

_____ Election Day

_____ the election campaign

_____ the "lame duck" period

_____ a party's selection of a vice presidential candidate

_____ the creation of a party platform

__1__ politicians announce they want to be president

_____ the opening of the political convention

_____ a party's selection of a presidential candidate

B. *Using information from this chapter and your opinions, in small groups discuss what's good and what's bad about the American system of choosing the president. Then fill in your answers.*

Good

1. _____

2. _____

Bad

1. _____

2. _____

II. Building Your Vocabulary

A. *These are the 15 key vocabulary words for this chapter. They are boldfaced in the reading. Pronounce these words after your teacher, and discuss their meanings.*

campaign*	demonstration	nominate
candidate	inauguration	opponent
conservative†	incumbent†	party
convention	issue	platform
delegate*	liberal†	primary†

B. *Complete these sentences with some of the key vocabulary words. Make the nouns plural if necessary, and put the verbs into the correct tense and form.*

1. Every 4 years, the two major political _____ hold a national

   _____.

2. At each convention, _____ vote to choose that party's candidates for president and vice president.

3. In general, the Democratic party appeals to more _____ voters and the Republican party to more _____ voters.

4. The planks of each party's _____ tell that party's viewpoints on important political and social _____.

5. The presidential candidates from each party _____ from September until the November election.

6. The Republican and Democratic presidential candidates run against one another. They are _____ in the election.

---

*These words can be nouns or verbs.

†These words can be adjectives or nouns.

(continued on the next page)

7. The president is elected in November but does not take office until the following January, immediately after the _____.

8. A president running for reelection is a(n) _____ candidate.

C. *What is the difference between a nominee and a candidate? Check the definitions in a dictionary. Then discuss these words in class.*

III. Sharpening Reading Skills

A. Making Inferences

Reread the paragraphs indicated after each statement and decide if the statement is true or false. Each paragraph either states or implies the information you need. After rereading each paragraph, mark each statement below true (T) or false (F).

_____ 1. Delegates at a national political convention belong to the same party. (2)

_____ 2. When a political convention comes to town, many businesses make money. (2)

_____ 3. The presidential candidate is expected to accept the party's platform. (3)

_____ 4. Being a delegate to a political convention could give a person a headache. (4)

_____ 5. A lot of compromises are made during a political convention. (5)

_____ 6. When delegates choose their party's presidential candidate, their main concern is to choose someone who will be a good president. (5)

_____ 7. When the convention votes, the candidate who wins the majority of the delegates' votes becomes the presidential candidate. (5)

_____ 8. The candidate with the second-largest number of delegate votes becomes the party's vice presidential candidate. (7)

_____ 9. This reading suggests that the U.S. needs more political parties. (11)

B. What Does the Chart Say?

Answer these questions based on the chart of popular and electoral votes on p. 159, and, where appropriate, the paragraphs indicated.

1. In 2000, which of the four listed states gave Bush more popular votes?

_____

2. Who got more popular votes in these four states combined, Gore or Bush?

_____

3. Who got more electoral votes in these four states combined?

_____

4. The chart says that Gore got all 11 of Wisconsin's electoral votes? Why? (17, 18)

_____

5. Why did Gore win more electoral votes in these four states even though Bush won more popular votes? (18) _____

_____

IV. Understanding Idioms and Expressions

A. *Complete each sentence with one of the expressions from the list. The numbers in parentheses give the paragraphs in which the expressions are used.*

cast ballots (16)   lame duck (21)
Electoral College (17)   raise money (10)
exit polls (16)   roll call (5)
in exchange for (5)   run for office (1)
in return for (10)   running mate (7)

1. At the conventions, each state announces how its delegates vote when a(n) _____ is taken.

2. Political candidates _____. They try to get elected to political jobs.

3. Candidates need to _____, in other words, get people to contribute to their campaign.

4. The _____ officially elects the president of the United States.

5. _____ are surveys conducted on Election Day to find out how people voted.

6. Another way of saying that people vote is to say that they _____.

7. Two of the expressions listed have the same meaning. They are _____ and _____.

8. In the last few months of his presidency, Bill Clinton was a(n) _____ president because a new president had been elected and he was leaving office.

9. In 1984, a woman ran for vice president. She was the _____ of Walter Mondale, the Democratic candidate for president.

B. *Discuss the meanings of the following expressions. The numbers in parentheses give the paragraphs in which they are used.*

quiet down (4)   get down to work (5)

V. Taking Words Apart

A. Compound Words

Discuss the meanings of the following compound words. The numbers in parentheses give the paragraphs in which the words are used.

long-standing (8)   soft-spoken (8)   outspoken (8)   outgoing (21)

B. Words with the Letters *ex-*

The letters ex- are sometimes pronounced [eks] and sometimes [egz]. Say these words aloud after your teacher. Then write [eks] or [egz] on each line. If you need help, look at a dictionary's pronunciation symbols.

1. example _____
2. extremely _____
3. expensive _____
4. executive _____
5. expect _____
6. exciting _____
7. exit _____
8. next _____
9. exchange _____
10. extent _____

C. Words Used as Nouns and Verbs: The Word *Support*

The word support appears in paragraphs 2, 4, 8, and 13. Indicate in which paragraphs it is used as a noun and in which it is used as a verb.

noun: _____

verb: _____

VI. Practicing Sentence Patterns

A. Passive Voice   In this chapter, many sentences use passive voice verbs. In *passive voice* sentences, the subject does not perform the action of the verb but receives that action: *An important law was passed by Congress yesterday.* On the other hand, in active voice sentences, the subject performs the action of the verb: *Congress passed an important law yesterday.*

Find two examples of passive verbs in paragraph 1 of the reading, and write them below.

_____   _____

Now write two sentences using the passive voice and the indicated words. Add any other words needed to make a good sentence.

1. American president / elected / the year 2000 (Use past tense.)

   _____

2. Vice presidential candidate / usually chosen / presidential candidate (Use present tense.)

   _____

B. Subjunctive Mood The last sentences in paragraphs 9 and 20 are in the subjunctive mood. The *subjunctive* is used to write about something that might—or might not—happen if some other condition were true: *If Abraham Lincoln were alive today, he probably wouldn't be elected president.* Notice that *were* is used after *if,* even when the subject is first person singular: *If I were old enough, I would vote in the next election.*

Write two of your own statements of this type. In the main clause, use would *plus an infinitive verb.*

1. If I were president of the U.S., _____

   _____.

2. If I had a million dollars, _____

   _____.

VII. Sharing Ideas

A. Issues

Debate these issues in small groups. Then choose one and write about it.

1. Besides being at least 35 years old and American-born, should there be additional requirements for presidential candidates? If so, what should they be?

2. What are some advantages and disadvantages of a two-party system?

3. Would it be a good thing for Americans to elect a woman president?

B. On a Personal Note

Write about one of these topics.

1. Almost all American parents dream of their child growing up to be president. Would you want to have that job? Would you want your child to have it? Explain why or why not.

2. In your opinion, what is good about the American system of choosing a president? What are some weaknesses of the system?

3. Write a letter to the current president of the United States. Give the president advice about how to handle a national or international problem. Address your letter to: The White House, 1600 Pennsylvania Ave. NW, Washington, D.C. 20500. (Add *U.S.A.* if you live outside the U.S.) Be sure to include your return address so your letter can be answered.

Citizenship: Its Obligations and Privileges

15

New American citizens at their swearing-in ceremony

BEFORE YOU READ

Discuss

1. What are some things that any government is expected to do for its citizens?

2. What are citizens expected to do for their government?

3. What are some advantages of being a citizen of the country you live in?

Guess

Try to answer the questions. Then look for the answers in the reading.

1. What is the range of income tax rates in the U.S.? Check (✓) one:

   _____ 5%–10.5%   _____ 15%–39.6%   _____ 22%–50%

2. Who is Uncle Sam? Check (✓) one:

   _____ a famous American president   _____ a symbol of the U.S. government

Citizenship: Its Obligations and Privileges

Becoming a Citizen

1   Every person living in the United States, citizen or not, is **entitled** to most of the nation's basic freedoms and protections. However, there are many **advantages** to becoming citizens for people who intend to live in the U.S.A. permanently. Of these, the most important are the right to remain in the U.S. and the right to participate in its government by voting. Once **aliens** become **naturalized** citizens, their rights are the same as those of any native-born citizen, except that they cannot become president or vice president.

2   With few exceptions, anyone born in the U.S. is automatically a citizen. Also, a person born outside the U.S. to parents who are both American citizens is a citizen. An alien who wishes to become a citizen must fulfill certain legal requirements. In most cases, a person must wait five continuous years after becoming a permanent resident. At least half of those five years must be spent in the U.S., and no trips outside the U.S. for more than six continuous months are permitted. The applicant must also have lived at least three months in the state in which the application is made.

3   In order to show the potential for being a good, productive citizen, it is necessary that the applicant show an understanding of the English language and of the history, principles, and form of government of the U.S. The applicant must also demonstrate good moral character and a belief in the principles of the U.S. Constitution, such as representative government and free speech. Once approved for citizenship, the applicant goes before a judge and swears loyalty to the United States of America. This swearing-in ceremony is usually attended by a group of people who become citizens at the same time.

✔ **Check Your Comprehension** *Name five requirements a permanent resident must fulfill in order to become an American citizen.*

Responsibilities of Citizens

4   Probably the most important right and responsibility of citizens in a democracy is to participate actively in government. One way that they participate is by voting. Unfortunately, in every election, a large percentage of those entitled to vote never come to the polls. In 1996, for example, fewer than 50% of those **eligible** voted for a presidential candidate. When a large number of citizens do not vote, those who do have a greater voice in determining the outcome of the election. If only 50% of the people vote, 26% of the total population can elect the president and members of Congress. The idea of majority rule is, thus, lost.

5   Another way that citizens can participate in government is by communicating with their representatives. In order for elected officials to represent their constituents properly, they must know what the voters think about current laws and **pending** legislation. Do they feel that certain laws are outmoded and should be discarded? Are they for or against a particular **bill**? Is there something their government should be doing but isn't (or shouldn't be doing but is)? Representatives who want to stay in office (be reelected) try to vote as their constituents desire. Voters can communicate with representatives by mail, phone, or e-mail or by attending town hall meetings. Unfortunately, very few voters take the time to communicate with their federal or state representatives. As a result, a small, active minority can influence legislation out of proportion to their numbers, and this leads to a distortion of the representative form of government.

6   Americans often exercise their right to protest government action (or inactions). The U.S. Constitution gives people living in the U.S. the rights to assemble peaceably, to petition the government (request changes), and to express opinions freely about the government's policies. Peaceful protests outside government office buildings (and many foreign embassies and consulates) are common. Groups (such as those **opposed** to the government's antidrug or abortion policies) march with signs, singing and chanting, to let their government know what they favor or oppose. However, in expressing dissatisfaction, people must respect the rights of others to express opposing views or be **neutral**.

7   One of a citizen's duties—military service—often leads to **controversy.** Although the U.S. does not now have **compulsory** military service, from time to time in its history, a military draft has been in effect. Of course, during World War II, citizens were required to serve in the armed forces, and most did so willingly. But in more recent times, the government has met with a great deal of **resistance** to its draft laws. During the Korean War and, especially, during the Vietnam War, many young men did everything they could to avoid military service. Some demanded noncombat assignments because they had strong personal or religious objections to killing. Some left the country to avoid the draft. Much of that resistance was due to the lack of support for the United States' fighting against countries that were not directly threatening its safety. American opposition to the war in Vietnam was so strong that the U.S. was finally forced to abandon its military efforts there.

8   Another duty of citizens is to serve on a **jury**, if selected. A jury is a group of people who are chosen to listen to evidence presented in court. In civil cases, members of the jury must decide which of the battling parties is right. In criminal cases, they must de-

cide whether the accused person has committed a crime. The jury is basic to the American system of justice. The right to a jury trial is guaranteed by the U.S. Constitution and by most state constitutions. Jury panels are usually selected from voter lists. From these panels, which may include several hundred people where courts are busiest, 12 jurors are usually selected to hear each trial. Many people find jury service an interesting and rewarding experience. Others consider it a nuisance. A jury summons means people are required to take time off from work (or their other daily activities) to appear in court and fulfill this civic duty—sometimes for days or even weeks.

> ✔ **Check Your Comprehension** *What are four ways that citizens can communicate their ideas to their representatives in government?*

Responsibilities of All U.S. Residents

9   Every individual, no matter how important or wealthy, must obey the laws. Of course, not all laws are perfect. Some are unwise, others are too harsh, many are foolish. But they cannot, for any of these reasons, be ignored. Anyone living in the U.S. who disapproves of a particular law has the right to try to persuade the government to get it changed through peaceful means.

10 The least popular laws are probably those requiring payment of taxes. For most people, the largest of these is the federal income tax. Since 1913, the U.S. government has been collecting income taxes. As the cost of running the government has increased, so have tax rates. When the federal income tax law was first enacted, people had to pay 1% on annual incomes of less than $20,000. Income of more than $500,000 was taxed at 7%. Today's income tax rates are between 15% and 39.6%. Currently, income taxes provide more than half the money collected by the federal government each year. In 1998, the federal government received about $960 billion in income taxes. These taxes are necessary to support a federal budget that, in 1998, was about $1.67 trillion. The money is used for many things. In addition to the cost of operating the government itself, there are expenses for defense, education, foreign aid, research, aid to the poor, and countless other services provided by governmental agencies.

11 Income tax is paid by nearly everyone who earns money in the United States—citizens, resident aliens, and visitors. Federal income tax rates are *graduated*, which means that people with larger incomes are taxed at a higher rate than those earning less. In addition, deductions and exemptions reduce the amount of income that is taxed. An unmarried person earning $25,000 a year pays about 11% of that in taxes, while someone earning $75,000 pays about 21%. (A married couple earning that amount would pay only 16%.)

12 Employers are required to withhold a percentage of their employees' salaries and pay it to the government to be applied toward the employees' taxes. Self-employed people and those earning a substantial amount in addition to their salaries must make quarterly payments toward their annual taxes. By April 15, each person whose income in the previous year exceeded a certain minimum must file a tax return—a statement, on

forms supplied by the government, listing income, expenses, number of dependents, and other information. After making calculations on the return, taxpayers can determine how much they owe. Those who have paid more than their share get a **refund**. Those who have paid less must pay the balance. Every year around April 15, millions of Americans complain, "Uncle Sam is taking all my money." Uncle Sam (the thin, bearded gentleman whose clothes resemble the American flag) is a symbol of the U.S. government. Uncle Sam knows a lot about each taxpayer and penalizes those who file false returns. Still, the income tax law could not be enforced without the honesty and cooperation of most taxpayers.

13   In addition to federal income tax, employers also withhold Social Security and Medicare taxes and state income taxes. Most states and many cities also collect income taxes. Besides income taxes, many other taxes are collected by federal, state, and local governments. The most common are those imposed on property and purchases. The owner of a car, for example, pays several taxes: a sales tax when buying the car, an annual vehicle registration tax, and a personal property tax. If the person who owns a car dies, the heirs may have to pay an inheritance tax on the car's value. Funds from these taxes are used to provide services and facilities such as courts, schools, roads, and parks.

14   Despite complaints about high taxes, Americans know that the taxes they pay make possible the valuable services they receive. Also, when all American taxes are added together, they total less than 32% of the nation's gross domestic product. This is one of the lowest percentages of all industrial nations.

✔ Check Your Comprehension   *What are four different taxes that most U.S. residents pay?*

Responsibilities of the Government

15   The government has many **obligations** to those who live in the U.S.A. For example, it must provide police services, courts, a legislative body (Congress), postal services, defense against foreign invaders, and the like. What additional services the federal government should provide has always been the subject of debate. Generally, conservatives feel that the federal government should not provide services much beyond the basics, while liberals want the government to provide assistance wherever it is needed.

16   Money for medical care for the poor and elderly, assistance for those who cannot afford decent housing, and aid to education at all levels are areas of controversy. During the twentieth century, the amount of direct assistance given to individuals generally increased. After considerable debate, Social Security was established in the 1930s to provide a modest pension for retired people. Today, Social Security also provides income to people who cannot work because of physical or mental disability. Most workers are required to contribute to the Social Security system by paying taxes into the fund. The amount of monthly pension payments a person receives depends upon past wages and age at retirement. Medicare provides payment of some of the medical expenses of those 65 or older and aid to those unable to work because of mental or physical disability.

17   Many people think that the government should provide more funds for college education for those in need, day care for preschool children of working parents, more help for nursing home expenses, a national health care program, and other benefits. But these are very expensive programs and there is some opposition to the government's spending a lot more money on social programs.

18   The most important characteristic of the American government does not concern what it does or doesn't do. It is the way in which governmental decisions are made—by people elected by citizens. Americans have the power to change their representatives (at the end of their term in office) if they are dissatisfied with the decisions being made. Representative government is slow and inefficient compared to a monarchy or dictatorship. But it has produced a government that Americans have no reason to fear and many reasons to admire. Most Americans believe that, in spite of its weaknesses, their system of government is the finest in the world.

19   In 1782, Americans chose as their national bird the bald eagle, one of the largest and most powerful of birds. This high-flying bird has long been a symbol of freedom and courage. Americans hope and believe that they will always have the courage and strength to protect the freedoms that their government provides. Protecting these freedoms is the ultimate responsibility of the American government and its citizens.

AFTER YOU READ

I. Getting the Message

Reread the paragraphs indicated after each question. Then answer each question by writing Yes *or* No *on each blank line.*

1. Can a resident alien ever become president of the United States? (1) _____

2. Can a naturalized citizen vote in an American election? (1) _____

3. Did the majority of eligible American voters vote in the 1996 presidential election? (4) _____

4. Is a person who is eligible to do something required to do it? (4) _____

5. Does a person who is neutral support one side in a dispute? (6) _____

6. Can the U.S. government require a person to serve in the military? (7) _____

7. Does everyone pay the same percentage of their income in income tax? (11) _____

8. Do most people pay their entire federal income tax in one payment per year? (12) _____

(continued on the next page)

9. Are American taxes high compared to those of other industrialized countries?
   (14) _____

10. Do conservatives favor less governmental help to citizens than liberals do? (15)
    _____

II. Building Your Vocabulary

A. *These are the 15 key vocabulary words for this chapter. They are boldfaced in the reading. Pronounce these words after your teacher and discuss their meanings.*

advantage	eligible	obligation
alien*	entitle	oppose
bill	jury	pending
compulsory	naturalize	refund†
controversy	neutral	resistance

B. *Complete these sentences with some of the key vocabulary words. Make the nouns plural if necessary, and put each verb into the correct tense and form.*

1. Mr. Brown's income tax return showed that he was _____ to a(n)
   _____ because he had overpaid.

2. Should we lower taxes? There is a lot of _____ about that issue.

3. Some people favor higher taxes, and some are against the idea. I have no opinion
   on the matter. I'm _____.

4. There are two types of American citizens: native-born and _____.

5. In the U.S., an 18-year-old citizen is _____ to vote, but a resident
   alien isn't.

6. A(n) _____ is a selected group of people who decide legal cases in
   court.

7. A proposed law being considered by a legislative body is called a(n)
   _____.

8. The government wants to raise the prices on postage stamps, but many people
   _____ this plan. Most people don't want to pay more for stamps.

9. This court case is delayed _____ the arrival of an important witness.

10. Citizens have the right and the _____ to vote.

Alien can be a noun or an adjective.
†*Refund* can be a noun or a verb.

11. Pedro is a permanent resident in the U.S., but he hasn't become a citizen yet. He is a(n) _____.

12. One of the _____ of becoming a citizen is that citizens can vote in local, state, and national elections.

III. Sharpening Reading Skills

Many English words have two or more meanings. To understand what you read, you need to consider the context in which these words are used.

Reread the paragraphs that the following words appear in. Then put a check (✓) before the sentence that uses the word as it is used in the paragraph.

Example

The word *neutral* in paragraph 6:

_____ a. The car is in <u>neutral</u>. It won't move.

_____ b. I want a new jacket in a <u>neutral</u> color: white, beige, or gray.

__✓__ c. I'm not siding with you or your wife in your divorce case. I'm <u>neutral</u>.

1. The word *alien* in paragraph 1:

_____ a. In that science fiction movie, the main character is an <u>alien</u> from the planet Mars.

_____ b. He has lived alone in a hut for 35 years. His behavior is <u>alien</u> to us.

_____ c. He's an <u>alien</u> now, but he wants to become an American citizen.

2. The word *voice* in paragraph 4:

_____ a. Her singing <u>voice</u> is beautiful.

_____ b. Should children have a <u>voice</u> in making family decisions?

_____ c. Is this verb in the active or passive <u>voice</u>?

3. The word *bill* in paragraph 5:

_____ a. The president won't sign that <u>bill</u>, so it will probably never become a law.

_____ b. Did you pay your electric <u>bill</u> yet?

_____ c. I don't have any change. Can I put a $1 <u>bill</u> in this coffee machine?

4. The word *draft* in paragraph 7:

_____ a. Please close the window. I don't like the cold <u>draft</u>.

_____ b. This isn't the final version of my paper. It's just the first <u>draft</u>.

_____ c. Some people were against the <u>draft</u> during the Vietnam War.

(continued on the next page)

5. The word *graduated* in paragraph 11:

_____ a. My sister <u>graduated</u> from medical school last month. Now she's a doctor.

_____ b. This is a <u>graduated</u> series of exercises. Each one is a little harder than the one before.

_____ c. My college <u>graduated</u> 525 students last year.

6. The word *return* in paragraph 12:

_____ a. Please <u>return</u> this book to the library.

_____ b. Seven percent is a good <u>return</u> on money in a savings account.

_____ c. The U.S. tax <u>return</u> is very complicated.

IV. Understanding Idioms and Expressions

Work with a partner. On each blank line, write the letter of the correct phrase to complete the sentence. The numbers in parentheses give the paragraphs in which the expressions are used.

1. *To stay in office* (5) means _____.
   a. to refuse to leave one's place of work
   b. to be reelected to a political job

2. *Uncle Sam* (12) is _____.
   a. your father's brother
   b. a symbol of the American government

3. *Gross domestic product* (14) means _____.
   a. a large item made and used in the U.S.
   b. the value of all goods and services produced in the U.S. in a particular year

4. *And the like* (15) means_____.
   a. and similar services
   b. and other services that people enjoy

5. *Social Security* (16) means _____.
   a. the protection of good friends
   b. a pension provided by the government

V. Taking Words Apart

A. *With a partner, write the abstract noun for each verb listed below. (An abstract noun is a word that refers to an idea rather than a concrete thing.) Use a dictionary for help if necessary. Some common endings for abstract nouns are -ment, -ance, -tion, and -sion. Sometimes the noun and verb are spelled exactly the same.*

Example

assist _____assistance_____

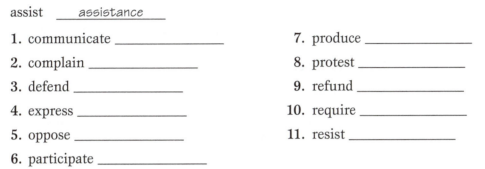

1. communicate _____
2. complain _____
3. defend _____
4. express _____
5. oppose _____
6. participate _____

7. produce _____
8. protest _____
9. refund _____
10. require _____
11. resist _____

B. *Pronounce these verb / noun pairs after your teacher. Note that a stress change may occur even when the spellings of the noun and verb are the same. In two-syllable pairs of this type, the noun is generally stressed on the first syllable and the verb on the second (as in items #8 and #9). Nouns ending with -tion or -sion are stressed on the next-to-last syllable.*

VI. Practicing Sentence Patterns

Paragraphs 5–7 in the reading talk about people having opposing ideas about a political issue. Here are some more examples of these phrases and patterns:

I'm <u>in favor of</u> strong gun-control laws. I'm <u>opposed to</u> allowing private citizens to own handguns.

I'm <u>for</u> more gun-control laws. I'm <u>against</u> private ownership of handguns.

I <u>support</u> stricter gun control. I <u>oppose</u> the easy purchase of handguns.

Try using some of these patterns. Then share your sentences with three classmates.

1. Write a sentence expressing your opinion about using federal money to help people pay for legal abortions.

   _____

2. Write a sentence expressing your opinion about a peacetime military draft.

   _____

VII. Sharing Ideas

A. Issues

Debate these issues in small groups. Then choose one and write about it.

1. Should voting be mandatory for all American citizens?

2. If there is a draft, should military service be mandatory for women as well as men?

3. Should people who refuse to serve in the military be sent to prison?

B. On a Personal Note

Write about one of these topics.

1. Summarize what a person has to do to become an American citizen. Do you think the requirements are reasonable?

2. Do you think the American government provides enough services and benefits to the nation's residents? If not, what additional help is needed? Should taxes be higher so that the government can provide more assistance to individuals and families?

3. Write about something you are opposed to. Explain why you oppose it.

16 Capitalism and the American Economy

" WELL, IF THE ECONOMIC BOOM BENEFITS EVERYONE, WHAT GOOD IS IT?!"

BEFORE YOU READ

Discuss

1. If we say that the economy of a country is strong or healthy, what do we mean? What does that say about employment, salaries, prices, production of goods, and so on?

2. What is capitalism? What are its main characteristics?

3. What is competition? When is it good? When is it bad?

Guess

Try to answer the questions. Then look for the answers in the reading.

1. How many Americans own shares of stock in companies traded on the two major stock exchanges? Check (✓) one:

   _____ 10 million _____ 60 million _____ 120 million

2. About how many Americans go bankrupt each year? Check (✓) one:

   _____ 500,000 _____ 1 million _____ 5 million

3. About how many women own their own businesses? Check (✓) one:

   _____6 million _____ 9 million _____ 12 million

Capitalism and the American Economy

The Basic Principles of Capitalism

1   The U.S.A. is a capitalistic country. In a capitalistic **economy**, businesses are privately owned and operated. The government's role in the business world is limited. Its main function is to protect each part of the economy—big business, small business, workers, and consumers—from abuse. In American **capitalism**, even such basic needs as transportation, communications, and health care are provided by private companies.

2   In a capitalist economy, prices vary with changes in supply and demand. When there are more apples available than people want to buy, the price of apples goes down; when there is a shortage, the price goes up. Of course, prices of **goods** and **services** are also affected by the cost of producing them.

3   Under ideal conditions, a free economy (with limited government controls) is good for everyone. Workers can choose their careers; they can change jobs to get higher wages, better working conditions, or professional advancement; and they can form unions with other workers to demand better treatment from their employer. Manufacturers, wholesalers, and retailers can also do well in a capitalist system. They **profit** when their businesses are successful.

4   Competition is an essential element of capitalism. In order to compete, businesses must operate efficiently, economically, and creatively. Because of competition, customers receive high-quality merchandise at the lowest possible prices. When there is a lack of competition in an industry, a **monopoly** may develop. This can happen when a company buys its competitors or when a company sells its products below cost for a while in order to drive competitors out of business. To prevent such abuses, there are national laws prohibiting most monopolies.

5   In a capitalistic economy, disagreements between employees and employers can lead to work stoppages called *strikes*. A strike occurs when unionized employees refuse to work until their demands are satisfied. A strike in a vital industry can disrupt the entire national economy. For example, if there is a strike in the transportation industry, companies that depend on trains or trucks to transport raw materials and / or finished products must shut down. Their employees are, therefore, laid off. When workers' incomes are greatly reduced, they do not spend as much. This, in turn, affects the income of businesses that usually sell to those workers. Also, when large numbers of workers go on strike, the public may be greatly inconvenienced. Strikes can shut down transportation or cut off food or fuel supplies to large areas.

6   Although capitalism has made most Americans prosperous, not all have benefited. Foreign competition and factory automation have caused many semiskilled workers who were earning good wages in manufacturing industries, such as automobile production, to lose their jobs. Many of those able to get new employment had to settle for lower-paying jobs.

7   At the end of the twentieth century, several multinational treaties greatly expanded the idea of competition to what is called a "free global economy." This means that businesses in different countries can export their goods to the U.S. and other countries without paying tariffs (taxes imposed upon imports in order to favor the goods of the importing country). A free global economy is good for the consumer who can purchase cheaper merchandise from countries where the cost of doing business is lower than it is in the U.S. However, it is not good for American workers who may lose their jobs as a result of that competition.

8   Today's American capitalism benefits most workers as well as business owners. However, not everyone is prosperous in the U.S. About 12% of the population have earnings below the poverty line established by the government. Some people cannot get a decent-paying job for reasons such as illness or disability, old age, drug or alcohol addiction, or lack of education or job-related skills. Most people with marketable job skills can earn a living in the U.S., and there are many opportunities for learning these skills.

✔ **Check Your Comprehension**   *What are three characteristics of capitalism?*
Who benefits from tariffs?

Stocks and Bonds

9   American businesses need huge amounts of money to develop new products, purchase new equipment, build factories, and pay other expenses of doing business. This money is known as *capital*. Much of it comes from **investors** (capitalists), who expect to receive a profitable return on the money that they invest. Without investors, the American economy would not be able to grow and produce the goods that consumers want. In other words, a capitalist economy depends on capitalists to keep it growing.

10   Most investments take one of two forms—**stocks** or **bonds**. Stockholders purchase **shares** of a business. If the business does well, they share in the profits of the company by receiving *dividends*. On the other hand, people who purchase bonds lend their money to a business in exchange for a fixed rate of return (a percentage of the face value of the

bond) known as **interest**. Both stockholders and bondholders hope that the value of their investments will increase. Stocks and bonds are traded on national exchanges. The New York Stock Exchange is located on Wall Street in New York City. As a result, the world of investors is commonly known as *Wall Street*. Stock prices are usually affected by the profits of the company, the general economic climate, and the outlook for the com-

The floor of the New York Stock Exchange

pany in the near future. Bond prices are primarily influenced by interest rates. If interest rates rise, bond prices usually fall and vice versa.

11   In recent years, there has been a huge growth in the volume of stock and bond sales. Between 1990 and 1999, the number of shares of stock traded on exchanges each year rose from about 4.5 billion to more than 350 billion. On an average trading day, more than a billion shares of stock change hands on the New York Stock Exchange and on the Nasdaq Stock Exchange. It is not unusual for each of those exchanges to handle more than 2 billion shares in a day. In 1987, the value of all stocks traded on stock exchanges was $1.9 trillion. By 1999, that figure had jumped to more than $14 trillion.

12   In 1980, only about 27 million Americans owned stocks. Today, more than 120 million individuals are stockholders. And many more are indirectly involved in the markets through their participation in pension plans, **credit** unions, and insurance plans. In fact, most of the stocks and bonds that are traded are owned not by individuals but by large investors such as banks, insurance companies, pension funds, and mutual funds (companies that invest in many different businesses in order to minimize risk).

> ✔ **Check Your Comprehension**   *What is the difference between stocks and bonds?*
> *Where are stocks and bonds traded?*

The Cashless Society

13   When people buy merchandise or services, they often do not pay for their purchases with cash. One very popular method of making payments is by check. Most Americans

have checking accounts and have access to their money at the many ATMs (automatic teller machines) found all over the country.

14   Another form of payment is the use of credit cards. One type of credit card is issued by a particular store to its regular customers. At the end of each month, the customer receives a bill showing the charge purchases made during that period and how much is owed. The customer must pay the balance within three or four weeks. If the payment is late, the customer is usually charged a late fee. Most credit cards permit the user to pay only a small portion of the total due. If the customer does this, interest is charged on the unpaid balance.

15   Yet another type of credit card is issued by banks or other financial institutions. Some of the most widely used are MasterCard, Visa, American Express, and Discover. These cards can be used for purchases at any business establishment that has agreed to accept them. The merchant sends the sales slip to the issuing institution, which pays the amount of the charge (less a discount) to the merchant and then bills the cardholder. As with store credit cards, interest is charged on any unpaid balance.

16   The easy availability of credit has given American consumers tremendous purchasing power. But it has also led to a huge amount of **debt**. Americans now owe more than $700 billion for credit purchases (not including mortgage loans). Most people pay their debts regularly. But if they have unexpected problems such as unemployment or an illness, there may not be enough money to make the payments. If payments are not made for several months, the seller may sue the debtor in court or take legal action to repossess the merchandise.

17   The debtor who thinks that there is little chance to repay the debts may choose to go into **bankruptcy** to be relieved of them. If the debtor has any sizable **assets**, these may be sold to partially pay the creditors. Then, the debtor no longer has the obligation to pay back the rest of the debts. While bankruptcy may sound like an attractive solution, it is available only once every 6 years, and it results in a loss of credit to the bankrupt person. That is, the person will be unable to get loans or credit cards for a long period of time, until he can show the ability and willingness to pay debts. About 1 million Americans go into bankruptcy each year. However, most people pay their bills regularly, and the economy is greatly strengthened by the billions of dollars of credit purchases made each year.

18   A recent development in the cashless society is the use of debit cards. Like credit cards, debit cards can be used to make purchases. However, they do not involve credit. When a debit card is used, money is immediately deducted from the user's bank account and paid to the seller. The use of a credit or debit card is necessary in purchases made by telephone or on the Internet. Debit cards are a way of doing business without increasing one's indebtedness.

19   Another way of making purchases without cash is by obtaining a loan. A person wishing to buy an expensive item such as a car or house can borrow the money and pay it back over a period of years. The payments are usually made each month until the amount due has been paid with interest. For example, a car may be paid for over a five-year period. A loan taken out to buy a house (a mortgage) may be paid back over 25 to 30 years. These loans enable Americans to buy the things they need and want before they have all the money to pay for them. Low-cost loans enable many Americans to go to college. Many college loans allow students to delay repayment until after graduation.

Why is the U.S. called a cashless society?
What is one advantage and one disadvantage of buying on credit?

Recent Trends in Business

20   Many changes in the way businesses operate have occurred over the past 50 years. Some of the most interesting are the increased use of computers; the increase in business ownership, especially of franchises; the increasing number of businesses owned by women and minorities; and the growing number of home-based businesses.

21   *Computers in Business*: Although computers have been used by businesses for many years, until recently only large companies could afford to own them. The 1980s saw a breakthrough in computer development when personal computers were introduced. They require little maintenance and can be operated by office personnel with a minimum of training. Because of their widespread use, mass-produced programs have been developed that can keep track of inventory and sales, keep payroll records, and even generate checks. Today, a business can hardly afford not to have its own computer. (See Chapter 18 for further discussion of computers.)

22   *Small Business Trends*: Every year, increasing numbers of Americans go into business for themselves. They are called *entrepreneurs*. In the 1960s, there were about 8 million individually owned companies; in 1999, about 17 million Americans owned their own businesses. For the person who wants to be his/her own boss, American capitalism provides the exciting (though risky) opportunity to try it.

23   Many people who want to become entrepreneurs do so by purchasing a franchise. A company that has developed a successful business may decide to license other companies to operate similar businesses under the same name. That license is called a *franchise*. The original company is known as the *franchisor*, and the licensed companies are *franchisees*. Each franchisee pays the franchisor for the right to use the franchise name and ideas. The franchisor assists its franchisees in selecting a site for the business, purchasing equipment, and learning how to operate the business. Advertising is done on a national basis. The franchisor controls the products sold, so consumers know the product will be the same whether they buy it in New York or California.

24   In the U.S., there are more than 500,000 franchised businesses with sales exceeding $700 billion annually. That is more than one-third of all retail sales in the U.S. Although the most well-known franchises are fast-food businesses, franchises are available in many industries, such as real estate brokerages, video rental stores, automotive parts stores, and travel and employment agencies. Why do so many people choose to buy franchises? A franchise is the least risky way to go into business for oneself. The franchise's national reputation, advertising, training program, and business experience give the franchisee a big advantage over independent businesses.

25   *Woman and Minority Business Ownership*: The growing trend toward business ownership by women and minorities is partly due to the influence of the civil rights and women's movements, which have encouraged these groups to go into fields offering greater opportunity for advancement. In 1999, about 9 million women owned businesses, while members of minority groups owned another 2 million.

26   *Home-based Businesses*: Home-based business and people doing their employers' work from home is also on the rise. This has been brought about largely by the expanded use of personal computers and their ability to connect with other computers to obtain information and relay data to a central business. There are now 4 million people operating their businesses out of their home, and it is estimated that that number will increase rapidly during the first decade of the twenty-first century.

✔ Check Your Comprehension *Name three recent developments in small-business ownership.*

27   American capitalism has proved to be one of the most productive economic systems in history. In a capitalistic system, people try to produce better goods and services because there are financial rewards for doing so. In addition, the freedom of choice that capitalism provides appeals to the independent American character. With few exceptions, no outside power tells an entrepreneur how much to charge for goods or services, and people are free to decide how they will earn and spend their income. The American economy is based upon the belief that every individual knows what is best for himself and must take responsibility for his decisions. Risks exist, but so do opportunities for advancement. Most Americans gladly accept both.

AFTER YOU READ

I. Getting the Message

On each blank line, write the letter of the correct phrase to complete the sentence.

1. Paragraph 1 says that the American government _____.
   a. is not allowed to regulate business
   b. regulates business to some extent

2. Paragraph 5 says that _____.
   a. workers shouldn't go on strike
   b. strikes sometimes create problems for the American public

3. According to paragraph 10, people who buy stocks and bonds _____.
   a. hope to make a profit
   b. usually become wealthy

4. According to paragraphs 16 and 17, buying on credit _____.
   a. usually leads to bankruptcy
   b. can lead to more debt than the consumer can handle

(continued on the next page)

5. The U.S. is called a cashless society because _____.
   a. most people don't have enough cash
   b. people use checks and credit cards instead of paper money to pay for many things

6. According to paragraphs 23 and 24, buying a franchise is _____.
   a. one common way to become an entrepreneur in the U.S.
   b. a form of business ownership used only in the fast-food industry

II. Building Your Vocabulary

A. *These are the 15 key vocabulary words for this chapter. They are boldfaced in the reading. Pronounce these words after your teacher, and discuss their meanings.*

asset	debt	monopoly
bankruptcy	economy	profit*
bond	goods†	service*
capitalism	interest*	share*
credit*	investor	stock

B. *Complete these sentences with some of the key vocabulary words. Make the nouns plural if necessary.*

1. The American _____ is sometimes called a cashless society because most people pay for things with checks and _____ cards.

2. People lend money to a business by buying _____, or they purchase a piece of a business by buying shares of _____.

3. A person can buy part of a business by purchasing _____ of a stock sold on a stock exchange.

4. When you get your hair cut at the barber or beauty shop or your coat cleaned at the dry cleaner's, you are purchasing a/an _____.

5. When you buy a jacket or some milk, you are purchasing _____.

6. _____ depends on competition to keep prices down and quality high.

7. When American Telephone and Telegraph was providing nearly all the telephone service in the U.S., it had a(n) _____.

8. A person who has a lot of _____ may decide to go into bankruptcy.

---

*These words can be used as nouns or verbs.
†This noun meaning "merchandise" is always plural.

9. Valuable things that you own (such as a car, a house, or stock) are your

_____.

10. If you buy 100 shares of stock for $45 a share and sell those shares a year later for $60 a share, you have made a nice _____ on your investment.

C. *Choose the correct word to complete each sentence. Then write it on the blank line in each sentence.*

1. You bought a pair of gloves using your credit card. A few days later, you returned the gloves to the store. The store _____ your account. (*credited / charged*)

2. Your mortgage application has been approved, so you can buy a condominium. The bank has agreed to _____ you the money for the purchase. (*borrow / lend*)

3. You purchased 100 shares of Delicious Candy Company stock. When the company had a jump in sales, you received _____. (*dividends / interest*)

4. You have $1,000 in your savings account. The bank pays you 4% _____ annually on this money. (*dividends / interest*)

5. You just won a million dollars on a quiz show. You also own three homes, four cars, a big diamond ring, and a painting by Picasso. You have a lot of _____. (*assets / debts*)

6. You own your own business, and two people work for you. They are your _____. (*employees / employers*)

7. The price of your Delicious Candy Company stock went down below what you paid for it. If you sell this stock now, you'll take a _____. (*profit / loss*)

8. A person who goes into _____ will have trouble getting credit for several years. (*debt / bankruptcy*)

III. Sharpening Reading Skills

Words in Context

Underline the meaning of the italicized word as used in the paragraph indicated.

1. What does *strike* mean in "to go on strike"? (5)
   a. to hit a person or an object
   b. to refuse to work until one's employer makes some improvement in working conditions, benefits, and/or salary

2. What does *return* mean in "a profitable return"? (9)
   a. to come back to a place
   b. income from an investment

3. What does *interest* mean in "interest rates"? (10)
   a. something someone wants to know about
   b. a fixed return on an investment

4. What does *stock* mean in "stocks and bonds are traded"? (10)
   a. shares of companies for sale to the public
   b. merchandise sold in a store

IV. Understanding Idioms and Expressions

Work with a partner. Match each expression in column 1 with its definition in column 2 by writing the correct numbers on the lines. The numbers in parentheses give the paragraphs in which the expressions are used. If you need help, use a dictionary.

1. change hands (11)   _____ a company has been permanently closed

2. cut off (5)   _____ original price of a bond when issued

3. earn a living (8)   _____ where stocks and bonds are sold

4. face value (10)   _____ closed, usually temporarily

5. laid off (5)   _____ accept less than you wanted or expected

6. out of business (4)   _____ transfer from one owner to another

7. settle for (6)   _____ how much of a product is available compared to the amount consumers want to buy

8. shut down (5)   _____ terminated, sometimes temporarily, from a job because one is not needed

9. supply and demand (2)   _____ make enough money to pay one's expenses

10. Wall Street (10)   _____ prevent access to something

V. Taking Words Apart

Work with a partner. Underline the correct word form (noun or adjective) to complete each sentence.

1. Capitalism is the (*economy / economic*) system of the U.S.

2. The American (*economy / economic*) depends on capitalists who invest in businesses.

3. In a (*capitalism / capitalistic*) economy, businesses are privately owned.

4. People buy stocks and bonds because they hope to make a (*profit / profitable*).

5. Sometimes their investments are (*profit / profitable*), and sometimes they lose money.

6. People who make a good living are (*prosperity / prosperous*).

VI. Practicing Sentence Patterns

To show the existence (or nonexistence) of something, use *there* and the verb *be*. Use the singular form of *be* if the complementary noun is singular or uncountable. Use the plural form if the noun is plural. Look at these examples.

Singular		Plural	
There has been	prosperity.	There have been	many strikes.
There was	a strike.	There were	debts.

Write there *plus the correct form of* be *in the following sentences. Add* not *where necessary.*

1. _____ about 3,000 companies listed on the New York Stock Exchange.

2. _____ 25 students in my English class last semester.

3. _____ a lot of rain so far this year.

4. _____ any snow here last summer.

Now complete your own sentences using this pattern.

1. There is _____.

2. There have been _____.

3. There weren't _____.

VII. Sharing Ideas

A. Issues

Debate these issues in small groups. Then choose one and write about it.

1. Which is better: to borrow money from a bank in order to start your own business or to wait until you have enough to go into business with your own money?

2. Is it better to be employed by a company or self-employed?

3. Should government employees (for example, teachers, police, and firefighters) be allowed to go on strike, or is this too harmful to society?

B. On a Personal Note

Write about one of these topics.

1. Would you like to own your own business some day? Why or why not?

2. Do you use a credit or debit card? Does it help you or create problems for you?

3. Do you think people should ever borrow money? Under what circumstances do you consider this a good idea?

4. Another trend in the American workplace concerns how people dress. In the 1990s, "casual Friday" became very popular. Do you think that the way people dress affects how they work? Explain.

17 | The American Worker

Workers on strike

BEFORE YOU READ

Discuss

1. If workers are not satisfied with their salary or working conditions, what can they do?

2. What is the difference between a blue-collar job and a white-collar job?

3. If you owned your own business, what kinds of benefits would you provide for your employees?

Guess

Try to answer the questions. Then look for the answers in the reading.

1. How many hours a week does the average American work? Check (✓) one:

   _____ 37   _____ 47   _____ 57

2. What percentage of the American work force is female? Check (✓) one:

   _____ almost 20%   _____ almost 35%   _____ almost 50%

3. About how many Americans earn more than $1 million a year? Check (✓) one:

   _____ 30,000   _____ 140,000   _____ 300,000

The American Worker

A Holiday That Honors Workers

1   It's called Labor Day, but it is certainly not a time for hard work. On the contrary, it's a day set aside for relaxation and fun, a time for parades and speeches honoring the achievements of the American work force (about 140 million people). Throughout the U.S.A., Labor Day is celebrated on the first Monday in September.

2   The origins of this holiday date back to a time when American employees did not have the kind of income, protections, and **benefits** that they do today. The story of Labor Day began with the dream of a man named Peter J. McGuire. McGuire was born in 1852, long before the U.S. had laws prohibiting child labor. He was the tenth child in a poor family. To help support his brothers and sisters, he went to work in a furniture factory when he was only 11 years old. He became a carpenter and, eventually, the president of a national **union** of carpenters. McGuire wanted to establish a holiday "to honor the industrial spirit, the great vital force of this nation." In 1882, he and a machinist named Matthew Maguire suggested that New York City hold a parade to honor workers. Some 10,000 people showed up to participate! In 1894, Labor Day became a federal holiday, and it was quickly adopted by all the states.

3   Parades and speeches are just one aspect of the Labor Day holiday. Since Labor Day is a 3-day weekend for most workers and students, many people use it to enjoy the outdoors with friends and family on this last summer holiday.

✔ **Check Your Comprehension**   *What is the purpose of Labor Day?*

The Role of Labor Unions

4   On Labor Day, when Americans celebrate the good fortune of the American worker, they are really honoring the achievements of labor unions. A labor union is a group of workers doing the same general type of work (a craft union) or employed in the same industry (an industrial union). Workers join unions to **negotiate** more effectively with management (to bargain with their employers for better contracts). There are unions for miners, musicians, public employees (such as teachers and police officers), janitors, nurses, plumbers, factory workers, construction workers, employees in the transportation industries, and many other groups.

5   Unions are democratic institutions. They have elected leaders (some are paid and some are **volunteers**) who try to carry out the group's goals. The union's leaders and important decisions are determined by a majority vote of the membership. Union members pay **dues** to support the activities of the union.

6   For more than 100 years, American unions have been representing workers. During the early years, there were many violent incidents because management considered unions illegal and tried to prevent workers from organizing. Later, unions became so powerful that federal laws were required to control union **abuses**. Today, unions are an accepted part of the workplace. Altogether, about 12% of the nation's workers—approximately 16 million Americans—belong to unions.

7   Unions have made great gains in getting employees greater job **security**, higher wages, a shorter workweek, extra pay for overtime work, paid vacations, sick leave, health insurance, pension plans, and safe, sanitary working conditions. Also, as a result of union efforts, many laws have been passed that protect and help workers. Federal laws prohibit employers from discriminating against workers because of race, religion, sex, age, or physical disability. Today, most workers must be paid at least the federal minimum hourly wage ($5.15 in 2000). Federal law also requires most employers to pay employees at least time-and-a-half (1½ times their regular hourly rate) when they work overtime. Unions have also fought to protect children in the workforce. In most states, children under the age of 14 are not allowed to hold jobs, though there are some exceptions to this restriction. For example, children are allowed to work part time to deliver newspapers or work as entertainers.

8   In attempting to achieve its goals, a union may employ its most powerful weapon: the **strike**. A strike occurs when union members decide not to return to work until their employer gives in to some or all of their demands. Workers on strike **picket** their employer by walking back and forth in front of their place of business, carrying signs stating their complaints.

9   In spite of the gains that unions have made for workers, in the last few decades of the twentieth century, American labor unions lost membership. The percentage of unionized workers in the workforce and the actual number of union members both declined. Labor unions have always been strongest in construction, manufacturing, mining, and transportation industries. In recent years, because of the **automation** of American factories and the shifting of many factories to foreign countries, the number of blue-collar employees (those whose jobs are mostly more physical) has greatly declined. However,

more white-collar workers (those whose jobs are mostly in offices) are becoming union-ized. For example, about 37% of government employees belong to unions.

10   Though the number of union members has been declining, unions remain important in the U.S. Collective bargaining agreements between labor and management also affect nonunion members in unionized businesses. These agreements cover not only salary schedules but also working conditions, workers' rights, and benefits. Moreover, labor unions have some political influence. The American labor movement does not have its own political party as in some other countries. However, union leaders influence legisla-tion and government policy by lobbying (talking to legislators in the state capitals and in Washington, D.C. about their goals). In election years, most candidates want the support of organized labor, so they must be concerned about the needs and interests of unions. Unions encourage their workers to contribute to the political campaigns of candidates they consider pro-labor and to vote for candidates who support workers' interests.

11   Most American unions belong to the AFL-CIO, an organization that combined the former American Federation of Labor and the Congress of Industrial Organizations. This federation, with some 13 million members, has a great deal of political influence.

12   Of course, many companies, institutions, and occupations are not unionized. Those that are cannot require prospective employees to join the union in order to be consid-ered for a job. However, in some industries, workers must agree to join the union after they are hired. In other places of business, union membership is **optional**. In some cases, workers who choose not to join must still contribute to the union because they, along with the union members, benefit from union achievements.

✔ **Check Your Comprehension**

List at least five ways in which unions have helped workers.

Protection for the American Worker

13   Most American workers have some protection against sudden stoppage of income. If workers are laid off (lose their jobs) through no fault of their own, they may be **eligible** for unemployment compensation—temporary payments from the government—until they find another job or their benefit period expires. Another way in which workers can protect their paychecks is by purchasing insurance that guarantees the family a regular income if the breadwinner(s) cannot continue working because of injury, illness, or death.

14   The most widespread type of financial protection of wages is a federal program called Social Security. It protects workers and their families against income loss due to retire-ment, illness, or death. About 44 million Americans (approximately one out of six) receive Social Security pension, disability, or survivors' benefits. Most U.S. workers (employees and self-employed persons as well) are required to participate in this pro-gram. Self-employed people pay contributions quarterly. Employees' contributions are **deducted** from their paychecks each payday. Most workers contribute about 7.65% of their wages; the employer contributes an equal amount. The government keeps a record of each worker's account under the person's Social Security number.

15   A worker must contribute to the fund for a specified length of time in order to be eligible for Social Security benefits. The amount of money received depends on the individual's average earnings during his working years. However, workers with low lifetime earnings collect benefits proportionally greater in relation to their contributions than do those with higher lifetime earnings. The average monthly Social Security check is about $830.

16   For many years, regular retirement age has been 65. However, a 1983 federal law provided for a gradual increase from age 65 to age 67 beginning in 2003 and ending in 2027. Workers may choose to **retire** and begin receiving pension payments a few years earlier than the regular retirement age, but then the amount received each month is smaller.

> **✔ Check Your Comprehension**
>
> *What different groups of people are eligible to receive money from Social Security?*

Living Standards

17   For most Americans, Labor Day is an occasion to count their blessings. The U.S. is a prosperous nation. Its unemployment rate (about 4%) is extremely low. Americans earning the median annual household income (about $41,000) or more can live comfortably, own a car, and buy appliances that save work and provide entertainment. Yet many people are dissatisfied with their earnings and their standard of living. Among those dissatisfied are the poor, some members of the middle class, and some women.

18   Who's poor in the prosperous U.S.A.? Nearly 12% of the population, according to 1999 statistics. (In that year, the U.S. government set the poverty level at $17,000 for a family of four.) Most poor Americans fall into one or more of these categories: the elderly retired, the physically or mentally ill, unskilled workers, the uneducated, the unemployed, single parents, children, and minorities. In 1999, those living in poverty included 17% of all American children and roughly 23% of African-Americans and Hispanics. Although the percentage of people living in poverty decreased from 1979 to 1999, the figure is still high. What can be done? More job training is needed so that unskilled workers can develop marketable skills. Also, many people feel that it would help to raise the minimum wage (the lowest hourly rate that most employers are allowed to pay employees). A family of three or four living on one person's minimum wage salary is quite poor.

19   The American middle class also has some discontented members. In the 1990s, the U.S. economy was booming, the stock market zoomed upward, and the rich got richer. Between 1992 and 1997, the number of Americans earning over $1 million a year more than doubled (from about 67,000 to about 142,000.) From 1994 to 2000, the number of households with a net worth of more than $1 million jumped from 3.5 million to 7.1 million. Meanwhile, some middle-class workers saw their purchasing power decline slightly; others made only modest gains.

20   Some of the nation's 64 million working women are also unhappy about the business environment. Since the women's liberation movement began in the 1960s, American women have struggled with two major disadvantages in the workplace: (1) men are, on the average, paid more than women to do the same job, and (2) women have more dif-

ficulty than men getting **promotions** to positions of more power and higher income. In recent decades, women have made great progress. The *glass ceiling*, which is the name for the barriers that hold back women and minorities in the workplace, is being broken in many areas. Still, although almost half of the American work force is female, only 4% of the top executives of corporations are women. Men outearn women substantially. For every dollar a man earns, a woman earns 76 cents. By the age of 50, the average American working woman has earned about $500,000 during her years of employment. For a man the same age, the comparable figure is about $1 million. However, women are narrowing the gap. More and more women are entering traditionally male-dominated high-paying professions such as medicine, law, engineering, and architecture. American women now earn 39% of the country's medical degrees and 43% of its law degrees. Women are also starting their own businesses in increasing numbers.

21   Though many Americans are not totally satisfied with the work they do or the money it brings in, on the whole the American workforce has adjusted well to enormous changes in the past 100 years. In 1900, about 20% of American women worked. Today, about 60% of women over age 16 are employed. During the twentieth century, the percentage of employed men age 65 or older fell from about 65% to about 15%. Social Security and other retirement benefits discourage older people from working full time. At the other end of the age spectrum, more young Americans are attending college now and are, therefore, beginning full-time employment at a later age. As a result, the number of years that the average American works full time has shrunk quite a bit since 1900. Also, during the twentieth century, the percentage of agricultural workers fell from 40% to about 2.6% of the workforce, and the percentage of other blue-collar workers also decreased. The majority of American employees are now white-collar workers. Years ago, it was common for workers to spend all their working years doing the same job for the same company. Today, conditions change rapidly, so people are often forced to relocate and learn new skills. From 1981 to 1985, about 11 million adult workers lost their jobs because of factory closings and cutbacks. Meanwhile, the number of jobs in high-tech fields has been growing rapidly.

22   One recent workplace change is causing some unhappiness. Americans are spending more hours on the job than they did a few decades ago. Americans think of a full-time job as being 40 hours a week—eight hours a day, five days a week. But, in fact, today the average American employee works about 47 hours per week, and about 37% of Americans are working 50 or more hours per week. Compared to 1980, Americans are working the equivalent of two additional weeks a year. Why? To increase profits, many companies have "downsized" (decreased their number of employees), and they expect to get more work out of those remaining. Also, to increase their incomes, many Americans "moonlight"—take on a part-time job in addition to a full-time job. Americans are now working more hours than people in any other highly industrialized nation. Even the Japanese, often called workaholics, spend slightly less time on the job than Americans. The average American works 1,966 hours per year, ignoring the well-known saying that tells them: "All work and no play makes Jack a dull boy." Nowadays, Americans really need that Labor Day holiday more than ever.

AFTER YOU READ

I. Getting the Message

A. *Discuss these questions with your classmates. On a separate piece of paper, write answers to two of them.*

1. According to the reading, what is good about working in the U.S.?

2. What three population groups have some dissatisfied workers? Why?

3. Why do today's Americans spend fewer years in the workforce than their parents and grandparents did?

B. *Reread the second section of this reading, "The Role of Labor Unions." Then put a check (✓) after each statement that tells about a benefit that workers get from a union.*

1. Unionized workers must pay dues to their union. _____

2. Unions negotiate contracts for their workers and can help them get higher pay. _____

3. Unions influence lawmakers to pass laws that protect workers. _____

4. Union members must go along with majority decisions even when they don't agree with them. For example, members are expected to go on strike if the group votes for one. _____

C. *On the job, the word* benefit *means something workers get from their employer in addition to their pay. Using this definition, put a check (✓) after each item that is a benefit.*

1. wages _____

2. the right to strike _____

3. union membership _____

4. paid holidays and paid vacations _____

5. private pension plans _____

6. medical, dental, and / or life insurance _____

II. Building Your Vocabulary

A. *These are the 15 key vocabulary words for this chapter. They are boldfaced in the reading. Pronounce these words after your teacher, and discuss their meanings.*

abuse*	eligible	retire
automation	negotiate	security
benefit*	optional	strike*
deduct	picket*	union
dues†	promotion	volunteer*

---

*These words can be used as nouns or verbs.

†As it is used in this chapter, *dues* is always plural.

B. *Complete these sentences with some of the key vocabulary words on page 195. Make the nouns plural if necessary.*

1. Labor _____ are organized groups of workers who do the same type of work or who work in the same industry.

2. Many past _____ of labor and management are now illegal because the federal government passed laws against them.

3. Union representatives often _____ with employers (management) and try, through compromise, to write a contract that satisfies both sides. This process is called *collective bargaining.*

4. Striking workers often _____ their employers, carrying signs expressing their complaints.

5. _____ are people who work for no pay.

6. Many Americans _____ at age 65 and receive a pension.

7. Social _____ provides disability protection and a pension after retirement.

8. Employers _____ Social Security payments from an employee's pay.

C. *Match each word in column 1 with its definition in column 2 by writing the correct numbers on the lines.*

1. employees   _____ individuals, businesses, or institutions that hire workers
2. employers   _____ workers who have a boss
3. self-employed   _____ work; a job
4. unemployed   _____ people who own their own businesses
5. employment   _____ not working

D. *Which pairs are synonyms (words having similar meanings) and which are antonyms (words having opposite meanings)? Write S for synonym or A for antonym after each pair.*

1. optional; required _____
2. hired; laid off or fired _____
3. security; freedom from danger or risk _____
4. prohibit; allow _____
5. labor; management _____
6. negotiate; bargain _____
7. decline; decrease _____

8. pension; retirement pay ___

9. volunteer; paid worker ___

10. deduct; add ___

III. Sharpening Reading Skills

Context Clues

On each blank line, write the letter of the correct phrase to complete the sentence.

1. In paragraph 1, *on the contrary* means ___.
   a. for this reason
   b. just the opposite

2. In paragraph 9, *in spite of the gains that unions have made* means ___.
   a. because of the progress of unions
   b. although unions have made progress

3. In paragraph 10, *organized labor* refers to ___.
   a. employees who organize their work well
   b. unionized employees

4. In paragraph 16, *workers may choose to retire* means ___.
   a. they may quit working permanently
   b. they may go to sleep on the job

5. In paragraph 19, *the U.S. economy was booming* means ___.
   a. there was a big explosion
   b. there was prosperity

IV. Understanding Idioms and Expressions

A. *On each blank line, write the letter of the correct phrase to complete the sentence. The numbers in parentheses give the paragraphs in which the expressions are used.*

1. The idiom *carry out* (5) is used here to mean ___.
   a. take something outside
   b. do or accomplish something

2. The expression *time-and-a-half* (7) refers to ___.
   a. a higher rate of pay for working overtime
   b. working half the usual time

3. *Minimum wage* (7, 18) means ___.
   a. the lowest hourly rate that most employers are allowed to pay
   b. the lowest annual salary that any worker can be legally paid

(continued on the next page)

4. *Give in* (8) means _____.
   a. refuse to accept
   b. stop arguing and do what someone else wants

5. *Blue-collar workers* (9) _____.
   a. wear blue suits and ties to work
   b. often do physical work

6. *White-collar workers* (9) _____.
   a. are all highly educated professionals
   b. usually work in offices

7. Workers get *laid off* (13) when they _____.
   a. behave badly on the job
   b. are not needed on the job

8. One's *standard of living* (17) is related to _____.
   a. one's moral values
   b. what one can afford to buy

9. *Purchasing power* (19) means _____.
   a. the right to buy a lot
   b. the value of money in terms of how much it will buy

10. A *workaholic* (22) is a person who _____.
    a. can't stop working and works too much
    b. drinks alcohol on the job

B. Discuss the meanings of the following expressions. The numbers in parentheses give the paragraphs in which the expressions are used.

on strike (8)
laid off (compare to being *fired*) (13)
glass ceiling (20)

V. Taking Words Apart

On each blank line, answer the questions about the word parts.

1. The prefix *de-* has several meanings, including "down," "removal," or "separation." Which meaning does *de-* have in *deduct, decline,* and *decrease*?

   _____

2. What does *auto-* mean in *automation* and *automobile*? _____
   What does *-mobile* mean? _____

VI. Practicing Sentence Patterns

Notice the use of *for example* in the following excerpt: *In most states, children under the age of 14 are not allowed to hold jobs, though there are some exceptions to this restriction. For example, children are allowed to work part time to deliver newspapers or work as entertainers.*

Write your own complete sentences after for example.

1. Most American employees enjoy many benefits. For example, _____

   _____

2. Workers may collect Social Security for several different reasons. For example,

   _____

VII. Sharing Ideas

A. Issues

Discuss these issues in small groups. Then choose one and write about it.

1. One hundred years ago, many people worked 10 hours a day, 6 days a week. Now Americans feel that 47 hours a week is too many hours to work. How many hours a week should a person have to devote to making a living?

2. When choosing a job, what's more important—the salary or the benefits?

3. Workplace privacy is a big issue in the U.S. Have you ever worked for an employer (in the U.S. or elsewhere) that intruded on your privacy, for example, by requiring drug and alcohol testing, asking about your income from other sources, reading your e-mail, monitoring your job performance, searching your desk, or enforcing a dress code. How much does an employer have a right to know about employees? What behavior should an employer be allowed to control?

B. On a Personal Note

Write about one of these topics.

1. Which gives a person a better life: working more hours and earning more money or working fewer hours and having more leisure time but less money?

2. Read the Help Wanted ads in local newspapers. Select an ad to answer. Write a job application letter and a résumé. Ask your teacher for help with the format.

3. Describe a job you once had. Write about the work and explain why you enjoyed it or hated it.

18 | High-Tech Communications

BEFORE YOU READ

Discuss

1. Do you use a computer? What do you do with it that's fun? How does it help get your work done?

2. Do you think the computer revolution has a downside? In other words, have computers created problems or increased risks for society?

3. Do you carry a cell phone with you? What are the advantages and disadvantages of doing so?

Guess

Try to answer the questions. Then look for the answers in the reading.

1. What percentage of U.S. households have computers? Check (✓) one:

   _____ about 25% _____ more than 50% _____ more than 75%

2. By the year 2010, which will probably be the larger number in the U.S.? Check (✓) one:

   _____ the number of computers _____ the number of people

High-Tech Communications

Computers

1   As the third millennium approached, people everywhere shivered with fear. A few worried that the year 2000 would fulfill an ancient **prediction** and bring the end of the world. Millions more feared a contemporary **calamity**—computer confusion. Would computers think that the year 2000 was 1900? As a result, would electricity, heat, water supplies, airplane service, banking, and food delivery all be disrupted? This widespread anxiety even had a name—Y2K (a symbol for the year 2000). Fortunately, the computer programmers who had predicted this potential problem figured out ways to avoid it. On January 1, 2000, there were amazingly few computer "glitches"—except for one very surprised man who was charged a $400,000 late fee on a rented videotape! But Y2K reminded the world just how dependent industrialized societies (and especially the U.S.) are on computers.

2   Computers control almost every part of American life. They are in places most people don't even realize. Computers regulate cars, microwave ovens, telephones, even newer models of refrigerators and dishwashers. The growth in computer usage came about only recently. In the 1970s, only large businesses and governments had computers. They were extremely expensive and very large. Shortly after the introduction of the smaller, cheaper personal computer, Ken Olson, the president of Digital Equipment Corporation, said, "There is no reason for any individual to have a computer in their home." Today, there are computers in 55 million American homes (more than half of all households), and the number is growing rapidly. About 30% of all computers are in the United States. About 92% of Americans under age 60 have used a computer. It has been predicted that, by the year 2010, there will be more computers than people in the U.S. What purpose do these computers serve? Among many other tasks, computers send and receive messages, do research, keep track of finances, make and check on investments, and purchase goods of all kinds—books, antiques, groceries, cars, homes, airplane tickets, and more computers. Almost anything that can be purchased at a store or by mail order can now be obtained by computer.

3   Businesses of all sizes now find computers a necessity. Computers keep track of inventory, record financial data, **transmit** credit card information, and receive immediate approval on credit card purchases. Products that are bought in person are also affected by computers. Most products sold today have a bar-code label that contains the name of the product, the price, and other information. An employee enters prices into a database that also contains product descriptions. A laser device reads the bar code at the checkout line, and the name of the product and price are automatically printed on a register tape. No matter what the job is, computer literacy is essential in today's business world.

4   Computers have revolutionized medicine. They have made possible such devices as the CT* scanner and the MRI† machine, both of which are used to diagnose medical conditions. An amazing new instrument is being developed that will be able to diagnose breast cancer long before a mammogram could detect it.

5   Home computers are useful to people of all ages. Children as young as 3 years old practice computer skills they will need in their school years and careers. Older children play exciting (and sometimes scary) computer games. Educational **programs** on CD-ROM **disks** teach reading, geography, and virtually all other academic subjects. Teenagers communicate with their friends by **e-mail** (electronic mail) and meet people with similar interests all over the world on the **Internet.** Many high school and college teachers give assignments to students by e-mail. Students research assignments on the Internet, use a word-processing program to type them up, and send them to their teachers via the Internet. Some teachers correct and grade work and return it electronically. Adults with money to invest study public companies and buy and sell stocks online. Older people use e-mail to communicate with their grown children and grandchildren who may live far away. Not only written material, but pictures, too, can be sent by computer anywhere in the world.

6   The computer revolution has had an enormous effect upon the economy. The computer, and especially the Internet, has produced a host of new businesses, such as companies that sell products exclusively on the Internet and companies that manufacture, develop, and improve software and hardware. When these companies sell their stock on stock exchanges, many people invest in them.

7   The growth of computer use has also created millions of new jobs, replacing those that were lost as manufacturing industries became more automated and companies built new factories outside the U.S. However, this new high-tech job market requires specialized skills and training.

8   Computers have even changed where workers do their jobs. Today, more than 20 million people are "telecommuting" (working at home and communicating with their offices by computer), at least part of the week.

---

*Computed tomography.

†Magnetic resonance imaging.

The Telephone and Associated Devices

9   In March of 1876, when Alexander Graham Bell called to his assistant on the telephone he had just invented, he could never have predicted what an important instrument he had just created. U.S. president Rutherford Hayes said, "That's an amazing invention, but who would ever want to use one of them?" However, he soon changed his tune. In 1878, he had a telephone installed at the White House. He immediately put in a call—to Alexander Graham Bell.

10   Perhaps no invention has affected daily life as much as the telephone. In its early years, it **enabled** people to talk to each other without having to travel long distances by foot or horseback. Later, it provided a means of transmitting news and other important information all around the world instantly. And today it provides the means for millions of people to communicate with each other directly or via the Internet.

11   Wireless portable phones (usually called *cellular* or *cell phones* in the U.S.) provide people with peace of mind because they can quickly contact others in case of an emergency even when no wired phone is nearby. People also use cell phones for less dramatic purposes. Many people chat with friends or check in on their kids as they walk along the street or shop. Ownership of these telephones greatly expanded between 1990 and 2000. In 1988, there were about 2 million in use, mostly by businesspeople and professionals who needed to keep in touch with their offices and clients. Today, more than 80 million cell phones are owned and used by people all over the U.S. Cell phone usage has increased because the cost has decreased to the point where most people can afford it. When first introduced, cell phones cost more than $1,000, and the per-minute rate made them impractical for most individuals. Today, many companies give the phones away or sell them at very low prices. The cost of air time also has dropped, to about 10 cents a minute.

"I TOLD YOU NEVER TO CALL ME HERE."

12   The quality of cell phones has also significantly improved. In the past, people speaking from wireless telephones were often difficult to hear and, frequently, the signal would be lost. Today's phones produce sound quality equal to wired telephones, and the connections are much more reliable. It is now even possible, with some new phones, to connect to the Internet.

13   Cell phones can also be **nuisances**. Many theaters and libraries have signs asking that cell phones be turned off. A famous Broadway actor actually stopped a performance when somebody's cell phone rang! People using cell phones while driving can be dangerous. They are engrossed in conversation instead of concentrating on their driving. Some states are considering laws to prohibit talking on the phone while driving.

14   Another popular method of high-tech communication is the **pager**, often referred to as a "beeper." It is a small device usually hooked onto one's belt or carried in one's purse. A person wishing to contact someone phones that person's pager. When the pager receives the message, it beeps to let the owner know that someone is trying to get in touch. A display on the pager shows the caller's telephone number. More sophisticated pagers display a message from the caller. Pagers were originally used primarily by physicians who needed to be reached in emergencies. Today, pagers are commonly used by many businesspeople to talk with customers. Parents also use them to relay messages to their children and vice versa.

15   Two other communication devices that have come into common usage are the answering machine and its cousin, voice mail. The answering machine gives callers a recorded message telling them to leave a name and telephone number. At one time, many people considered the use of answering machines rude. Today, most people consider the lack of an answering machine inconsiderate since, without it, the caller cannot leave a message for a person who is away. Voice mail also provides a message and a chance to leave a message. It is more often used by businesses because it can also channel callers through a series of messages to the department that will best serve the callers' needs. Voice mail can be very frustrating to people who want to speak to an actual person immediately.

✔ Check Your Comprehension

Why are cell phones so popular? List four uses of them.

The Internet

16   Perhaps the most radical changes in American communications involve the widespread use of the Internet, a vast network of **connected** computers. The Internet was originally created by the U.S. government to enable research scientists to communicate with one another. The original experiment involved just four computers. The Internet began to expand in the 1980s when the National Science Foundation provided funding to involve more computers at more sites. During the 1990s, the Internet grew to connect computers all over the world. As more computers became available, the use of the Internet grew at a very rapid rate. In 1994, about 3 million people were using the Internet. By 1999, that number had grown to 200 million, mostly in the U.S. At the turn of the cen-

tury, it was estimated that within 5 years, a billion people would communicate in cyberspace (a name commonly used to mean the Internet).

17   To use the Internet, one must subscribe to an Internet service provider (ISP). By far the largest of these is America Online, which has a membership of more than 20 million. Most people connect to the Internet through their telephone line. A subscriber, using a computer and modem, dials a local telephone number and is connected to the ISP. From there, the user can connect to computers all over the world or communicate by e-mail with other Internet users. People who need faster Internet service can subscribe to a DSL (digital subscriber line), which uses copper wiring with special hardware and is more expensive. High-speed Internet connections are also available through cable from the same companies that furnish cable TV service. Even higher speeds are available to businesses over superfast telephone lines called T1 and T3.

18   One of the most popular features of the Internet is e-mail. E-mail provides a means of communicating with people all over the world almost immediately. To do so, the person sending the message types the recipient's e-mail address and a message into a computer program that looks like a form. The message is then sent over telephone lines to the ISP, which transmits it to the recipient, who can log on to his ISP and receive the message. In addition to text messages, **graphics** and computer programs can be sent by e-mail. About two-thirds of all e-mail comes from the U.S. It is estimated that the number of e-mail messages sent from the U.S. exceeds the number of letters delivered by the U.S. Postal Service (often called *snail mail*). Thanks to e-mail and the World Wide Web, people all over the world can receive news from anywhere else without censorship. Governments can no longer hide behind their propaganda. The truth is available to anyone with Internet access.

19   Another very popular and important feature of the Internet is the World Wide Web (WWW). It can connect a computer anywhere in the world with a vast number of other computers that contain a world of information (not all of it accurate, however). You can find the text of all of Shakespeare's plays and read them on your computer screen, download them to your computer's hard drive, or print them on your printer. Recently, the entire *Encyclopedia Britannica* was made available on the Web to anyone with a computer, a modem, and an ISP. Using the Web, one can look into the Library of Congress or find the opinions of the U.S. Supreme Court. The amount of information on the Web is enormous and growing daily. It is often referred to as the "Information Superhighway." It is estimated that, by the end of the twentieth century, there were more than 1 billion Web pages available to "Web surfers," most of them free.

20   To reach a Web site, it is necessary to know the address. For example, to reach the White House you would enter www.whitehouse.gov. This is pronounced "www dot whitehouse dot gov."

21   Probably the fastest-growing part of the Web is called *e-commerce*. Most retail businesses have Web sites where prospective customers browse among the company's merchandise, finding pictures and prices of the products available. To order something on the Web, a customer fills in an order form with his name, address, credit card information, and a list of the products to be purchased. The customer's account is charged, and the merchandise is delivered to his door. Many companies without retail stores have set up shop on the Web, and the number of such companies is growing rapidly. There are

also companies that sell goods by **auction** (a sale where people offer to buy an item at a certain price, and the one making the highest bid gets to buy the product). Some Web sites search the Web and find their customers the best price for a particular product, for example, life insurance policies, airplane tickets, and home mortgages.

22   The importance of the Web to research cannot be overemphasized. President Clinton proposed that every classroom in America be equipped with Internet access and that every teacher be instructed in the use of the Internet. The amount of material available on the Web is much greater than any library's resources. All this information is also available in many foreign languages from sites around the world.

23   While computers have greatly expanded communications, computer usage has created a whole new language that must be learned. Some call it *computerese*. *Online* (being connected to a network), *surf* (searching through the World Wide Web), *download* and *upload* (receiving and sending data from or to another computer), *laptop* (a **portable** computer), and *mouse* (a device for performing operations on the computer) are just a few of the new words (or new meanings of old words) used in computerland.

✔ **Check Your Comprehension**   *What are three major activities that can be done on the Internet?*

The Future of Technology

24   What new inventions will technology bring by the year 2010? While it is difficult to predict the future, it is likely that computers will continue to become smaller, faster, and cheaper. Here are some additional predictions. Smaller and longer-lasting batteries and wireless access to the Internet will enable people to take computers (probably pocket-sized) wherever they go. Cell phones will also become smaller and more reliable and will be usable anywhere in the world. Cell phones will have paging capability, so today's pagers will become **obsolete**. Faster computers and cheaper DSL and cable will eliminate the frustration of waiting for a Web page to appear. The Internet will become an essential tool for research, shopping, and communication. Finally, worldwide use of communication tools will help people around the globe better understand and interact with each other.

AFTER YOU READ

I. Getting the Message

A. *Reread paragraphs 2, 3, 6, 8, and 21. Discuss with a partner the various ways that computers are used in the business world. Then list three uses you consider very important.*

1. _____

2. _____

3. _____

B. *Reread paragraphs 5 and 19. Then list three ways in which computers can help students.*

1. _____

2. _____

3. _____

C. *Reread paragraphs 11–14. Then explain the difference between a pager and a cell phone.*

_____

_____

II. Building Your Vocabulary

A. *These are the 15 key vocabulary words for this chapter. They are boldfaced in the reading. Pronounce these words after your teacher and discuss their meanings.*

auction*	e-mail*	pager
calamity	graphic	portable
connect	the Internet	prediction
disk	nuisance	program*
enable	obsolete	transmit

B. *Answer or complete these questions with some of the key vocabulary words.*

1. What would you use to send your friend a letter via the Internet?

   _____

2. The word *cyberspace* is another name for what? _____

3. Where can you save what you have written on the computer? _____

4. When you create a picture on your computer, what are you creating?

   _____

5. What is another word for *send* often used when referring to computer messages?

   _____

6. A cell phone has no wires, so you can carry one around with you. What word

   describes that characteristic of cell phones? _____

---

*These words can be used as nouns or verbs.

(continued on the next page)

7. If you don't have a cell phone, what else could you carry that would allow people to communicate with you anytime, anywhere? _____

8. People can buy things on the Internet by bidding (offering a certain amount of money for an item). What do we call this way of offering merchandise for sale?

   _____

9. What would you call your cell phone if it rings while you're at a concert?

   _____

10. What do you think computers will be able to do 10 years from now? What is your _____ about the future of high-tech communications?

III. Sharpening Reading Skills

Making Inferences

Mark each statement true (T) or false (F). The paragraphs indicated in parentheses will not give you the answers directly, but you can make inferences based upon their content.

_____ 1. The word *glitches* means everything is working perfectly. (1)

_____ 2. *Revolutionized* means "caused major changes." (4)

_____ 3. Cell phones are noisy. (13)

_____ 4. You can talk to a caller on your pager. (14)

_____ 5. Voice mail is more complicated than an answering machine. (15)

_____ 6. *Turn of the century* means "the end of one century and the beginning of another." (16)

_____ 7. The U.S. Postal Service is called *snail mail* because it's much faster than e-mail. (18)

_____ 8. You need a credit card to make Internet purchases. (21)

IV. Understanding Idioms and Expressions

"Computerese" has given English a lot of new words and phrases. Match each one in column 1 with its definition or description in column 2 by writing the correct numbers on the lines. The numbers in parentheses give the paragraphs in which the words or phrases are used. If necessary, find a computer-literate classroom partner to help you.

1. CD-ROM (5)   _____a plastic disk, similar to a compact disk, that can store a great deal of information and loads programs onto the computer's hard drive

2. computer literacy (3)   _____a device inside the computer for permanently storing data

3. e-commerce (21)   _____automatic recorded phone messages that help callers leave a message for the right person or department

4. log on (18)   _____the ability to use a computer

5. hard drive (19)   _____used to type text, such as letters or essays, on the computer

6. surf (23)   _____connect with an ISP

7. voice mail (15)   _____part of the Internet, often used for doing research

8. Web site (20, 21)   _____not a spider's home—an exact Internet location, for example, of a particular, business, person, or publication

9. word processing (5)   _____search the Web to find information

10. World Wide Web (18, 19)   _____the buying and selling of products and services via the Internet

V. Taking Words Apart

A. *Use the correct word part listed below to make the opposite of each word listed below.*

    de-   *dis-*   *down-*   *un-*

Example

wired   _____*unwired*_____

Add the Prefixes

1. civilized _____

2. connect _____

Change the Prefixes

3. increase _____

4. upload _____

B. *Discuss the difference between the* Internet *and an* intranet.

VI. Practicing Sentence Patterns

A. Time Expressions with *when* Phrases or clauses with *when* can begin or end a sentence. When the time clause begins the sentence, a comma is used to separate it from the main idea.

Examples

When I got home, I sent an e-mail.

I sent an e-mail *when I got home.*

Write your own sentences with time clauses that tell when something happened:

1. When _____ .

2. _____ when _____ .

B. The Pronoun *one* In formal writing, the author may not want to address the reader directly with an informal *you* or an imperative form. Instead, *one* is often used to refer to a nonspecific person (meaning people in general). Examples of its use are in paragraphs 14, 17, and 19.

Change these sentences from second person to third person. Use one *and a singular verb.*

Example

You need to be computer literate if *you want* a good job in the United States.

One needs to be computer literate if *one (he, she) want*s a good job in the U.S.

1. If you have a cell phone, you can make calls from your car.

   _____

2. If you are computer-literate, you'll find a job more easily.

   _____

VII. Sharing Ideas

A. Issues

Debate these issues in small groups. Then choose one and write about it.

1. Everyone knows how to use a telephone. Some people say that everyone should also know how to use a computer. Do you agree?

2. The Internet is a sociable place. It has chat rooms, special-interest groups, auctions, and games. Some people become computer addicts. They communicate with people from all over the world via the Internet, but they forget to communicate with family members in their own living room. Have computers encouraged Americans to substitute virtual (online) relationships for real, personal human relationships? What will be the results of this?

3. When people put messages on the Internet, do they risk a loss of privacy? Is it risky to send credit card information on the Internet?

B. On a Personal Note

Write about one of these topics.

1. Some people imagine a world in which everyone is carrying a cell phone (perhaps worn like a wristwatch) at all times. Do you think that would be a good or a bad development?

2. Some people treat their computer like a person. They get angry when it doesn't follow orders. They praise it when it produces good work. How do you feel about the computer you use? Do you like it, hate it, or distrust it? Do you ever talk to your computer? Do you ever hit it or curse it? Write a humorous piece about your relationship with your computer.

3. Where do you think high technology will take us in the future? Write your predictions.

UNIT 7

American

Holidays:

History

and

Customs

19 | Christopher Columbus: A Controversial Hero

Christopher Columbus's first landing in the Western Hemisphere in 1492

BEFORE YOU READ

Discuss

1. Have you heard of Christopher Columbus? Tell what you know about him.

2. Some people think of Columbus as a great man. Others consider him a villain. What's your opinion?

3. Have you ever traveled by ship? Where did you go? Was the water rough?

Guess

Try to answer the questions. Then look for the answers in the reading.

1. On his first voyage, how many days did it take Columbus to cross the Atlantic Ocean? Check (✓) one:

   ____ 18 ____ 36 ____ 64

2. In what year did Columbus make his first voyage? Check (✓) one: ____

   1492 ____ 1541 ____ 1620

Christopher Columbus: A Controversial Hero

His Accomplishments, His Holiday

1   He was called *Cristoforo Colombo* in Italian and *Cristóbal Colón* in Spanish. Today, Americans call him *Christopher Columbus*. Worldwide, he's commonly called the discoverer of America. Some people might wonder why. After all, Columbus didn't set out in search of new **continents**, and he never realized that he had found any. Moreover, he wasn't the first European to set foot in the Western **Hemisphere**. Human skeletons with European characteristics—bones that may be 10,000 years old—have been found in North America. About A.D. 1000, Vikings (Scandinavian sailors) probably reached the New World and lived for a while on the coast of North America. Historians also believe that, in the fourteenth century, Portuguese and English fishing boats crossed the Atlantic Ocean and landed in Newfoundland and Labrador. But these contacts didn't last long and didn't change anything. Only Columbus's **voyages** resulted in permanent links between the Eastern and Western Hemispheres and the widespread colonization of the Americas. Columbus's historic landing on an **island** in the Bahamas on October 12, 1492, was a turning point in world history.

2   In the U.S.A., this event is celebrated on Columbus Day, the second Monday in October. The holiday is also celebrated in Italy and in most Spanish-speaking countries. In some places, it's called *Landing Day* or *Discovery Day*. In many Latin American countries, it is called *Día de la Raza* (*Day of the Race*). Columbus Day celebrations often involve parades, patriotic speeches, and dramatizations of the landing.

3   In 1992, the year of the quincentennial celebration of Columbus's discovery, there were many debates about who should honor Columbus and even whether he should be honored. In *Columbus and the Age of Discovery*, the author (Zvi Dor-Ner) describes some of these disputes: "The Spaniards and the Italians argued over how to divide the national honor. [Columbus was born in Genoa, which is now part of Italy, but Spanish money paid for his **expeditions**.] The Scandinavians contended that if any man should

be honored for discovering America, it should be Eric the Red. [Eric the Red, from Norway, explored Greenland in the year 985. His son, Leif Ericson, was one of the first explorers to visit mainland America.] The Third World countries insisted that there was no need to honor a rank colonialist. And the nations in the Caribbean basin resented the notion that they had been discovered at all. As the joke has it, they knew where they were; it was Columbus who was lost."

4   The consequences of Columbus's voyages were most tragic for the native peoples of the Americas. For them, Columbus Day is not a festive occasion but a day of mourning. As Europeans took over the New World, Native Americans lost their lives by the millions. They died from European illnesses or were killed in battles with colonists. Those who survived were forced to live like prisoners in special areas called *reservations*. So today, when Americans honor the bravery and the genius of Columbus, they also remember the pain that resulted from his ventures. (Chapter 21 provides more information about Native Americans in the U.S.)

> ✔ **Check Your Comprehension**
>
> *Why do some people object to a holiday honoring Columbus?*

Preparations for a Great Journey

5   Young Columbus lived in the perfect place at the perfect time for the role he was destined to play in history. He was born in 1451 in Genoa, a seaport now part of Italy. In the fifteenth century, maritime **exploration** was common. By 1453, the Ottoman Turks had conquered much of southeastern Europe, and they controlled Constantinople (now Istanbul, Turkey), a major trade center between Europe and Asia. This made it difficult for Europeans to **import** the Asian **luxuries** they wanted—such as gold, jewels, silks, perfumes, and spices. A land journey with these goods was risky and expensive. Europeans wanted a safe sea route to allow trade with the countries of the Far East—India, China, Japan, and the Indies. That was an important goal in Columbus's time.

6   As a boy, Columbus helped his father in his wool-weaving business. His father soon pushed him into a business career. At the age of 14, Christopher began sailing on trading ships in the Mediterranean. In 1476, when he was 25 years old, he found out firsthand how dangerous life aboard ship could be. On his first voyage on the Atlantic Ocean, off the coast of Portugal, his group of five ships was attacked by 13 French and Portuguese pirate ships. Seven ships went down, and hundreds of men were killed. Columbus, a sailor on one of the ships that sank, held onto a floating oar until he reached the Portuguese shore.

7   Columbus stayed in Portugal for about 10 years. He settled in Lisbon, an important maritime power, and he joined his brother's mapmaking business. He also worked as a seagoing businessman, buying and selling goods. He married a Portuguese woman, and his first son, Diego, was born in 1480. Columbus's wife died in 1484.

8   The Portuguese were trying to reach the Far East by sailing around the southern tip of Africa. Columbus thought he had a better route, and he tried to "sell" his idea to the king of Portugal. Columbus claimed that a ship could reach the East by sailing west. He

was right, but he also made three important mistakes. First, he underestimated the size of the Earth. Second, he thought that a much greater percentage of the Earth's surface was land than actually is—he didn't realize how large the oceans were. Third, of course, he didn't know that the huge continents of North and South America lay between Europe and Asia. These mistakes were understandable. Columbus was familiar with the writings and maps available to educated people of his time. His studies led him to these geographical errors.

9   In 1485, after the king of Portugal refused to finance Columbus's expedition, Columbus and his son traveled to Spain to ask King Ferdinand and Queen Isabella for ships and sailors. Columbus promised them wealth and new territory. A religious man, Columbus also promised that his expedition would bring Christianity to new areas of the world. Columbus was a good salesman. Isabella and Ferdinand put him on the royal payroll. However, they could not afford to equip him for the voyage while the Spanish were fighting the Moors (North African Arabs who had conquered and ruled much of Spain for many centuries). Columbus waited about 7 years.

10   Finally, in 1492, the Spanish conquered Granada, the last Moorish stronghold. Isabella was then able to give more thought to Columbus's idea. King Ferdinand didn't want to spend the money because the recent wars had been very expensive. Legend says that Isabella offered to pawn her jewels to finance the trip. But this **sacrifice** was not necessary. The treasurer of Spain supplied most of the funds from the national treasury and his own savings. Some of Columbus's wealthy supporters also contributed. What would Columbus receive for undertaking this difficult and dangerous voyage? His written agreement with the king and queen gave him a good salary, a percentage of the riches his discoveries brought to Spain, the right to be governor of any lands he discovered, and aristocratic titles that he could hand down to his descendants. Columbus asked for so much that Ferdinand got angry and almost rejected the arrangement. But, in the end, they made an agreement that was very generous to Columbus.

✔ Check Your Comprehension   *What were Columbus's goals?*

Four Important Voyages

11   Most of the information we have about Columbus's voyages comes from his journals and letters, which were written in Spanish. For his first voyage, Columbus had three ships: the *Niña*, the *Pinta*, and the *Santa Maria*. Columbus was the captain of one of the ships, and his two brothers were in charge of the others. The entire **crew** of all three ships numbered about 90. The ships had good compasses to tell direction but no instruments to measure distance. Fortunately, Columbus was a very skillful sailor and could navigate well by looking at the stars. He also understood wind patterns and how to use them to his advantage. Although he was wrong about what part of the world he had reached, Columbus's great skill enabled him to find his way back to the same general area on four expeditions.

12   The ships sailed from the Canary Islands on September 6, 1492. The crew lost sight

of land on September 9, and the men began to sigh and cry. Columbus wrote in his journal, "I comforted them with great promises of land and riches."

13   Weeks went by, and there was still no land in sight. The sailors became even more frightened. They knew that the world was round, not flat, and they weren't afraid of falling off the edge. But they were afraid that they would die at sea. The crew begged Columbus to turn back; there were even whispers of **mutiny.** On October 10, Columbus and his crew agreed to sail on for 3 more days and then turn around if no land was seen. Columbus was optimistic. They saw land birds flying overhead and some carved wood floating on the water. He felt certain that land must be nearby.

14   In the middle of the night, just 36 days after leaving the Canary Islands, the sailors were overjoyed to see pinpoints of light in the darkness and then white sand shining in the moonlight. Columbus's ships were approaching an island in the Bahamas, an island that Columbus named *San Salvador*. Which island was it? Historians don't all agree, but most think it was the one once called *Watling Island* and then renamed *San Salvador*.

15   When dawn came, Columbus and some of his men came ashore in small boats. The landing party found themselves in a strange, beautiful tropical environment. They placed a Spanish flag and banner in the ground and declared the island a Spanish possession. They were greeted by timid but friendly people who wore no clothes. Because Columbus thought he had landed on an island in the Indies near Japan or China, he called these natives *Indians*. Today, the islands that Columbus explored are called the *West Indies*.

16   The three ships spent only a few days at San Salvador. They then sailed on to Cuba and Haiti, where the *Santa Maria* was wrecked. On January 16, 1493, the *Niña* and *Pinta* set sail for Spain. They took with them some samples of unusual findings—trinkets, plants, and birds. They also brought back some New World natives. The voyage home was extremely rough, and some of the Indians died en route. On March 15, Columbus's ships arrived safely in Palos, Spain.

17   After his first voyage, Columbus was very popular and in favor with the king and queen. For his second expedition, he was given 17 ships and about 1,500 men. Columbus's second expedition sailed through the Lesser Antilles and past Puerto Rico. He also explored Cuba. On his third voyage, he landed on Venezuela, finally reaching the mainland of South America.

18   His later explorations didn't live up to expectations. There was less gold and more trouble. Some Spanish settlers remained in the new land to form a **colony** called *Hispaniola* (where Haiti and the Dominican Republic are now located). These settlers had expected to find huge supplies of gold and other riches. Instead, they found difficult living conditions, strange foods, hard work, and constant danger. They blamed Columbus for their disappointment. Many went back to Spain and complained about him. Others stayed and rebelled against his leadership. The king's representative came from Spain to settle the trouble in Hispaniola. He put Columbus and his brothers in chains and sent them back to Spain for trial. On board ship, the captain offered to release Columbus from his chains, but Columbus refused this offer. When he arrived in Spain, the king and queen freed him, but they replaced him as governor of Hispaniola.

19   In an attempt to regain his good name, Columbus began his fourth and last voyage. With four ships, he left Spain in 1502. On this voyage, his ships sailed along the east coast of Central America—past the present-day countries of Honduras, Nicaragua,

Costa Rica, and Panama. During the journey, his ships were badly damaged. As a result, he and his crew were stranded on Jamaica for a year before being rescued and returned to Spain in 1504. Columbus was, at that point, considered an unsuccessful explorer. He had not brought back riches from the Far East. (Later, in the sixteenth century, Spain took huge profits from the Americas, but that was after Columbus's death.) To make matters worse for him, Queen Isabella, his great supporter, died.

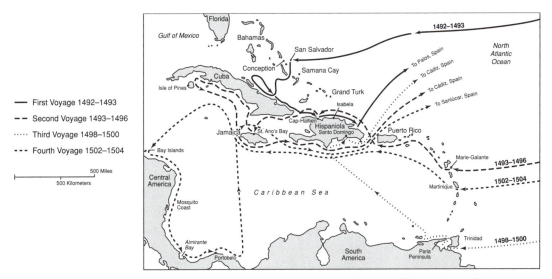

First Voyage 1492–1493
Second Voyage 1493–1496
Third Voyage 1498–1500
Fourth Voyage 1502–1504

Routes of Columbus's four voyages

20   During his last years, Columbus had a comfortable income from his share of the gold that was found in Hispaniola. However, he was unhappy because King Ferdinand denied him some of the other rewards he had been promised. Moreover, he was sick and in great pain from arthritis. He died in 1506 at the age of 54 and was buried in Spain. In 1542, his body was moved to the Dominican Republic, once part of "his" colony, Hispaniola. He may still be buried there.

21   Was this controversial man a hero or a villain? Probably both. He was certainly ambitious. That trait motivated him to work hard, take risks, and accomplish something of significance. However, many would say he was also greedy, wanting too much in return for his efforts. His **persistence** was a virtue. But he was so persistent that he was often stubborn. Despite evidence to the contrary, he never faced the fact that he had not reached the Far East. Admitting that would have meant his expeditions failed. Most disturbing, however, is the evidence that Columbus was harsh, even cruel, in dealing with his crew, the colonists in Hispaniola, and the Native Americans. He had an **autocratic** manner with his crew. Trying to make his colony more profitable, he sometimes ordered the killing of Spanish colonists who were troublemakers in Hispaniola. He sent some Indians to Spain to be sold into slavery and forced others to find a certain quantity of gold per day or face death.

22   Still, Columbus continues to be admired for his courage, self-confidence, ability, and, perhaps most of all, his persistence. In school, children read Joaquin Miller's famous poem about Columbus. The closing lines say, "He gained a world; he gave that world / Its grandest lesson: 'On! Sail on!'"

What were Columbus's character strengths? What were his flaws?

Why "America"?

23   If Columbus is considered the most important European explorer of the Western Hemisphere, then why are citizens of the U.S. called *Americans*, not *Columbians*? And who were the continents of North and South America named after? These are questions that some newcomers to the U.S. ask.

24   Columbus's name appears many times on a map of the Western Hemisphere. Several cities in the U.S. are named after him, as is the Columbia River, one of the chief rivers in the U.S.A. and Canada. The nation's capital city is called Washington, D.C., with the initials standing for *District of Columbia*. However, the two continents of the Western Hemisphere are named after Amerigo Vespucci, another Italian explorer. He made at least two (and possibly four) voyages to the Americas, the first only a few years after Columbus's first voyage. Vespucci's 1499 voyage was undertaken for Spain and led by a Spanish explorer. It brought Vespucci to Brazil, Venezuela, and Hispaniola. Then, in 1501, he sailed to Brazil again, this time with the ships of a Portuguese captain. The 1501 voyage **convinced** Vespucci that he had reached a new continent. He was the first person to claim this.

25   About 1503, Vespucci's account of his discovery of a new continent was published in English under the title *New World*. It was also translated into many other languages and published in many European countries. Its fame established Vespucci as the discoverer of the New World. Columbus never disputed this claim.

26   In 1507, a German mapmaker who read Vespucci's writings became the first person to use the name *America* to describe the area that Columbus and Vespucci had explored. Vespucci received many honors and important jobs. After his death, it was discovered that this so-called great explorer was not really so great. After all, Columbus had reached the Western Hemisphere before Vespucci did. In addition, despite his claims, Vespucci was probably not the leader of the expeditions he was on. Therefore, it is appropriate that Amerigo Vespucci is the forgotten explorer, while Columbus is honored annually in many countries.

AFTER YOU READ

I. Getting the Message

On each blank line, write the letter of the correct word or phrase to complete the sentence. The numbers in parentheses give the paragraphs you can reread if you need help.

  1. Columbus was born in 1451, in the middle of the _____ century. (5)
      a. fourteenth
      b. fifteenth

2. Columbus left Portugal and went to Spain because _____. (9)
   a. the Portuguese king wanted to finance his voyage
   b. he hoped that the Spanish government would pay for the ships and crew he needed

3. From 1485 to 1492, Columbus was trying to get ships for an expedition so he could _____. (8)
   a. find new continents
   b. reach the East by sailing west

4. Columbus's goal was to _____. (10)
   a. help his native country get colonies in the Far East
   b. become rich and famous

5. Columbus made this mistake: _____. (8)
   a. He thought the world was round
   b. To the west, he thought that there was only water, not land, between Europe and Asia

6. Columbus's first voyage was important because _____. (1)
   a. he was the first European to land in the Western Hemisphere
   b. his landing led to European development of the Americas

7. Columbus's life was similar to Vespucci's in this way: Both men _____. (10, 18, 19, 24)
   a. crossed the Atlantic Ocean
   b. led voyages for Portugal

II. Building Your Vocabulary

A. *These are the 15 key vocabulary words for this chapter. They are boldfaced in the reading. Pronounce these words after your teacher, and discuss their meanings.*

autocratic	expedition	luxury
colony	exploration	mutiny*
continent	hemisphere	persistence
convince	import*	sacrifice*
crew	island	voyage*

B. *Discuss the answers to the following questions with a classmate. Then choose four of the questions to answer on a separate piece of paper. Use a dictionary for help if necessary.*

1. What behavior shows that Columbus was persistent?

2. What kinds of sacrifices do parents often make for their children?

---

*These words can be used as nouns or verbs.

(continued on the next page)

3. In what way is a mutiny similar to a revolution?

4. Have you ever taken a voyage (a long boat trip)? Where did you go?

5. Which continent is Central America a part of—North America or South America?

6. What is an island surrounded by?

7. What are some countries in the Far East?

8. What country did the colony of Hispaniola belong to?

9. What's the difference between importing and exporting merchandise?

C. *Arrange these words in order of the size of the place, starting with the smallest.*

| city | continent | country | hemisphere | world |

1. _____   3. _____   5. _____

2. _____   4. _____

III. Sharpening Reading Skills

A. Punctuation Tips

1. *Reread paragraph 3. Notice that it contains a quotation of several sentences. Within the quotation, there are two pairs of brackets, which look like this: [ ]. The brackets contain information that the authors have added to explain something in the quotation. Compare brackets to parentheses, also used in this paragraph. Parentheses look like this: ( ). Discuss some uses of parentheses.*

2. *Reread paragraph 20. Why is the word his in quotation marks? Discuss.*

3. *In the last sentence of paragraph 22, note the use of single quotes within double quotes. The single quotes refer to Columbus's words, which are quoted in the poem. Practice writing a sentence that has a quotation within a quotation.*

B. Map-Reading Practice

Find the following on a map of the world:

1. the seven continents

2. all the countries mentioned in the reading (Scan the reading for the countries.)

3. Columbus's general route on his first and fourth voyages

IV. Understanding Idioms and Expressions

A. *On each blank line, write the letter of the correct word or phrase to complete the sentence. The numbers in parentheses give the paragraphs in which the expressions are used.*

1. *After all* (1) means _____.
   a. after many events
   b. considering these facts
   c. a surprising outcome

2. The *New World* (1) means _____.
   a. North America
   b. the Western Hemisphere
   c. the Eastern Hemisphere

3. The *Third World* (3) means _____.
   a. Europe and Asia
   b. the Far East
   c. developing, less industrialized countries

4. *Lost their lives* (4) means _____.
   a. died
   b. got lost
   c. lost their freedom

5. *Find out* (6) means _____.
   a. find
   b. get information about
   c. go out

6. *Lost sight of land* (12) means _____.
   a. lost their way
   b. couldn't see land anymore
   c. lost their eyesight

7. This *so-called* great explorer (26) implies that Vespucci _____.
   a. deserved to be called great
   b. called himself great
   c. wasn't really so great

B. *Discuss the meanings of the following expressions. The numbers in parentheses give the paragraphs in which the expressions are used.*

turning point (1)   live up to expectations (18)   face the fact that (21)

V. Taking Words Apart

A. Adjective Hunt

In small groups, make lists of adjectives that describe Columbus. Scan the reading for adjectives used there or for nouns that you can make into adjectives (for example, skill into skillful). Put the lists on the board. See which group has the longest list of appropriate words. Write a G after the words that describe good traits and a B after the ones that are bad. Finally, tell why each adjective fits Columbus.

B. Names of Places and Groups of People

Fill in the missing words.

Examples

Europe _____European_____   _____China_____ Chinese

1. Italy _____   4. France _____

2. Asia _____   5. _____ Portuguese

3. _____ Spanish   6. U.S. _____

C. Prefixes

A quincentennial is a 500th anniversary. Fill in the correct prefix, where needed, for each of the following expressions. Use bi-, tri-, and sesqui-.

1. 100 years = _____centennial   3. 200 years = _____centennial

2. 150 years = _____centennial   4. 300 years = _____centennial

D. Compound Words

Find these compound words in the paragraphs indicated: underestimated (8) and overjoyed (14). From the context, guess their meanings. Then check the dictionary definition to see how close you were.

1. What does *under* mean in *underestimate*? _____

2. What does *over* mean in *overjoyed*? _____

VI. Practicing Sentence Patterns

Reread the first sentence in paragraph 23. Note that it begins with a condition (If . . .) and then asks a question. Here is another example of a sentence that begins with a condition:

If you have very little money, then why did you buy a new car?

Now write your own sentences using this pattern.

1. If you're tired, then why _____?

2. If _____, then why _____?

VII. Sharing Ideas

A. Issues

Debate these issues in small groups. Then choose one and write about it.

1. Should there be a holiday to honor Columbus?

2. Is it fair to blame Columbus for what happened to Native Americans after his death?

3. People seem to need two opposing elements in their lives: adventure and security. Columbus seemed to prefer adventure. Which is more important to you?

B. On a Personal Note

Write about one of these topics.

1. It is ironic (the opposite of what is expected) that Columbus became famous for something he never knew he did. Look up the word *irony* in the dictionary. Then write about something ironic that occurred in your life.

2. Search the Internet for more information about Columbus. Summarize some of the new information you discovered.

3. Tell about a time when you were blamed for something that wasn't your fault.

20 | Halloween: A Time for Scary Fun

Children in costume trick-or-treating on Halloween

BEFORE YOU READ

Discuss

1. Why are the children in the picture dressed in costume? Can you find the witch, the pirate, and the monster?

2. Are some holidays more important to children and others more important to adults? Explain.

3. What other holidays do you know of on which people wear special clothing?

Guess

Try to answer the questions. Then look for the answers in the reading.

1. European immigrants from what country brought Halloween to the U.S.? Check (✓) one:

   _____ Spain _____ Italy _____ Ireland

2. A jack-o'-lantern is made from what vegetable? _____

3. How much have the heaviest pumpkins ever grown weighed? Check (√) one:

   _____ about 150 pounds   _____ about 500 pounds

   _____ more than 1,000 pounds

   (*NOTE*: 2.2 pounds = 1 kilogram)

Halloween: A Time for Scary Fun

A Typical Halloween Scene

1   It was a cool autumn evening. Mrs. Brown was sitting in her living room, reading. Suddenly, there was a loud knock on her door, then two or three more knocks. Mrs. Brown put the safety chain on her door. Then she opened the door a little and looked out. There stood three children wearing masks and **costumes**. When they saw her, they all shouted, "Trick or treat! Money or eats!"

2   Mrs. Brown dropped a candy bar into each child's bag. One boy was wearing a big hat, a plaid shirt, blue jeans, and high boots. The holster on his belt had a toy gun in it. Mrs. Brown asked him, "Who are you?"

3   "I'm a cowboy," he answered.

4   "And I'm a **ghost**," shouted the child next to him, hidden under a white sheet.

5   "And I'm a **skeleton**," said the third child. The "skeleton" was wearing a black shirt and black pants with strips of white tape on them.

6   "Thanks for the candy," shouted the children as they ran off to ring another doorbell.

7   "You're welcome," said Mrs. Brown. "Have fun, and don't play any pranks."

*   *   *

8   Every year on October 31, Halloween scenes like this occur throughout the U.S.A. American children love to dress up in costumes and go trick-or-treating. If an adult refuses to supply a treat—candy, cookies, fruit, or money—the children may play a trick. Typical Halloween pranks are soaping windows, writing on doors with crayons, overturning garbage cans, sticking pins into doorbells to keep them ringing, throwing raw eggs, and spraying shaving cream on cars and friends.

Why does Mrs. Brown give the children candy?

The Origins of Halloween Customs

9   The name *Halloween* is a short way of saying *All Hallows' Eve*, which means "the night before the Roman Catholic holiday of *All Saints' Day.*" Although Halloween got its name from a Christian festival, its customs are of pagan origin. They come from two different sources: an ancient Celtic festival in honor of Samhain, lord of death, and a Roman festival in honor of Pomona, goddess of gardens and orchards. The Halloween colors, black and orange, suggest both ideas: death and **harvest**.

10   Masquerading, begging, and other Halloween customs are now mainly enjoyed by children. But many hundreds of years ago, these customs were performed quite seriously by adults as part of their religion. The scary part of Halloween comes from the Celts, who lived in the British Isles and northern France during ancient and medieval times. The Celts worshiped gods of nature. They feared the coming of winter, associating it with death and **evil spirits**. Every year on October 31, the last day of the year on the old pagan calendar, the Druids (Celtic priests and teachers) built huge bonfires to scare away the bad spirits of evil and death. They threw animals and crops into the fire as gifts for the evil spirits. The Celtic people also dressed in ugly, scary costumes. They believed that, if they **disguised** themselves, the spirits wouldn't harm them. According to traditional beliefs, ghosts rose from their graves on this evening, and **witches** flew through the air on broomsticks or black cats. Also, the spirits of dead relatives and friends were expected to return to Earth for a visit. The Druids built bonfires on hilltops to guide these spirits back home.

11   From the Druid religion come the custom of masquerading and the symbols of Halloween: ghosts, skeletons, devils, witches, black cats, and owls. The jack-o'-lantern is also of Celtic origin. It was an Irish custom to **hollow** out turnips and place lighted candles inside them to scare evil spirits away from the house. In the U.S., people now use the native **pumpkin**. Pumpkins grow in a great variety of sizes—up to 1,092 pounds! To make a pumpkin into a jack-o'-lantern, remove the pulp and seeds. Then, cut holes in the hollow pumpkin to make the eyes, nose, and mouth. Put a candle inside it, light the candle, and put the jack-o'-lantern by the window. Why is this light called a *jack-o'-lantern*? An Irish story tells about an unhappy man named Jack. He wasn't welcome in heaven because he was **stingy**, and he couldn't go to hell because he had played jokes on the devil. So he had to walk the Earth forever, carrying a lantern.

12   The Irish also introduced the trick-or-treat custom hundreds of years ago. Groups of farmers would travel from house to house asking for food for the village Halloween party. They would promise good luck to **generous** contributors and threaten those who were stingy.

13   The Druid holiday of Samhain also celebrated the harvest. This part of the celebration became even more significant after 55 B.C., when the Romans invaded England and brought with them their harvest festival of Pomona. After that, nuts and fruit—especially apples—became part of the Samhain ceremonies. Today, at Halloween time,

Americans honor the harvest by displaying cornstalks and pumpkins; eating nuts, autumn fruits, and pumpkin pies; and playing games with apples. One of the most popular Halloween games is bobbing for apples. In this game, apples float in a large tub of water. One at a time, children bend over the tub and try to catch an apple in their mouths without using their hands.

14   The Druid religion lasted longest in Ireland and Scotland, and Halloween was most important in these two countries. In the 1840s, Irish immigrants brought their Halloween customs with them when they came to the U.S.A.

✔ Check Your Comprehension   *Today's Halloween customs come from what two ancient holidays? What are the two main themes and colors of Halloween?*

Halloween Celebrations Today

15   Halloween is celebrated by nearly all American children, and over 70% of adults also participate in some Halloween activity. College students and other young adults may attend **masquerade** parties or Halloween parades. Many families carve pumpkins and decorate the outside of their homes with the traditional Halloween symbols. Businesses get into the act, too. Store windows display jack-o'-lanterns, **scarecrows**, and witches. Servers in restaurants and salespeople in supermarkets and bookstores are often in costume. Many nightclubs and bars encourage customers to come in costume by offering prizes for the best disguises.

16   Part of the fun of Halloween is to get scared out of your wits. This can easily be done by visiting a **haunted** house. Supposedly, the spirits of dead people "live" in haunted houses. These spirits try to scare away living residents or visitors so that the spirits can enjoy their afterlife (which really means a life after death) in peace. Why do spirits hate the living? The living always want to clean up and brighten their surroundings, while ghosts and skeletons prefer dust, spiders, cobwebs, and darkness. These days, it's hard to find a real haunted house. But every year shortly before Halloween, many charities and communities create fake haunted houses. They hire actors to dress up in scary costumes and hide inside. Customers pay a few dollars each to walk through these places and have "ghosts" surprise them with a loud "Boo!" and "skeletons" clang chains in their ears. Children usually love these haunted houses, but sometimes their parents are scared to death! For those who have no haunted house nearby, another way to share a good scare is to go with friends to see a horror movie in a theater or rent one and watch it together on Halloween night (in a dark room, of course).

17   Most American children have a wonderful, exciting day on Halloween. If Halloween falls on a schoolday, they sometimes bring their costumes to school and spend the last few hours of the schoolday with spooks instead of with books. After school and perhaps on into the evening, they go trick-or-treating. Often, there's a party at a friend's home or at the local community center. At most Halloween parties, prizes are given for the best costumes. Bobbing for apples, telling fortunes (predicting the future), playing scary games, and snacking on caramel-covered apples, candy, apple cider, and pumpkin pie are all part of the fun. Some communities build a bonfire, just as the Celts did. Children

may sit around the bonfire telling scary stories while roasting hot dogs or toasting marshmallows. Halloween, which began hundreds of years ago as an evening of terror, is now an occasion of great fun.

18   However, some words of warning are needed. Halloween is a time when children can become overexcited and careless, and it is a time when care is especially needed. To be sure that cars will see children after dark, parents should dress them in light-colored costumes or put reflecting tape on their clothing. To be sure that the kids see the cars, parents should enlarge the eye-holes in masks by cutting them with scissors. When trick-or-treating, children should go in groups. Younger children should go with older children or an adult. Kids should be told never to go inside the house or apartment of a stranger but to wait outside for their treats. Even if no treat is given, children should be told not to damage property. Kids should stop trick-or-treating by 8:00 P.M. When they get home with their candy, parents should inspect it and throw out anything not wrapped and sealed. (There have been rare incidents of harmful ingredients found in Halloween treats.)

19   On Halloween night, adults should be careful, too. Robbers could take advantage of the casual, open-door Halloween spirit to gain access to strangers' homes. Note that Mrs. Brown (the woman at the beginning of this reading) did not completely open her door until she was sure that her uninvited visitors were children.

AFTER YOU READ

I. Getting the Message

A. *Mark each statement true* (T) *or false* (F).

_____ **1.** In the U.S. today, Halloween is an important religious holiday.

_____ **2.** Pagan religions had many gods.

_____ **3.** Halloween is celebrated by nearly all American children, no matter what their religion.

_____ **4.** Some costumes are disguises, but others are not.

_____ **5.** A scarecrow is put in a field to scare away people.

_____ **6.** Skeletons and ghosts are symbols of a good harvest.

_____ **7.** The Irish made jack-o'-lanterns from pumpkins.

_____ **8.** When children go trick-or-treating, they usually collect a lot of apples.

B. *Name four things American children usually do to celebrate Halloween.*

1. _____

2. _____

3. _____

4. _____

C. *The reading compares and contrasts two holidays, the ancient holiday of Samhain and modern-day Halloween. Working in small groups, make a list of all the customs shared by these two holidays. Then make a second list of differences between these holidays. Compare lists and see which group has the longest list of correct comparisons and contrasts.*

II. Building Your Vocabulary

A. *These are the 15 key vocabulary words for this chapter. They are boldfaced in the reading. Pronounce these words after your teacher, and discuss their meanings.*

costume	harvest*	scarecrow
disguise*	haunt	skeleton
evil	hollow†	spirit
generous	masquerade*	stingy
ghost	pumpkin	witch

B. *Complete these sentences using some of the key vocabulary words. Make the nouns plural where necessary.*

1. If you give a trick-or-treater a penny, you are _____. If you give the child 50 cents, you are _____.

2. At Halloween parties or _____, some people don't recognize their friends when they are wearing masks over their faces.

3. On Halloween, it is an American custom for children to dress up in

    _____.

4. The Halloween colors, orange and black, relate to the holiday's two major themes, which are _____ and death.

5. A(n) _____ protects a farmer's harvest because it stands in the fields and scares away birds and animals that might otherwise eat seeds or crops.

6. To make a jack-o'-lantern, take the insides (the pulp and seeds) out of a

    _____ and then cut a face into the orange shell.

7. A ghost is the invisible _____ of a dead person.

---

*These words can be nouns or verbs.
†*Hollow* can be an adjective or a verb.

C. *Underline the correct word to complete each sentence.*

1. (*Which / Witch*) one of you wants to wear this scary costume?

2. I don't like that bright-red devil (*costume / custom*).

3. On Halloween, I wear makeup or a (*mask / masquerade*) to disguise myself.

4. After I take the insides out of this pumpkin, it will be (*hallow / hollow*).

5. People say a ghost lives in that house. They say it's (*haunted / hunted*).

D. *Label each item listed to tell which Halloween theme it symbolizes. Write D for darkness and death and H for harvest. If a word relates to both themes, write both D and H.*

Example

witch _____D_____

1. apple _____
2. ghost _____
3. haunted house _____
4. jack-o'-lantern _____

5. owl _____
6. pumpkin _____
7. scarecrow _____
8. skeleton _____

III. Sharpening Reading Skills

A. Inferences and Implications   Sometimes an author does not tell readers something directly but just implies (hints at or suggests) an idea. When readers figure out what a writer is saying indirectly, they *infer* or *make inferences* about the meaning.

Try making some inferences about this reading. Discuss your ideas in small groups.

1. In paragraph 1, what does the text imply when it says, "Mrs. Brown put the safety chain on her door"?

2. Make inferences about why some adults don't like Halloween.

3. If you live in the U.S., what does the text imply that you buy before Halloween?

4. In paragraph 16, what is implied by the sentence "These days, it's hard to find a real haunted house"?

B. Quotation Marks   Quotation marks have two main uses: (1) to show that a writer is repeating the exact words spoken or written by someone else, or (2) to indicate that a word or phrase is being used in a special way, instead of its usual meaning.

Answer the following questions about quotation marks.

1. In the first sentence in paragraph 5, why are there quotation marks?

_____

2. In the second sentence in paragraph 5, why are there quotation marks around *skeleton*?

_____

3. In the third sentence in paragraph 16, why are there quotation marks around *live*?

_____

C. Map-Reading Practice

Find the following on a map of the world.

1. Great Britain (which includes England, Scotland, and Wales)
2. the British Isles (which include Great Britain, Ireland, the Isle of Man, and adjacent small islands)
3. the United Kingdom (which includes Great Britain and Northern Ireland)

D. Dictionary Skills

Look at the dictionary pronunciation symbols to find the answers to the following questions.

1. In *Celtic,* is the first *c* pronounced like a *k* or an *s?* _____ (Check in two dictionaries. Do they agree? Is there more than one correct pronunciation?)
2. What letters are silent in *guide* and *disguise?* _____

IV. Understanding Idioms and Expressions

A. On each blank line, write the letter of the correct word or phrase to complete the sentence. The numbers in parentheses give the paragraphs in which the expressions are used.

1. *"Trick or treat; money or eats!"* (1) means _____.
    a. "I'd like either a trick or a treat"
    b. "if you give me a treat, I'll play a trick on you"
    c. "give me a treat, or I'll play a trick on you"

2. To *play a prank* (7) means to _____.
    a. play a game
    b. trick someone
    c. beg for candy

(continued on the next page)

3. A *jack-o'-lantern* (11) _____.
   a. haunts houses
   b. is carried around on Halloween night
   c. has a light in it

4. When you are *bobbing for apples* (13), you can _____.
   a. get wet
   b. get scared
   c. carve a pumpkin

5. *Scared out of your wits* (16) means _____.
   a. too scared to think clearly
   b. scared of being witty
   c. too scared to talk

6. *Scared to death* (16) means that someone _____.
   a. died of fear
   b. was very frightened
   c. was afraid of dying

7. *Telling fortunes* (17) means _____.
   a. predicting what will happen in the future
   b. telling scary stories
   c. telling people how to get rich

8. *Gain access to* (19) means _____.
   a. rob
   b. get into
   c. unlock

B. *Discuss the meanings of the phrasal verbs* dress up *and* make up. *Also discuss the meaning of* makeup *as a noun.*

V. Taking Words Apart

Sometimes present participles and past participles are used as adjectives. Present participles—such as *exciting*—describe the quality or a characteristic of something. Past participles—such as *excited*—are often used to describe the feelings or responses of a person or animal.

Underline the correct adjective to complete the following sentences.

Example

The Halloween party will be fun. I'm very (*excited* / *exciting*) about going.

1. Winning the prize at the costume party was very (*excited* / *exciting*).
2. Reading about Halloween is (*interested* / *interesting*).

3. I'm (*interested / interesting*) in learning about American holidays.

4. I thought the fortune-telling game was (*bored / boring*).

5. Were you (*bored / boring*) by that game, too?

VI. Practicing Sentence Patterns

A. Direct and Indirect Speech   In paragraphs 1–7, the conversation between Mrs. Brown and the children is dialogue, or direct speech. The speakers' exact words are in quotation marks. Here are pairs of sentences expressing the same idea in direct and then indirect speech:

Direct Speech	Indirect Speech
He said to Mary, "I like your costume."	He told Mary that he liked her costume.
He asked, "Are you a witch?"	He asked if she was a witch.
He said, "Don't fly away."	He told her not to fly away.

Now change some of the statements at the beginning of the reading from direct to indirect speech. Reread paragraphs 1–7. Then complete the following statements.

Example

The children asked Mrs. Brown to _____ *give them a treat* _____ .

1. Mrs. Brown asked one boy _____.

2. The boy wearing the big hat told Mrs. Brown _____.

3. Mrs. Brown told the children to _____ and not

_____ .

B. *Would* for Repeated Past Actions

In paragraph 12, sentences 2 and 3, would *plus an infinitive verb form is used to describe repeated past actions. Write a sentence using* would *to tell about something you did often when you were a child.*

When I was a child, _____.

VII. Sharing Ideas

A. Issues

Debate these issues in small groups. Then choose one and write about it.

1. Is Halloween good or bad for children? What kinds of behavior does it encourage?

2. Should American Halloween customs be changed to make the holiday safer and less destructive? If so, what changes should be made?

B. On a Personal Note

Write about one of these topics.

1. Besides Halloween, do you know of any other holidays on which people wear masks and / or costumes? Describe the holiday and its customs.

2. Have you ever dressed up in costume? Write a paragraph telling why, and describe what you wore. Did you wear makeup or a mask? Could your friends recognize you, or were you disguised?

3. Write a short dialogue that repeats a funny or unusual conversation you had with another person. Use quotation marks around the spoken words. Indent (begin a new paragraph) whenever there is a change in who is speaking. Use the dialogue at the beginning of the reading as a model for correct indenting and punctuating.

21 Thanksgiving and Native Americans

"Colonists" at Plimouth Plantation, recreating the 1627 village of Plymouth, Massachusetts

BEFORE YOU READ

Discuss

1. Were the Native Americans and the European colonists friends or enemies?

2. What do you know about Native Americans from movies? How accurately do these films portray contemporary Native Americans?

3. What foods are served at a traditional American Thanksgiving feast? Have you ever eaten any of these foods? Do you like them?

Guess

Try to answer the questions. Then look for the answers in the reading.

1. When did the Pilgrims come to America to establish a colony? Check (✓) one:

   _____ 1620   _____ 1685   _____ 1725

2. The Pilgrims did not have this piece of silverware: Check (✓) one:

   _____ knife   _____ fork   _____ spoon

Thanksgiving and Native Americans

Thanksgiving: Origin and Customs

1   Thanksgiving Day is on the fourth Thursday in November. It is a time for big family **reunions** and big dinners, a time to eat turkey, stuffing, corn, cranberry sauce, and pumpkin pie. But between endless bites of food, Americans also take time to feel grateful for whatever is good in their lives. Some people thank God; others thank fate or their loved ones. And most people remember the small group of English colonists who gave Americans this delicious and meaningful holiday.

2   Today's Thanksgiving holiday was inspired by a harvest festival in Plymouth, Massachusetts, almost 400 years ago. The small group of colonists, residents of the second permanent English settlement in the New World, had very little by today's standards, but they were thankful for receiving what they valued most—a good harvest and the freedom to live and worship as they pleased.

3   The Plymouth colonists began their journey to America in September of 1620 on a ship called the *Mayflower*. Some of the passengers were members of a **persecuted** religious sect. They were called *Separatists* because they had separated from the Church of England in order to practice their religion in ways they considered closer to the message of the Bible. In search of greater religious freedom, some members of this group went to live in Holland for several years, but they were unhappy there, too. So they made plans to come to America, where they would be free to live as they chose. They returned to England to prepare for the journey. Many years later, the Separatists came to be called *Pilgrims* because of their travels in search of religious freedom. Today, Americans commonly refer to all of the Plymouth residents as *Pilgrims*, but only about half of the colonists were Separatists. The others came to America, not for religious reasons, but for adventure or new opportunity.

4   The journey to the New World was paid for by English businessmen in return for furs and other goods to be sent back to England from the new colony. The *Mayflower* was very crowded with 102 passengers (men, women, and children), about 25 sailors, two dogs, and probably some chickens, cats, and pigs. At times, the trip was very rough. Yet, during the voyage, the travelers suffered only one death. Since there was also one birth aboard ship, the *Mayflower* was still carrying 102 passengers when, after 65 days at sea, it landed in Provincetown Harbor, on the tip of Cape Cod, Massachusetts. The *Mayflower*

passengers had planned to settle near Jamestown, Virginia, where the first permanent English colony in America had been established in 1607. However, winds pushed the *Mayflower* farther north, where the climate was much colder.

5   The Pilgrim leaders knew that, in order to **survive**, every society needed rules for proper behavior. So 41 men aboard the *Mayflower* held a meeting. They chose their first governor and signed the *Mayflower Compact*, an agreement to make laws for their colony and to obey them. It was the first formal agreement for self-government in America.

6   For about a month, the Pilgrims lived aboard ship and sent out a few men to explore the coastline. At Plymouth, the men found a harbor with some cleared land and fresh water. The men went back to the *Mayflower* and reported their discovery. A few days later, the *Mayflower* sailed across Cape Cod Bay to Plymouth Harbor. According to a traditional story, when the *Mayflower* passengers came ashore in their small boat, they landed on a large rock later named *Plymouth Rock*. In Plymouth, that rock is still on display for tourists to see.

7   The Pilgrims were not trained and equipped to **cope** with life in the **wilderness**. During their first winter, they suffered tremendously. Diseases, cold weather, and insufficient food killed about half of them. Still, from this small group of about 50 colonists, there are thousands of descendants alive today. Among them is former American president George Bush.

8   One spring morning in 1621, a friendly Native American walked into the little village of Plymouth and introduced himself. Later, he brought the chief (Massasoit). The colonists gave gifts to their new friends. The members of Massasoit's **tribe** taught the Pilgrims how to hunt and fish; how to plant pumpkins, beans, and corn; and how to fertilize the corn with fish. Because of this help, that fall the colonists had a good harvest. To celebrate, they decided to have a harvest festival. Massasoit and about 90 of his men came to share the celebration.

9   The Indians sent hunters out to bring back deer meat for the **feast**. Some of the Pilgrim men also went hunting and returned with wild birds such as ducks, geese, and turkeys. The women of Plymouth prepared dishes from corn, squash, and pumpkins. The meal was cooked and served out-of-doors. The holiday combined feasting and entertainment. The colonists performed a military display with their guns, and the Indians probably danced. The celebration lasted three days and was a great success.

10   Today, when Americans celebrate Thanksgiving, they like to think that they are imitating that 1621 harvest festival in Plymouth. And in some ways they are. The foods that are eaten are those that were part of the Plymouth diet—such as turkey, squash, corn, and pumpkin. But in many ways the modern Thanksgiving dinner is quite different from the meal that the Plymouth colonists shared with their Indian neighbors. To start with, the wild turkey that the Pilgrims hunted was somewhat different from today's domesticated turkey. (Wild turkeys, for example, can fly, but today's commercially produced turkeys cannot.) Next, the Plymouth colonists didn't have enough sugar to make the sweetened cranberry sauce that is considered an essential part of today's Thanksgiving meal. If they had cranberries at all, they were probably in the turkey stuffing. If they had pumpkin, it was probably cut into pieces, not mashed and served in a pie. Also, for today's Thanksgiving dinner, most Americans set a beautiful table with a fancy tablecloth and the finest dishes, glassware, and silverware they have. The Pilgrims (like most early-seventeenth-century people) didn't have forks. They picked up most of their food with

their fingers, and then wiped their hands on very large napkins. And, of course, few Americans eat their Thanksgiving dinner outside, as the Pilgrims did.

11   Every year, about 500,000 tourists take a journey into early American history by visiting Plymouth, Massachusetts. This modern city offers many opportunities for reliving the Pilgrim experience. In Plymouth Harbor, sightseers tour *Mayflower* II, a recently built ship similar to the original *Mayflower*. They see the famous Plymouth Rock. Then they spend a few hours walking through a recreation of the original Plymouth village as it looked in 1627. The site, called Plimoth Plantation, is just a few miles from the location of the original village. Plimoth Plantation is "inhabited" by role-playing costumed guides who speak in many different English dialects, as the real Plymouth residents did. They also demonstrate a wide range of activities that were part of village life in the 1620s.

✔ **Check Your Comprehension**   *Compare the Plymouth Thanksgiving of 1621 with today's typical American Thanksgiving.*

A Famous Pilgrim Story

12   In 1858, Henry Wadsworth Longfellow, a famous American poet, wrote a long poem about the Pilgrims of Plymouth Colony. He called it "The Courtship of Miles Standish." The colonists Longfellow wrote about were real people. However, the story he told, about two men in love with the same woman, was invented. Still, it is a famous American story and well worth retelling.

13   Captain Miles Standish came to America with the Pilgrims, but he was not a Puritan. He was a soldier. Although he was very brave in battle, Standish was timid with women. After his wife died, he was lonely and wanted to marry a Puritan girl named Priscilla Mullens. But he was too shy to ask her. Instead, Standish asked his best friend, John Alden, to **propose** marriage for him. Never were two friends so different. Standish was a short, stocky, middle-aged man. John Alden was a young man and very handsome. While Standish was a man of action, Alden was a scholar. In only one way were these two men alike: They both loved the same woman.

14   Poor John! He also loved Priscilla, but he wanted to be a loyal friend. Hiding his own feelings, he went to Priscilla and asked her to marry Miles Standish. He told her how kind the captain was. He talked about Standish's bravery in battle and about his fine family. When John finished talking, Priscilla asked him a question: "Why don't you speak for yourself, John?"

15   John didn't take Priscilla's advice. Instead, he returned to his friend and told him what Priscilla had said. The captain became very angry. "You have **betrayed** me!" he shouted. A short time later, Standish left for a battle against hostile natives. While the captain was gone, John and Priscilla grew to love each other more and more. However, John did not ask her to marry him because he did not want to be an unfaithful friend. Then a message arrived saying that Standish had been killed in battle. After that, John proposed marriage to Priscilla.

16   As the wedding ceremony ended, the guests saw a familiar figure standing in the doorway, a figure they thought was a ghost. It was Captain Miles Standish! He hadn't

been killed after all. He had come to apologize for his anger. At the end of the story, John, Priscilla, and Miles were reunited as friends. What about the real colonists? Standish eventually remarried, and John and Priscilla had 11 children. One of their descendants was the famous poet Henry Wadsworth Longfellow.

✔ **Check Your Comprehension**

Was John Alden a loyal friend, or did he betray Miles Standish?

Friends and Enemies

17   In the past, the earliest residents of the Americas were called *American Indians*. Today, some members of this group prefer to be identified as *Native Americans*. Others still call themselves *Indians*. Whichever name is used, on Thanksgiving Day, the **indigenous** peoples are remembered with gratitude. Many tribes helped early European **settlers** adjust to life in the American wilderness. In addition, Native American cultures have contributed much to modern American life.

18   Of all the Indians' gifts to the settlers, food was probably the most important. Indian foods and methods of planting, hunting, and fishing helped settlers survive in their new home. Two of the most important **crops** in the world—corn and white potatoes—were first planted by American Indians. They also introduced European settlers to more than 80 other foods, including the sweet potato, pumpkin, squash, peanut, tomato, banana, pineapple, and avocado. Native Americans showed the new arrivals how to cook these unfamiliar plants to make grits, popcorn, succotash, and tapioca. Cacao (for chocolate), chicle (for chewing gum), and tobacco were also among their crops. In addition, many of the drugs that Indians extracted from plants are still used in modern medications.

19   Indians also introduced settlers to various **utensils**, clothing, trails, and methods of transportation. Native American inventions adopted by settlers include hammocks, canoes, dogsleds, toboggans, pipes, rubber balls, snowshoes, and moccasins.

20   The colonists also adopted words from Native American languages. In the Western Hemisphere, thousands of mountains, lakes, rivers, cities, states, and countries have Native American names—*Chicago, Massachusetts, Oregon,* and *Mexico,* to mention just a few. Other Indian words in English include *skunk, moose, tobacco, succotash,* and *squash.*

21   The most famous Native American friend of the white settlers was a young princess named Pocahontas. She was only 12 years old when English settlers came to Jamestown, Virginia, in 1607. Captain John Smith, one of these early colonists, wrote that he owed his life to Pocahontas. She threw her arms around Smith to prevent her father, the chief, from killing him. Pocahontas visited the English fort often, bringing food and other necessities. Despite her kindness to the settlers, she was kidnapped by them at the age of 17 to guarantee the good behavior of her tribe. The following year, Pocahontas married one of the colonists. She later traveled with him to England, where she became very popular in British society. While in London, she died of smallpox at the age of 21. She had a son from whom many Virginians claim descent. Her fascinating story inspired a number of books and a popular animated Hollywood movie.

22   Another well-known Native American woman was Sacagawea. Her name, usually pronounced "Sak-uh-juh-WEE-uh," means "bird woman." She was the guide and interpreter

who accompanied the Lewis and Clark expedition. At the request of President Thomas Jefferson, in 1804, this group set out to explore the West. They traveled some 8,000 miles, exploring territory from the Mississippi River to the Pacific Ocean. Their safe return (in 1806) and fascinating reports encouraged further exploration and settlement of the West. In 2000, the U.S. government created a gold-colored $1 coin in honor of Sacagawea. On the coin, she is shown carrying her baby on her back.

23   Although the Native Americans helped the European settlers in many ways, because both groups wanted the same land, they became **enemies**. The result was a long history of bloodshed and cruelty. The Indians were doomed to defeat since the settlers had guns, while the Indians fought mostly with bows and arrows. Also, the settlers were able to unite, while the Indians were divided into hundreds of different tribes that were hostile to one another.

24   As early as 1786, the U.S. government began setting aside special territories, called **reservations**, for Indian resettlement. The Native Americans were pushed onto land that was considered undesirable, mostly in the Southwest and the Northwest. During the mid-nineteenth century, they were forbidden to leave these areas without a permit. When Columbus arrived in 1492, about 700,000 natives lived in the area that later became the U.S.A. By 1890, as a result of wars, diseases, and poor living conditions, the U.S. Indian population was down to about 240,000.

25   In the 1920s, American treatment of Native Americans began to improve. As a result, the population grew. Today, about 2.5 million Native Americans live in the U.S., including the Aleuts and the Inuits (Eskimoes) of Alaska. About half of the Native Americans in the U.S.A. live on or near federal reservations. Those who leave usually move to a big city. Most American Indians live in the West—Arizona, New Mexico, Montana, Wyoming, and California. However, a number of tribes are in the South and Midwest—Oklahoma, North Dakota, and South Dakota. There are also dozens of small Indian communities along the East Coast.

Crazy Horse, a mountain carving in progress
(South Dakota)

26   On reservations, traditional Indian customs, languages, and styles of dress have survived. Tourists visit these reservations to observe traditional ways of life. Various tribes make baskets, pottery, woven blankets and rugs, wood sculpture, beadwork, and silver jewelry. Because of their beauty and fine workmanship, these goods are often purchased by tourists.

27   Native Americans have been among the most deprived of U.S. minority groups. Their education, income, employment levels, housing, health, and life expectancy are all below national averages. However, their quality of life is beginning to improve. Every year, the federal government's Bureau of Indian Affairs (BIA) spends millions of dollars to improve Native American living conditions. The BIA has also responded to Indian demands for more control of their own affairs. Today, the majority of Native American young people complete high school, and about 9% of those age 25 or older are college graduates. Many tribes have made money from oil discovered on their land or by operating gambling casinos on reservations. Some tribes have gone into business, for example, making automotive or electronic parts. There is now an Indian middle class that includes many professionals, and there are well-known Native American writers and artists. After centuries of suffering, Native Americans are finding something to be thankful for in a land that was once their own, among people to whom they have given so much.

AFTER YOU READ

I. Getting the Message

A. *On a separate piece of paper, complete the following sentences with information from the reading.*

1. The Separatists came to America because _____.

2. It isn't historically correct to refer to all the Plymouth colonists as *Pilgrims* because _____.

3. The colonists were grateful to Massasoit and his tribe because _____.

4. Priscilla Mullens didn't want to marry Miles Standish because _____.

5. The settlers and the Native Americans became enemies because _____.

6. Pocahontas was kidnapped by the Jamestown colonists because _____.

B. *Put these events in chronological order. Number them 1–5, starting with the earliest.*

1. Native Americans were forced to move to reservations. _____

2. Pocahontas saved John Smith. _____

3. The *Mayflower* crossed the Atlantic Ocean. _____

4. Longfellow wrote "The Courtship of Miles Standish." _____

5. John Alden married Priscilla Mullens. _____

II. Building Your Vocabulary

A. *These are the 15 key vocabulary words for this chapter. They are boldfaced in the reading. Pronounce these words after your teacher, and discuss their meanings.*

betray	indigenous	settler
cope	persecute	survive
crop	propose	tribe
enemy	reservation	utensil
feast*	reunion	wilderness

B. *Answer the following questions using a few words. You don't need to write full sentences.*

1. Is a fork a utensil, a wilderness, or a crop? _____

2. Are indigenous people original residents or newcomers? _____

3. Do Americans feast or fast on Thanksgiving Day? _____

4. Was a tribe a group of Indians or a colony of settlers? _____

5. At a reunion, are people getting together for the first time? _____

6. Are there cities in the wilderness? _____

7. Should you be loyal to your enemy? _____

8. Did John persecute Priscilla or propose to her? _____

9. If you cope with your problems, do you handle them well? _____

C. *Work with a partner. After each word listed, there is a paragraph number. Look in that paragraph for an antonym (opposite) of the word.*

Example

temporary (4) ____permanent____

1. die (5) _____

2. enough (7) _____

3. ancestors (7) _____

4. original (11) _____

5. was faithful to (15) _____

6. immediately (16) _____

7. united (23) _____

8. allowed (24) _____

---

*Feast can be used as a noun or a verb.

III. Sharpening Reading Skills

A. General and Specific Meanings

Sometimes the same word can have a general meaning and also a more specific, related meaning. Discuss the following italicized words.

1. What is a *pilgrim*? Who were the *Pilgrims*?

2. What does it mean to make a *reservation* at a hotel or restaurant? What is an Indian *reservation*? How are these word meanings related?

3. What is the general meaning of the word *propose*? What type of proposal is mentioned in paragraphs 13 and 15?

B. Context Clues

Reread the paragraph indicated to determine what each underlined word means. Underline the correct definition.

1. inspire (2):
   a. cause someone to want to do something
   b. require someone to do something

2. voyage (4):
   a. a short hike or car ride
   b. a long trip, usually on water

3. courtship (12):
   a. visiting the court of a king
   b. seeking romance and / or marriage

4. timid (13):
   a. courageous
   b. shy and frightened

5. alike (13):
   a. friendly
   b. similar

6. hostile (15):
   a. showing the desire to help someone
   b. showing the desire to hurt someone

7. apologize (16):
   a. say you're sorry for doing something wrong
   b. express your anger

8. bloodshed (23):
   a. injury and / or death
   b. a shed full of blood

C. Making Inferences

To infer means to figure out what is being suggested but not stated directly. Make inferences about these questions. Discuss your inferences with a partner.

1. What can you infer about Priscilla from her question, in paragraph 14, "Why don't you speak for yourself, John?" Which man did she want to marry? Was she a timid or an assertive person?

2. What can you infer about Pocahontas's character from the description of her actions in paragraph 21?

D. Map-Reading Practice

On a map, point out the Mayflower's journey from England to Provincetown to Plymouth.

IV. Understanding Idioms and Expressions

On each blank line, write the letter of the correct meaning of each expression. The numbers in parentheses give the paragraphs in which the expressions are used.

1. *On display* (6) means _____.
   a. put out for people to see
   b. on a big ship

2. If you have your Thanksgiving dinner *out-of-doors* (9), you eat it _____.
   a. with the doors of your house open
   b. outside

3. *Role-playing* (11) means _____.
   a. rolling a ball around in a game
   b. pretending to be someone else

4. If you *take advice* (15) from a friend, you _____.
   a. take your friend's possessions
   b. do what your friend suggests

5. *After all* (16) means _____.
   a. after a long time
   b. what happened was a surprise

6. John Smith *owed his life* (21) to Pocahontas because she _____.
   a. lent him money
   b. protected him from death

V. Taking Words Apart

A. Practice with Word Parts

Study the meanings of these word parts. Then use them to complete the words defined below. Use a dictionary for help if necessary.

un-, in- = not   *re-* = again, back   *ex-* = out, beyond   *-less* = without

1. _____sufficient (not enough)

2. _____create (make again)

3. end_____ (without end)

4. _____union (to come together again)

5. _____desirable (not good, not wanted)

6. _____tract (remove something from something else)

B. Noun Endings for People's Occupations, Nationalities, and Activities

To tell about a person's identity, occupation, nationality, or activity, English words usually add one of these endings: -r, -er, -or, - ist, - an, or -ant. Put the correct ending on each noun listed below.

1. a person who comes to see sights in a particular place: a tour_____ or a

   sightsee_____

2. a person who lives in a colony: colon_____

3. a person traveling in or on a moving vehicle but not operating it:

   passeng_____

4. someone born in Europe: Europe_____

5. the chief political leader in a colony or American state: govern_____

VI. Practicing Sentence Patterns

Priscilla Mullens asked John Alden a question beginning, "Why don't you . . . ?" This type of question can be:

(1) <u>A suggestion or offer:</u>
"Why don't you come over to my house for dinner tonight?"
<u>Answer:</u> "Thanks, I'd love to."

(2) <u>A question asking why a person does not do something:</u>
"Why don't you own a car?"
<u>Answer:</u> "I don't know how to drive."

(continued on the next page)

Answer the following question.

In your opinion, was Priscilla making a suggestion or asking a question when she said, "Why don't you speak for yourself, John?" _____.

Complete these questions beginning with "Why don't . . ." and "Why doesn't . . .?"

1. It's raining out. Why don't you _____?
2. Joe got a low grade on his math test last week. Why doesn't _____

_____?

VII. Sharing Ideas

A. Issues

Debate these issues in small groups. Then choose one and write about it.

1. Everybody loves a love story. That's why the poet Longfellow invented one to tell about the Pilgrims. And when Hollywood made a movie about Pocahontas, it added a fictitious romance between John Smith and the young Indian princess. Should writers change historical facts to make a more interesting story? Is it okay to blend fact and fiction?

2. Do newcomers to an area have a right to push earlier residents off the land? Does land really belong to any particular group of people?

B. On a Personal Note

Write about one of these topics.

1. If you had lived in the seventeenth century, would you have left your country and come to America? Explain why or why not.

2. Pretend you are John Alden or Priscilla Mullens. Write a letter to a friend telling about your life in Plymouth. Use the form for a social letter that your teacher gives you.

3. Find a recipe (in a cookbook, magazine, or newspaper) for something traditionally eaten on Thanksgiving. Try the recipe. Then write a paragraph about your experience cooking it. (Did it taste good? Did you make any mistakes?) Exchange recipes and paragraphs with four classmates.

22 | The Winter Holiday Season

A family enjoying the winter holiday season

BEFORE YOU READ

Discuss

1. The picture shows a typical winter scene in a cold part of the United States. Do you like this type of winter weather? Tell why or why not.

2. The winter holidays are special for many people. What holidays are celebrated at this time of year, and why are they special?

3. Discuss new year's holidays in different cultures.

Guess

Try to answer the questions. Then look for the answers in the reading.

1. What percentage of Americans are Christian? Check (✓) one:

   _____ 32 %   _____ 52 %   _____ 86 %

2. How many time zones are there in the 50 American states? Check (✓) one:

   _____ 2   _____ 4   _____ 6

The Winter Holiday Season

Merry Christmas!

1   Santa Claus, snowmen, bright lights, colorful decorations, bells, and traditional songs—all these help to make December the most **festive** month of the year. As the month progresses toward the winter **solstice** (December 21), the daylight hours grow shorter and shorter. In the northern part of the U.S., winter weather can be (as one seasonal song says) "frightful." Yet even winter snowstorms cannot bury that contagious feeling of festivity. Why does almost everybody feel so good? It's gift-giving time, party time, and vacation time. Students from elementary school through college have about 2 weeks' vacation, beginning shortly before Christmas and ending soon after New Year's Day. Many families go away for the holidays to visit relatives in another state, ski in the mountains, or sunbathe on the beaches in the South. But those who stay home have fun, too. Parties abound to celebrate the birth of Christ and the arrival of the new year. Even the workplace is festive, thanks to the traditions of office parties and holiday (or end-of-the-year) **bonuses** (extra money given to employees).

2   Christianity, the major religious faith in the U.S., the Western Hemisphere, and the world, is based upon the teachings and life of Jesus Christ. There are about 2 billion Christians worldwide. They believe in Jesus's ideas of equality, caring for the weak and needy, generosity, forgiveness, and love and kindness to all. They also believe that Jesus Christ is the Son of God, born to the Virgin Mary, and that he was sent to Earth to save the human race. The word *Jesus* means "savior" or "help of God." The word *Christ* means "anointed one," someone set apart for special honor.

3   Jesus was born in Bethlehem in ancient Judea. The year A.D. 1, from which most modern calendars are dated, is supposed to be the year of his birth. However, Jesus was actually born several years earlier. No one knows the exact year or day, but Christians have celebrated his birth on December 25 since the fourth century. This date was probably selected so that Christmas would replace pagan celebrations of the beginning of winter.

4   In the U.S., the spirit of Christmas arrives at least a month before the holiday itself. Starting in November, street lights and store windows begin to display the traditional Christmas colors, red and green. Santa Claus, shepherds, angels, and Nativity scenes appear in shop windows. Winter scenes with snowmen, sleds, skaters, and skiers decorate greeting cards and store windows.

5   The manufacture and sale of Christmas items is big business. Stores depend on Christmas shoppers for about one-fourth of their annual sales. Smart shoppers buy their gifts far in advance, before the Christmas rush makes shopping a chore. Some shop on the Internet to avoid crowds. Christmas is often very expensive. To earn extra money for gifts, in December many Americans get part-time jobs delivering mail or selling gifts, trees, **ornaments**, or greeting cards.

6   Since 86% of Americans are Christian, December 25 is both a religious and a legal holiday. Most businesses are closed on Christmas Day. Although all Americans can enjoy the **commercial** aspects of Christmas, for Christians, the most meaningful parts of the holiday occur at home and in church. Many families go to church on Christmas Eve or Christmas morning. After services, they gather around the tree and open their gifts. Then they enjoy a traditional Christmas dinner—turkey or ham, sweet potatoes, vegetables, and cranberry sauce. Dessert is usually fruit cake, plum pudding, or mince pie.

7   Most of the Christmas customs that Americans enjoy today are variations of traditions brought here by European immigrants. Some go back to ancient times.

8   *Exchanging Gifts.* The first Christmas gifts were birthday gifts that the three Wise Men brought to the infant Jesus. In the U.S., it is customary to **exchange** gifts with family members and close friends. Both children and adults get Christmas presents, although children usually get many more.

9   *Receiving Toys from Santa Claus.* Many American children believe that on Christmas Eve, Santa Claus (a fat, jolly man who wears a red suit and has a long white beard) slides down their chimney to bring them gifts. According to the story, Santa Claus flies through the air in a sleigh (a fancy sled) pulled by eight reindeer. Several days or weeks before Christmas, children tell Santa what toys they want by writing him letters or visiting him in a local department store. Then, on Christmas Eve, many youngsters lie awake listening for Santa and his sleigh. Some children even leave him a snack of milk and cookies.

10   Where did this **legend** come from? Santa Claus is the American name for St. Nicholas, a generous fourth-century bishop who lived in what is now Turkey. It was his custom to go out at night and bring gifts to the poor. After his death, his fame spread throughout Europe. Dutch immigrants brought the idea of St. Nicholas, whom they called *Sinter Klaas*, to the U.S., where the name was mispronounced and finally changed to *Santa Claus*. Then, nineteenth-century American artists and authors changed St. Nick's appearance and created the roly-poly man in red that we know today. Santa's sleigh and reindeer came from an old Norse legend. So, today's Santa Claus is a blend of several different cultures.

11   *Hanging Stockings.* As in Great Britain, American children hang stockings hoping that Santa will fill them with candy and toys. Traditionally, stockings were hung near the fireplace, but today children hang them wherever they think Santa will see them!

12   *Decorating the Home with Holiday Plants.* The winter custom of **decorating** homes and churches with **evergreens** began in ancient times. Branches of fir or spruce were thought to bring good luck and guarantee the return of spring. The early Germans believed that in winter, evil spirits killed plants and trees and caused green leaves and flowers to disappear. Bringing evergreens into their homes was supposed to protect them from death.

13   Germans of the sixteenth century probably started the custom of decorating trees. In the nineteenth century, the idea spread throughout Europe and the U.S. Now, at Christ-

mastime, decorated trees stand in about two-thirds of American homes. Every year, Americans spend about $460 million buying Christmas trees. The modern American tree is usually covered with colored glass balls and strings of colored lights. The star on top represents the star in the East that guided the three Wise Men to Bethlehem.

14   In ancient times, mistletoe was hung over doorways for good luck. Today the custom continues, but now it is for fun. Anyone standing under the mistletoe is supposed to get kissed.

15   The poinsettia plant is another familiar Christmas decoration. Its star-shaped red leaves symbolize the holiday. This plant is native to Central America and Mexico. It was named after Joel R. Poinsett, who served as the first U.S. ambassador to Mexico (from 1825 to 1829). An amateur botanist, he brought the plant back with him when he returned to the United States.

16   *Going Caroling.* In the early days of the Christian Church, the bishops sang carols on Christmas Day. Now, soloists and choirs on the radio, on TV, in church, and in school all help fill the winter air with beautiful music. Copying an old English custom, many Americans go caroling—walking with friends from house to house singing the traditional holiday songs.

17   *Sending Christmas Cards.* The custom of sending Christmas cards began in London in 1843 and came to the U.S. in 1875. Today, most Americans (Christians and non-Christians) send dozens of season's greetings cards to relatives, friends, and business associates.

18   *Attending Traditional Christmas Theatrical Productions.* Americans of all religions enjoy performances of three traditional Christmas works. One of these is *Messiah*, an oratorio written by the German composer George Frederick Handel and performed by a chorus, orchestra, and solo singers. Another classic work performed during the Christmas season is the Russian composer Peter Ilich Tchaikovsky's ballet *The Nutcracker*. It is a favorite with children because it tells the delightful story of a little girl's Christmas dream about her toys coming to life. Finally, there is A *Christmas Carol*, a story written by the nineteenth-century English author Charles Dickens. It is traditionally performed as a play and tells the tale of a mean old man named Ebenezer Scrooge. Scrooge is selfish, lonely, and rich. With the help of ghosts from his past, present, and future life, he regains the spirit of Christmas—the ability to care about others and enjoy helping them.

✓ Check Your Comprehension

What event does Christmas celebrate?
How does gift-giving relate to the birth of Christ and the spirit of the holiday?
Name five other American Christmas customs.

Happy Hanukkah!

19   While Christians brighten winter with Christmas color and lights, Jews throughout the world celebrate their Festival of Lights—Hanukkah. This holiday celebrates the **triumph** of religious freedom. In 168 B.C., the Syrian king conquered Judea and tried to force the Jews to worship pagan gods. Three years later, a small group of Jews defeated the powerful Syrian armies.

20   When the Jews recaptured Jerusalem and rededicated their holy temple, they relit the eternal lamp. They had only one day's supply of the special oil needed for that lamp. But miraculously, the light burned for eight days, until fresh oil was available. In memory of this **miracle**, Jews celebrate Hanukkah for eight days and light candles in a special holder called a *menorah*. The date of Hanukkah is determined by the Hebrew calendar, but the holiday always occurs in December. So, for Americans of both the Christian and Jewish faiths, the year ends in a spirit of joy.

✔ Check Your Comprehension

What does Hanukkah celebrate? Why are lights important?

An African Festival

21   During the winter holiday period, African-Americans, along with Africans in many other countries, celebrate Kwanza. This holiday was developed in the U.S.A. in 1966 but is based in part upon a traditional African harvest festival. The name *Kwanza* means "first fruits of the harvest" in Swahili, an East African language. The festival begins on December 26 and lasts for 7 days. Each day is dedicated to discussion of one of these principles: unity, self-determination, collective responsibility, cooperative economics, purpose, creativity, and faith. Kwanza customs include lighting candles and exchanging gifts, especially handmade ones.

22   On December 31, community members dress in African clothing and share a feast of traditional African foods. This celebration includes musical and dance performances, an assessment of the past year, and commitments for the coming year.

23   Kwanza provides an opportunity for African-Americans to reestablish their links to an African past and their connections to their contemporary community. It is celebrated by about 5 million African-Americans and about 10 million others in Africa, Canada, the Caribbean, and parts of Europe.

✔ Check Your Comprehension

Where did Kwanza originate?

Happy New Year!

24   "Ring out the old, ring in the new," wrote Alfred, Lord Tennyson, the nineteenth-century English poet. And that's exactly what Americans do every December 31. New Year's Eve is a time for noise and fun. At home or in restaurants, most Americans drink and dine with friends. One popular New Year's Eve drink is eggnog, made with eggs, milk or cream, nutmeg, and sugar. Throughout the Christmas season, eggnog is a popular party beverage. Another is, of course, champagne—the drink that symbolizes a celebration. At midnight on New Year's Eve, bells ring, horns blow, and friends toast each other with champagne. It's also customary to exchange kisses. Everyone celebrates the disappearance of old Father Time, replaced by the baby New Year. New Year's Eve festivities

often continue until two or three o'clock in the morning. Many people travel from one party to another to celebrate with several different groups of friends.

New Year's Eve in New York City's Times Square

25   The country's most crowded New Year's Eve celebration takes place in New York City's Times Square. Since 1907, the famous ball-lowering ceremony has been a holiday highlight. To celebrate the arrival of the year 2000, an estimated 2 million people crowded into Times Square, and hundreds of millions viewed the scene on TV. The huge, 1,070-pound lighted crystal ball began its descent from a 77-foot flagpole at 11:59 P.M. and reached the bottom at exactly midnight. Simultaneously, confetti, balloons, and fireworks brightened the night sky. It was the biggest public event ever held in the city.

26   The new year arrives earlier in the East than in other parts of the country. When midnight comes to New York, it is 11 P.M. in Chicago, 10 P.M. in Denver, and only 9 P.M. in Los Angeles. The contiguous (connected) 48 states span four time zones; Alaska and Hawaii add two more.

27   What do Americans do on New Year's Day? Many sleep late because they stayed up all night long. Many watch TV, which offers spectacular parades and football games between champion college teams. From ancient times to the present, New Year's customs have been connected with saying good-bye to the past and looking forward to a better future. Therefore, New Year's Day often inspires people to start new programs and give up bad habits. Some people make New Year's **resolutions**, promises to themselves to improve their behavior. People talk about "turning over a new leaf," referring to a clean, blank page or a fresh start. Typical New Year's resolutions are to spend less money, give up smoking, begin a diet, or be nicer to others. It's safe to assume that about half of them are forgotten by January 31!

28   Although the theme of the New Year's holiday has not changed much from one century to the next, the date of the celebration has been changed many times. The ancient

Egyptians started their year on September 21, while the ancient Greeks began theirs on June 21. The old Roman calendar contained only 10 months, and New Year's Day was March 1. In 46 B.C., Julius Caesar introduced an improved calendar containing two additional months, January and February. January was named for the Roman god Janus, whose name comes from the Roman word for *door*. Like a door, Janus looks both ways; he is usually shown with two faces, one looking backward and the other forward. Julius Caesar's calendar, called in his honor the Julian calendar, was revised in 1582 by Pope Gregory XIII. This Gregorian calendar is the one in use today.

Check Your Comprehension *What is the major theme of the New Year's holiday? How do Americans celebrate?*

Chinese and Jewish New Year's Holidays

29   Many Chinese-Americans celebrate the New Year holiday established by China's ancient lunar calendar more than 4,000 years ago. The 15-day Chinese New Year begins with Yuan Tan and concludes with the Festival of Lanterns, held at the time of the full moon between January 21 and February 19. During this period, Chinatown sections in major American cities look very festive, with paper and glass lanterns decorating the houses and colorful marchers parading in the streets.

30   Rosh Hashanah (which means "head of the year") is the traditional Jewish New Year. It occurs in September or October. Rosh Hashanah is a very solemn holiday, marking the beginning of 10 days set aside for self-**appraisal**, **repentance**, and promises to be a better person in the coming year.

31   In most cultures, the closing of one calendar year and the opening of another is a happy, yet serious, occasion. To Americans, it is a time for fun and reflection, a time to look both ways, to review the past with **nostalgia** and look forward to the future with hope.

AFTER YOU READ

I. Getting the Message

Put a check (✓) in the column if the custom is associated with that holiday. Some customs may be traditional on both holidays.

Customs	Christmas	New Year's
1. exchanging gifts around a tree		
2. kissing under the mistletoe		
3. promising to improve oneself		
4. helping the poor		
5. going caroling		
6. attending church services		
7. watching the ball drop on TV		
8. drinking champagne at midnight		
9. blowing horns		
10. talking or writing to Santa Claus		
11. sending season's greetings cards		
12. watching the Bowl games on TV		

II. Building Your Vocabulary

A. *These are the 15 key vocabulary words for this chapter. They are boldfaced in the reading. Pronounce these words after your teacher, and discuss their meanings.*

appraisal	exchange†	ornament
bonus	festive	solstice
commercial*	legend	repentance
decorate	miracle	resolution
evergreen	nostalgia	triumph†

---

*Commercial can be a noun or an adjective.

†These words can be used as nouns or verbs.

B. *Discuss the following questions with a partner. Then choose any five questions to answer on paper.*

1. If your boss gives you a holiday bonus, will you be happy or unhappy?
2. What miracle is associated with the birth of Christ?
3. What do people use to decorate a Christmas tree?
4. What do we mean by the commercial aspects of Christmas?
5. What is exchanged under the mistletoe? What is exchanged around the Christmas tree?
6. What triumph does Hanukkah celebrate?
7. What miracle do Jews celebrate on Hanukkah?
8. Does a person repent after doing something bad or something good?
9. What New Year's resolution will you make this year?
10. When is the winter solstice?

III. Sharpening Reading Skills

A. Making Inferences

On each blank line, write the letter of the correct word or phrase to complete the sentence.

1. Most American Christmas customs originated in _____.
   a. the U.S.
   b. other countries
   c. Bethlehem

2. Christ was actually born _____.
   a. on December 25, A.D. 1
   b. several years before A.D. 1
   c. in the fourth century A.D.

3. Christmas is celebrated by _____.
   a. all Americans
   b. Christians everywhere
   c. Christians and Jews everywhere

4. Which would *not* be a good New Year's resolution? _____.
   a. I'll spend more time with my family
   b. I'll stop smoking
   c. I'll buy some groceries

5. The year A.D. 500 was about _____.
   a. 1,500 years ago
   b. 500 years ago
   c. 2,500 years ago

B. Map-Reading Practice

On the map of the U.S. on page 287, find the lines indicating the time zones. Then answer the following questions.

1. Are these straight lines? _____

2. Can you make an inference about why they aren't? _____

   _____

3. Write the names of the four time zones in the contiguous 48 states:

   a. _____   c. _____

   b. _____   d. _____

IV. Understanding Idioms and Expressions

On each blank line, write the letter of the correct word or phrase to complete the sentence. The numbers in parentheses give the paragraphs in which the expressions are used.

1. The *Christmas rush* (5) refers to _____.
   a. shoppers
   b. churchgoers
   c. carolers

2. *Roly-poly* (10) means _____.
   a. fat
   b. jolly
   c. slender

3. Greeting cards containing "season's greetings" (17) are usually sent to _____.
   a. strangers
   b. Santa Claus
   c. relatives, friends, and business associates

4. *Turning over a new leaf* (27) means _____.
   a. buying a new poinsettia plant
   b. decorating your home with new evergreens
   c. making a fresh start and improving one's behavior

5. When you *look forward to* (31) an event, you _____.
   a. expect and want it to happen
   b. fear it
   c. make it happen sooner

V. Taking Words Apart

A. Pronunciation of the Letters *ch* The letters *ch* are usually pronounced as in the words *child* and *cheese*. But, in some words, *ch* is pronounced like a *k* and in others like *sh*.

Say the following words after your teacher:

[ch]	[k]	[sh]
chore	chorus, choir	champagne
chimney	school, orchestra	Chicago
church	Christmas, Christ	Michigan
China	ache, character	machine

B. Pronunciation and Spelling of Ordinal Numbers Ordinal numbers tell position or order. They begin with *first, second, third*. After that, add *-th* to change the cardinal number to the ordinal. More spelling changes to note:

1. Just add *h*: eight, eigh<u>th</u>; twenty-eight, twenty-eigh<u>th</u>

2. Change final *-y* to *-ie*: twent<u>y</u>, twent<u>ie</u>th; thirt<u>y</u>, thirt<u>ie</u>th

3. Change *ve* to *f*: fi<u>ve</u>, fi<u>f</u>th; twel<u>ve</u>, twel<u>f</u>th

Ordinal numbers are used for calendar dates, floors of a building, rows in a theater, and many other things.

Practice ordinal number pronunciation with a partner by saying the following dates. Look on a calendar or in the holiday sections of this book for dates you don't know.

1. New Year's Day
2. Flag Day
3. Columbus Day
4. Halloween
5. Thanksgiving Day
6. Christmas Day
7. the last day of the year
8. your birthday

VI. Practicing Sentence Patterns

In the first sentence of paragraph 19, *while* is a transitional word connecting two events that happen at the same time. However, the second sentence in paragraph 28, *while* is a word of contrast, similar to *although* in the first sentence of the paragraph.

Study these examples carefully. Then write two sentences with while, *one of each type.*

1. (Use *while* to connect simultaneous actions.)

   _____

2. (Use *while* to contrast two ideas.)

   _____

VII. Sharing Ideas

A. Issues

Debate these issues in small groups. Then choose one and write about it.

1. Christmas is a religious holiday, and American law and tradition require separation of church and state. Should tax dollars (from a local, state, or the federal government) be spent to put Christmas decorations in and around public buildings? In public schools, should children sing Christmas carols in music class and make Christmas decorations in art class?

2. Every year during the holiday season, some people develop a psychological problem called *Christmas blues* (a feeling of great sadness). Why might some people be depressed at this time of year?

B. On a Personal Note

Write about one of these topics.

1. Pretend you are building a snowman. To have a well-dressed snowman, what clothing and props would you use? Describe your snowman.

2. Pretend that you are dressed up as Santa Claus to give out gifts at a party for hospitalized children. What are you wearing? How do you feel in the costume?

3. Pretend that you have a neighbor who has no relatives and few friends living in the same city. What can you do to help this person avoid the "Christmas blues"?

4. Do you believe in miracles? If so, write about one you think really happened.

23 | Two Presidents and Two Wars

Mount Rushmore National Memorial (South Dakota)

BEFORE YOU READ

Discuss

1. What do you know about Presidents George Washington and Abraham Lincoln? In the picture, which two are Washington and Lincoln?

2. What is a revolutionary war? What is a civil war? What causes these types of wars?

3. What sections of the present-day U.S. fought in the American Revolutionary War? In the American Civil War? Point these areas out on a map of the U.S.

Guess

Try to answer the questions. Then look for the answers in the reading.

1. Which of these former presidents has an American state named after him?
   Check (✓) one:

   _____ George Washington   _____ Abraham Lincoln

2. Whose portrait is on these coins?

   the penny _____ the quarter _____

3. Who's on these American bills?

   the $1 bill _____ the $5 bill _____

Two Presidents and Two Wars

1   George Washington and Abraham Lincoln are the only American presidents whose birthdays are widely celebrated as legal holidays. Why are these two presidents especially **honored**? Without their wise leadership, the United States of America would probably not exist today. Both men lived during critical periods in American history, and both met the challenge of their times with great courage and **wisdom**. Washington faced the dangers of a **revolutionary** war to help the 13 American **colonies** win their independence from England. Less than 100 years later, Lincoln **declared** war on the southern states to keep the young nation from dividing in two.

2   But Washington and Lincoln are remembered not only for their political accomplishments. Both men are American heroes. They are symbols of traits and **ideals** that are greatly admired by Americans. Among these admirable traits are honesty, courage, and love of freedom.

George Washington

3   George Washington, commonly called the father of his country, was born in 1732. The son of a wealthy Virginia planter, he was privately educated and trained to be a surveyor (a person who measures land boundaries). But when serving as an officer in the French and Indian War (from 1753 to 1758), he gained an interest and experience in military leadership.

4   In 1759, Washington married a widow named Martha Custis, who later became famous as a wonderful hostess in the first president's home. After his marriage, Washington returned to his Virginia plantation, Mount Vernon, to live the life of a gentleman farmer. However, he soon became involved in colonial **opposition** to British **policies** in America. In 1763, the British government began to tax its American colonies more heavily and also tried to increase its control over the colonies. England wanted to sell the

colonies all the manufactured goods the colonists needed, so it tried to restrict the colonists' trade with other countries. England also prohibited westward expansion into American territories reserved for the Indians. But the increased taxation caused the most trouble. Eventually, the colonists refused to pay the new taxes on stamps, tea, and other imports. As a result, relations between the mother country and its colonies went from bad to worse.

5   In 1774, the First Continental Congress met. It was attended by 56 delegates from 12 of the 13 colonies. This group told Great Britain what kind of treatment the colonies demanded concerning taxation, trade, and the right to make their own laws. But British colonial policies did not change. In 1775, the Second Continental Congress declared war on Great Britain and named Washington commander in chief of the Revolutionary Army. Washington's job was very difficult. His army was small, poorly fed, and inadequately clothed. The men suffered greatly during terribly cold winters. Washington had to fight the Revolutionary War with poorly equipped, untrained soldiers. He never asked for and never received any salary for the job he performed. In fact, he often spent his own money to buy clothes for his men and send aid to their families.

6   Before the colonies declared their independence, celebrations honoring the birthdays of British rulers were customary. After the Declaration of Independence, the American people **ignored** royal birthdays and began instead to celebrate General Washington's birthday. This custom started in 1778 during the army's cold, snowy winter at Valley Forge, Pennsylvania, when one of the military bands marched to Washington's headquarters and played for him.

7   With help from the French government, Washington's army was able to defeat the British. By 1781, it was obvious that the British had given up. It was then suggested that a monarchy be set up, with Washington as king. Washington viewed this idea "with abhorrence" (hatred). He was not an ambitious man. He didn't want political power. He only wanted to go home. When the peace treaty was finally signed in 1783, Washington eagerly returned to Mount Vernon. But his quiet life as a farmer was again interrupted. When the new country formed a stronger national government, George Washington was **unanimously** chosen as its first president. He took office in 1789 and was reelected in 1792. In 1796, he refused a third term and retired from political life. He died 2 years later and was buried at Mount Vernon. Today, more than a million tourists visit this beautiful site every year.

8   Shortly after his death, Washington was praised in these famous words: "First in war, first in peace, and first in the hearts of his countrymen." To the American people, Washington symbolizes dignity, statesmanship, and, above all, honesty. The famous cherry tree story, which was invented by Washington's first biographer, has become a lesson in morals for all American schoolchildren. The story says that when George Washington was about 6 years old, his father gave him a hatchet, which the little boy loved to play with. One day, he hit the edge of his hatchet against his father's favorite young cherry tree. He did enough damage to kill the tree. The next morning, his father noticed the damage and ran into the house shouting, "George, do you know who killed that beautiful little cherry tree . . . in the garden?" George's famous reply was, "I can't tell a lie, Pa, you know I can't tell a lie. I cut it with my hatchet." His father, pleased with the boy's courage and honesty, quickly **forgave** him. Because of this cherry tree story, traditional

desserts on Washington's birthday are cherry pie or a log-shaped cake decorated with cherries.

9   The birthday of the nation's first president has been declared a holiday by the federal government and by all the individual states. In 1968, the federal government moved the holiday to the third Monday in February and also renamed it *Presidents' Day*. In some states, it is an occasion to honor both Washington and Lincoln, and some states call the day *Washington–Lincoln Day*. In other states, the holiday honors all former presidents.

✔ **Check Your Comprehension**   *What caused the American Revolution?*
What two important jobs did George Washington have?

Abraham Lincoln

10   Although Americans admire George Washington, the greatest American hero is certainly Abraham Lincoln. Why? Americans like to believe that people who are honest and hardworking can achieve success no matter how humble their beginnings. Lincoln is a perfect example of what Americans call a *self-made man*.

11   Lincoln was born on February 12, 1809, in a log cabin in Kentucky. His parents were uneducated and poor. Stories about Lincoln's youth demonstrate his honesty. (In fact, he earned the nickname "Honest Abe.") Although Lincoln eventually became a lawyer, he had very little formal education. But he did have a brilliant mind and great moral strength. He had the courage to do what he felt was right, no matter how great the sacrifice. In 1860, shortly before the Civil War began, he said, "Let us have faith that right makes might; and in that faith let us, to the end, dare to do our duty as we understand it."

12   Elected to the presidency in 1860 and reelected in 1864, Lincoln was the first successful presidential candidate nominated by the Republican party. During his presidency, the American Civil War was fought. The issues were slavery and **secession**. In the agricultural southern states, blacks forcibly brought from Africa were used as slaves to work on tobacco and cotton farms and do housework. In the industrial North, slavery was illegal. In the northern states, where there were only small farms, the economy had little use for large numbers of agricultural workers. Moreover, Northerners opposed slavery as inhumane. In order to protect their right to keep slaves, the southern leaders decided that the southern states should secede (separate) from the Union and form a new nation—the Confederate States of America.

13   Lincoln felt that the Union had to be saved. In 1858, Lincoln had said, "A house divided against itself cannot stand. I believe this government cannot **endure** permanently half slave and half free." In 1860, the U.S.A., was, indeed, "a house divided." At that time, the U.S. was the only important democracy in the world. Self-government would be proved a failure if the nation could be destroyed by a minority of its own citizens. Lincoln chose to lead the country into civil war rather than allow the South to secede.

14   There were 33 American states when the Civil War began. Eighteen of them did not allow slavery, and 15 did. During the Civil War, 11 states fought for the Confederacy (Virginia, North Carolina, South Carolina, Georgia, Florida, Tennessee, Alabama, Missis-

sippi, Arkansas, Louisiana, and Texas). On the Union side there were 23 states, after a section of Virginia that wanted to remain in the Union separated from the rest of the state and became West Virginia (in 1863). Seven western territories also fought on the Union side. Among the states that bordered the North and the South, some sided with the Confederacy and others with the Union. For some, it was a difficult decision. Kentucky and Missouri, for example, remained in the Union, but secessionist groups within these states set up their own state governments and sent representatives to the Confederate Congress.

15   The Civil War began in April of 1861, only a few months after Lincoln's inauguration as president. It began when Lincoln declared secession illegal and sent military troops to keep federal possession of a U.S. government fort located in the harbor of Charleston, South Carolina. In terms of human suffering, the Civil War was by far the most painful the U.S. has ever been involved in. About 620,000 soldiers died in **battle** and another 500,000 suffered from war-related injuries or illnesses. The number of Civil War deaths was almost as high as the total number of American lives lost in all other wars that the U.S. was involved in from 1775 to 1995. In addition, the Civil War caused the breakup of many friendships and even families when loyalties were on opposite sides. By the end of the war, the economy of the South was in ruins and a great deal of property had been destroyed. On April 9, 1865, General Robert E. Lee, the Confederate commander in chief, **surrendered** to General Ulysses S. Grant, the Union commander. It took until May 26 before the word reached all the generals in the field, and the battle between the North and the South finally ended.

16   During the war, Lincoln's Emancipation Proclamation declared all slaves in the Confederate states to be free. After the war, the Thirteenth Amendment to the Constitution was adopted. It freed all slaves throughout the nation.

17   Lincoln was an excellent writer who could express his beliefs clearly and with great emotional force. For example, in 1863, Lincoln dedicated a national cemetery in Gettysburg, Pennsylvania, the site of one of the Civil War's bloodiest battles. He ended his shortest and most famous speech with the following wish: ". . . that this nation, under God, shall have a new birth of freedom, and that government of the people, by the people, for the people shall not perish from the earth." These words, as well as other parts of Lincoln's speeches, are still memorized and recited by schoolchildren and actors because they express in beautiful language the highest ideals of American democracy.

18   On April 14, 1865, less than a week after Lee's surrender, Lincoln, his wife, and some friends attended a play at Ford's Theatre in Washington, D.C. Shortly after 10:00 P.M., a gunshot was heard in the crowded auditorium. John Wilkes Booth, a well-known actor and southern sympathizer, had shot the president in the head. Lincoln was carried unconscious to a neighboring house, where he died early the following morning. He was the first American President to be assassinated, but, unfortunately, not the last.

19   Because Lincoln had spent most of his adult years in Illinois, his body was brought back there and buried in the state capital, Springfield. Now there is a large monument where Lincoln, his wife, and three of their four sons are buried. Visitors to Springfield can also tour the home where the Lincolns lived before moving to the White House.

20   Lincoln's birthday, February 12, is celebrated as a legal holiday in 14 states. Another 15 states honor him on Presidents' Day or Washington–Lincoln Day. Arizona celebrates

Lincoln's birthday on the second Monday in February. Most of the southern states do not celebrate Lincoln's birthday since he was their enemy during the Civil War.

✓ **Check Your Comprehension**

What were the two main causes of the American Civil War?
How many men were killed or wounded in this war?
How did Lincoln die?

21   The names and faces of both Washington and Lincoln are an important part of American culture. Washington is the only president for whom a state is named. The state of Washington is in the northwest part of the United States. On the other side of the country lies the nation's capital city, Washington, D.C. The nation's capital has beautiful monuments honoring these two great presidents. The Washington Monument—more than 555 feet high—is the capital city's only skyscraper and the tallest masonry (stone) tower in the world. The Lincoln Memorial contains a beautiful marble sculpture (larger than life-size) of a seated Lincoln. Throughout the U.S.A., cities, towns, streets, schools, bridges, and other structures are named for both Washington and Lincoln. Portraits of both these national heroes decorate the walls of many public buildings. In addition, portraits of Washington and Lincoln

The Lincoln Memorial (Washington, D.C.)

(like those of other presidents) appear on the front of U.S. coins and bills. Washington's picture is on the quarter and the $1 bill; Lincoln's is on the penny and the $5 bill. To Americans, the faces of Washington and Lincoln are as familiar and inspiring as their courageous leadership.

AFTER YOU READ

I. Getting the Message

A. Some of the sentences in this chart describe Washington, some describe Lincoln, and some describe both men. Put checks (✓) in the appropriate boxes.

	Washington	Lincoln
1. He was born into a poor family.		
2. He was known for his honesty.		
3. A state is named after him.		
4. His face is on American money.		
5. He was married.		
6. He was president during a war.		
7. He was a skillful military leader.		
8. He opposed secession.		
9. He was assassinated.		
10. Tourists can visit his home.		

B. *On each blank line, write the letter of the correct phrase to complete the sentence.*

1. In the Revolutionary War, the American Revolutionary forces fought against
   _____.
   a. each other
   b. France
   c. Great Britain

2. In the Civil War, the American states fought against _____.
   a. the Native Americans
   b. Great Britain
   c. each other

3. If the colonies had lost the Revolutionary War, they might still, even today, be
   _____.
   a. a communist country
   b. governed by England
   c. two countries

(continued on the next page)

4. If the South had won the Civil War, today the southeastern part of the U.S. would be _____.
    a. the Confederate States of America
    b. a British colony
    c. a part of the U.S.

5. In the Civil War, the Confederacy fought against the rest of the United States, commonly called _____.
    a. the Union or the North
    b. the South
    c. the colonies

II. Building Your Vocabulary

A. *These are the 15 key vocabulary words for this chapter. They are boldfaced in the reading. Pronounce these words after your teacher, and discuss their meanings.*

battle*	honor*	revolutionary‡
colony	ideal‡	secession
declare	ignore	surrender*
endure	opposition	unanimously
forgave†	policy	wisdom

B. *Complete these sentences with some of the key vocabulary words. You may need to use some words twice. Make the nouns plural if necessary, and put each verb into the correct tense and form.*

1. In the story about George Washington and the cherry tree, the boy's father _____ his son for disobeying him because his son told the truth.

2. The British _____ the colonists' complaints about high taxes.

3. In 1776, during the Revolutionary War, the American colonies _____ their independence from England.

4. George Washington was _____ chosen as the first president of the new nation.

5. A(n) _____ war is fought to make a complete change in the government.

6. Slavery and _____ caused the American Civil War.

---

*These words can be nouns or verbs.
†*Forgave* is the past tense of *forgive*.
‡These words can be adjectives or nouns.

7. Northern _____ to slavery was one of the main causes of the American Civil War.

8. Washington and Lincoln were men of great _____ and honor.

9. In Washington, D.C., beautiful monuments _____ the memory of these two great presidents.

10. Five uncountable nouns in this vocabulary list are _____, _____, _____, _____, and _____.

C. *Answer these questions by writing* Yes *or* No.

1. Was secession tried as a way for the South to keep slavery? _____

2. If you forgive someone for hurting you, do you stay angry? _____

3. If you ignore something, are you paying attention to it? _____

4. Does the side that loses a war surrender? _____

5. Is a colony an independent country? _____

6. Does an honorable person have high ideals? _____

7. If you declare your opposition to something, are you in favor of it? _____

8. Does a person with wisdom usually make good decisions? _____

III. Sharpening Reading Skills

A. Making Inferences

Work with a partner. On each blank line, write the letter of the correct answer to the question.

1. The famous cherry tree story (paragraph 8) illustrates which two good character traits? _____
   a. strength and modesty
   b. courage and honesty
   c. wisdom and kindness

2. What's the meaning of "Let us have faith that right makes might"? (paragraph 11) _____
   a. If we are strong, we will also be morally right.
   b. If we are morally right, that will give us strength.
   c. Right and might are the same.

(continued on the next page)

3. When Lincoln said "A house divided against itself cannot stand," (paragraph 13) what was he comparing? _____
    a. an old house and a new house
    b. a house cut in half with a country that allowed slavery in some areas but not others
    c. the U.S. and Great Britain

4. In the quotation in paragraph 13, what did Lincoln predict would happen to the U.S. if it continued to have both slave states and free states? _____
    a. It would not survive.
    b. It would have slavery everywhere.
    c. It would have no slavery.

B. The Ellipsis   Note the use of three dots in paragraphs 8 and 17. This punctuation is called an *ellipsis*. What is its purpose? It means that one or more words have been omitted from the quotation.

IV. Understanding Idioms and Expressions

A. *Answer the following questions about expressions used in the reading. The numbers in parentheses give the paragraphs that contain the answers.*

1. Why is Washington called *the father of his country* (3, 5, 7)? Give two reasons.

   _____

   _____

2. Why is Lincoln called a *self-made man* (10, 11)?

   _____

B. *Discuss the meanings of the expressions listed below. Then use them to complete the sentences. The numbers in parentheses give the paragraphs in which the expressions are used.*

>   above all (8)   give up (7)   side with (14)
>   break up (15)   no matter (11)

1. Through difficult times, the Revolutionary Army kept fighting. The soldiers didn't _____.

2. The revolutionary forces wanted to win their independence, so they kept fighting, _____ how difficult and dangerous it was.

3. Lincoln was intelligent, humble, and, _____, honorable.

4. Did Lincoln _____ the North or the South?

5. The South wanted to _____ the U.S. into two countries.

V. Taking Words Apart

A. Look-Alike Words

Discuss the meanings and practice the pronunciation of the following groups of words. Then underline the correct words to complete the sentences. Finally, read the sentences aloud.

a *desert*, to *desert*, a *dessert*

to *separate* (verb), *separate* (adjective)

to *face* (verb), a *face* (noun)

human, humane

1. Sometimes soldiers become frightened and run away or (*desert / dessert*) from the army. A (*desert / dessert*) is a dry, sandy area. Cherry pie is a traditional (*desert / dessert*) on Washington's birthday.

2. The southern states wanted to (*separate / separated*) from the rest of the U.S. and become a (*separate / separated*) country, so they seceded, or (*separate / separated*) from the Union.

3. Washington and Lincoln both (*facing / faced*) difficult decisions. Today, their (*face / faces*) are familiar to all Americans.

4. The Civil War led to a great deal of (*human / humane*) suffering. The war was fought because people in the North thought that slavery was not (*human / humane*).

B. Silent *h* At the beginning of a word, sometimes the letter *h* is silent, especially when it is followed by the letter *o*.

Say these words after your teacher.

Silent *h*: honest, honor, hour

Pronounced *h*: holiday, home, hostess, humane, humble

C. Negative Prefixes

Three prefixes that mean not are il-, in-, and un-. Use the correct prefix to make each word from the reading negative. Use a dictionary for help if necessary.

Example

____un____happy

1. _____legal

2. _____conscious

3. _____humane

4. _____fortunately

5. _____adequate

D. Nouns and Verbs That End in -y   To make plurals, third person singular present tense, and past tense forms of words that end in -*y*, follow these rules:

If a consonant precedes the -*y*, change the *y* to *i* before adding -*es* or -*ed*.

Examples

city: _____cities_____   I try: he _____tries_____   study: _____studied_____

If a vowel precedes the -*y*, don't make this change. Just ad -*s*.

Examples

key: _____keys_____   I enjoy: he _____enjoys_____   play: _____played_____

Write the plural.

1. policy: _____   2. country: _____   3. cherry: _____

Write the third person singular (present tense).

1. hurry: _____   2. stay: _____

Write the past tense.

1. try: _____   2. bury: _____   3. enjoy: _____

VI. Practicing Sentence Patterns

A. The Emphatic Past Tense   These two sentences seem very similar:

Lincoln had very little schooling, but he <u>had</u> a brilliant mind.
Lincoln had very little schooling, but he <u>did have</u> a brilliant mind.

The two sentences have the same meaning, but the second emphasizes the contrast.

Discuss in class various times when emphatic forms are used. Then complete the following sentences with emphatic past tense verbs.

1. We didn't have any milk in the house, but we _____.
2. I didn't need help with my math class, but I _____.

B. *Let us* or *Let's*   *Let's* is the contraction for *let us*. This sentence pattern is used to make a suggestion that the speaker and the listener do something together. Lincoln used it in his famous statement "Let us have faith that right makes might." *Let us* is very formal. In ordinary conversation, *let's* is usually used. After *let's,* a base verb (with no ending) is used.

Write two sentences beginning with Let's.

1. Let's _____.

2. Let's not _____.

VII. Sharing Ideas

A. Issues

Debate these issues in small groups. Then choose one and write about it.

1. Is a revolutionary leader a hero or a traitor? When is it morally right for people to revolt?

2. Did the South have the right to secede? Can part of a country declare independence?

3. Washington, who worked so hard for freedom, was himself a slave owner. (He did, however, free his slaves in his will.) Does that make Washington less of a hero?

B. On a Personal Note

Write about one of these topics.

1. Describe your ideal hero or heroine. What character traits and goals must this person have?

2. Read more about one of these people, and then write your reaction to their decisions and / or actions: Mary Todd Lincoln, Robert E. Lee, or John Wilkes Booth.

3. Do you think it's important for political leaders to be moral people in their personal lives?

4. Tell about a revolution or a civil war that you know about.

24 | Four Patriotic Holidays

Three symbols of the United States of America

BEFORE YOU READ

Discuss

1. Why do you think the flag, the bald eagle, and Uncle Sam are symbols of the United States?

2. Do you know the meaning of *patri-* in English or another language? Have you heard people refer to their native country as their *fatherland* or *motherland*? What does this suggest about people's feelings for their country?

3. Who were the opposing sides in the American Revolution and the Civil War?

Guess

Try to answer the questions. Then look for the answers in the reading.

1. Whose signature is the biggest and fanciest on the Declaration of Independence? Check (✓) one:

   _____ Benjamin Franklin   _____ John Hancock   _____ George Washington

2. What is the national bird of the U.S.? Check (✓) one:

   _____ the turkey   _____ the bald eagle   _____ the robin

Four Patriotic Holidays

Why Patriotism?

1   The Scottish author Sir Walter Scott (1771–1832) wrote a famous poem called "Love of Country." It begins with this question: "Breathes there the man, with soul so dead / Who never to himself hath said: / 'This is my own, my native land. . . .'" At the end of the poem, Scott predicts that a man who does not love his country will die "unwept, unhonored, and unsung."

2   **Patriotism** is encouraged, expected, and commonplace worldwide. Why? Love of country seems to serve the needs of nations as well as their individual citizens. After all, in order to survive, a nation needs **loyal** citizens who will support and defend its interests until death if necessary. On the other side of the coin, citizens need to feel linked to an honorable and enduring nation. Holidays that celebrate a nation's birth, military victories, significant accomplishments, and great leaders make people feel proud of their national heritage. Patriotic holidays are also occasions for telling the nation's "story" to the next generation and to new immigrants. In the U.S.A., national memories give a multi-ethnic nation a common culture.

3   In February, Americans celebrate the greatness of George Washington and Abraham Lincoln. Four other patriotic holidays span the year from spring through late fall. Memorial Day was inspired by the Civil War and **Veterans** Day by World War I. The two other patriotic holidays—Independence Day and Flag Day—are related to the American Revolution and the birth of the U.S.

> ✔ **Check Your Comprehension**   *What are some reasons why countries have patriotic holidays?*

Memorial Day

4   Memorial Day, originally established to honor the Civil War dead, now honors all Americans who lost their lives in military service. Unofficially, the holiday has been

extended beyond its military connection to become a day of general **tribute** to the dead. On Memorial Day, cemeteries are crowded with families who come to decorate the **graves** of their loved ones.

5   Shortly after the bitter and bloody Civil War between the northern and southern states, the women of Columbus, Mississippi, put flowers on the graves of both Confederate and Union soldiers. By doing so, they honored the war dead who were their enemies along with their Confederate defenders. Northerners saw this gesture as a symbol of national unity. In 1868, Decoration Day—now called Memorial Day—became a legal holiday. Today, in every state except Alabama, Memorial Day is celebrated on the last Monday in May. Parades and military exercises mark the occasion. Also, in much of the country, Memorial Day is the first warm-weather holiday. People get out the barbecue grill and start planning outdoor fun. But, hopefully, they remember the meaning behind the day.

Check Your Comprehension *On Memorial Day, who is remembered?*

Veterans Day

6   Veterans Day, like Memorial Day, is a serious holiday honoring men and women who have served in the military. Originally, the holiday was called **Armistice** *Day*. It was established by President Woodrow Wilson in 1919 to commemorate the signing of the armistice (on November 11, 1918) that brought an end to World War I. In 1954, President Dwight Eisenhower signed a bill changing the name of the holiday to *Veterans Day* and extending its significance so that it now honors American veterans of all wars. The holiday is celebrated on November 11 throughout the U.S. and in other countries as well. The armistice between the opposing forces in World War I was signed in the eleventh month, on the eleventh day, at 11 A.M. Some people still observe two minutes of silence at that time.

7   On Veterans Day, the flag is displayed, and veterans march in parades in many communities. Special services are held at the Tomb of the Unknowns in Arlington National Cemetery. The Tomb of the Unknowns is special to Americans because the unidentified members of the military buried there symbolize everyone who has died in defense of the U.S. Large crowds also gather for services at the Vietnam Veterans Memorial (commonly called *The Wall*) in Washington, D.C.

8   On this holiday, veterans' organizations in many countries sell paper poppies (red flowers) to raise money for needy veterans. Poppies became associated with World War I because of a famous poem by John McCrae. He wrote about a World War I Belgian battle site, now an American military cemetery: "In Flanders fields the poppies blow / Between the crosses, row on row." The poppies symbolize the contrast between the beautiful, peaceful landscape and the bloody battlefield it once was.

Check Your Comprehension *What are four Veterans Day customs?*

Independence Day

9   Independence Day, the most important patriotic holiday in the U.S., celebrates the birth of the nation. In 1776, the 13 American colonies were in the midst of the Revolutionary War against Great Britain. On July 2, the Second Continental Congress (which had representatives from all 13 colonies) passed a resolution of independence. Two days later, this body adopted the Declaration of Independence—a **document** that declared the colonies free and independent. In taking these actions, these revolutionary leaders were risking their lives, and they knew it. If the colonies had lost the war, these leaders would probably all have been executed for treason. Ben Franklin told the other members of the Continental Congress, "We must all hang together, or assuredly we shall all hang separately."

10   The Declaration of Independence was written by Thomas Jefferson, who later became the young nation's third president. The document listed the abuses that the colonists had suffered at the hands of Great Britain and its king, George III. Its most famous paragraph summed up ideals that are still held by Americans today:

> We hold these Truths to be self-evident, that all Men are created equal, that they are endowed by their Creator with certain unalienable Rights, that among these are Life, Liberty, and the Pursuit of Happiness—That to secure these Rights, Governments are instituted among Men, deriving their just Powers from the Consent of the Governed.

These words implied, among other things, that government should be the servant of the people, not the other way around.

11   After making a few changes on Jefferson's draft, on July 4, 1776, the members of the Continental Congress accepted the revised version. The document was quickly printed and announced to the public on July 8. The news of independence was greeted enthusiastically by most colonists. The following day, in New York City, an excited crowd pulled down a statue of King George III. Later, its lead was melted down to make bullets for the war.

12   On July 19, Congress ordered the Declaration of Independence written on parchment in special script. The members of the Continental Congress signed this fancy document. Today, this **original** signed copy is on display in the National Archives in Washington, D.C. Among the 56 signatures, one name stands out. It is the large, fancy signature of John Hancock, president of the Second Continental Congress. Today, his name is often used as a synonym for the word *signature*. When asked to sign a legal document, Americans are sometimes told, "Put your John Hancock right here."

13   Since Independence Day is a summer holiday and a day off from work for almost everyone, many families enjoy picnics or beach outings. The occasion is also commemorated by colorful and noisy **fireworks** displays, parades, and, in some communities, patriotic speeches. The flag is flown, and red, white, and blue ribbons are used for decoration at public ceremonies.

14   On the Fourth of July weekend of 1999, Americans heard good news. On the nation's birthday, President Bill Clinton announced the rebirth of the national bird, the bald eagle. (No, this majestic bird isn't bald. The white feathers on its head just make it look that way.) Like the nation it represents, the bald eagle has survived good times and bad. At one time, about half a million of these huge birds flew in the skies of North America.

By 1963, bald eagles were close to extinction. Only 417 breeding pairs remained in the contiguous 48 states. Hunters, pesticides, power lines, and loss of habitat caused this decline. Then DDT was banned, and the Endangered Species Act led to protective measures. Today, the U.S.A. is home to about 6,000 pairs of these powerful birds, and they are being taken off the endangered species list. Americans are delighted. They laugh when they recall that Benjamin Franklin wanted the national bird to be the turkey. The high-flying bald eagle seems much more appropriate for a nation so proud of its power and independence.

✔ Check Your Comprehension

Why is the Fourth of July an important American holiday? What happened on July 4, 1776?

Flag Day

15   Flag Day, June 14, is the birthday of the American flag. It is a minor holiday honoring a major American symbol. On this date in 1777, the Continental Congress adopted a resolution stating that the flag of the new nation should have 13 **horizontal stripes** (7 red ones and 6 white ones) to symbolize the 13 colonies and 13 white stars on a blue background to symbolize the unity and equality of these colonies. According to George Washington, the red stripes symbolized Great Britain and the alternating white stripes represented the separation between Great Britain and its former colonies. White was also the symbol of liberty.

16   Who made the first American flag? A young widow, who was a Philadelphia seamstress and flag-maker, probably did. Almost 100 years later, Betsy Ross's grandson went public with this family story: Early in 1777, George Washington and two other men came to the Philadelphia home of Betsy Ross with a design and asked her to make a flag for the new country. She followed their plan except for making the stars five-pointed instead of six-pointed. When Betsy Ross's story became known throughout the country, more than 2 million people contributed to a fund for the preservation of her home. Today, it remains a popular tourist attraction.

Betsy Ross making the first American flag

17   The American flag has been redesigned many times. Today, it still contains 13 stripes in honor of the original colonies. But now there are 50 stars (one for each state) arranged in 9 rows, alternating 6 stars in one row and 5 in the next. Because of its design, the American flag has been nicknamed the *Stars and Stripes*. It is sometimes also called *Old Glory*.

18   In school, children memorize and often **recite** the following Pledge of **Allegiance** to the flag: "I pledge allegiance to the flag of the United States of America and to the Republic for which it stands, one Nation under God, indivisible, with liberty and justice for all." Americans recite this pledge while standing and holding the right hand over the heart to show devotion to the flag and the nation it represents.

19   In 1814, the American flag inspired a lawyer and amateur poet named Francis Scott Key to write "The Star Spangled Banner," the poem that was later set to music and became the national **anthem**. During the War of 1812 between Great Britain and the United States, Key was on a ship in Baltimore Harbor watching the British attack Fort McHenry. As long as Key saw the American flag flying over the fort, he knew his country had not lost the battle. He wrote, "the bombs bursting in air / gave proof through the night / that our flag was still there." (The bombs lit up the sky and allowed him to see the flag.) When this terrible night ended and dawn finally came, to his great joy, Key saw that the Stars and Stripes still flew "o'er the land of the free and the home of the brave." Key set his poem to music, using the melody of an old British song. More than 100 years later, in 1931, Congress declared "The Star Spangled Banner" the national anthem.

20   The American flag is a symbol of the country—its government, its people, and its ideals. As such, most people agree that it should be handled with respect. There are many rules and customs about proper handling of the flag. It is usually displayed only between sunrise and sunset. If displayed after dark, it must be lit up. It can be flown at half-mast to honor someone who has just died. It should never touch the ground nor be stepped on. Occasionally, people who are angry about some government action or critical of American life in general show disrespect to the flag by burning it in public or stepping on it. There have been many efforts to pass laws or amend the Constitution to make it illegal to **desecrate** the flag. However, objectors to such laws say that handling the flag disrespectfully is a form of free speech and should be allowed. It is an interesting debate, which goes to the basic question of what American rights are and what they should be. On patriotic holidays, the American flag flies in front of many homes and reminds many Americans of their valuable Constitutional rights and freedoms.

AFTER YOU READ

I. Getting the Message

A. *Discuss these questions with a partner. Then write your answers on a separate piece of paper.*

1. Two of the four holidays described in the reading are birthday celebrations. Which are they, and what do they celebrate?

(continued on the next page)

2. Of the four holidays discussed in the reading, which two seem most similar to you? Why?

3. Paragraph 10 quotes a part of the Declaration of Independence. According to this section, what is the purpose of government? Where does the government get its power?

4. Reread the Pledge of Allegiance, quoted in paragraph 18. When Americans recite this pledge, what are they promising to do?

B. *Reread paragraphs 15–19. Then mark each statement true (T) or false (F).*

_____ 1. The American flag has more white stripes than red stripes.

_____ 2. Today's American flag looks exactly like the one that Betsy Ross made.

_____ 3. Today's American flag has 50 five-pointed stars.

_____ 4. Francis Scott Key wrote the words and music to the national anthem.

II. Building Your Vocabulary

A. *These are the 15 key vocabulary words for this chapter. They are boldfaced in the reading. Pronounce these words after your teacher, and discuss their meanings.*

allegiance	fireworks†	patriotism
anthem	grave‡	recite
armistice	horizontal	stripe
desecrate	loyal	tribute
document*	original	veteran

B. *Complete these sentences with some of the key vocabulary words. Make the nouns plural if necessary, and put each verb into the correct tense and form.*

1. When you are standing up, your body is vertical. When you are lying down, you are in a(n) _____ position.

2. A country's national _____ usually expresses love of one's country.

3. In a cemetery, the bodies of the dead are buried in _____.

4. The Declaration of Independence is a very important _____ in American history.

5. People who once served in the military but are no longer in active service are called _____.

---

*Document can be a noun or a verb.

†*Fireworks* is always plural. It can be a noun or an adjective.

‡*Grave* is used as a noun in this reading.

6. When Americans _____ the Pledge of Allegiance to the Flag, they say it aloud with the right hand over the heart.

7. Noisy and colorful _____ are a traditional part of an Independence Day celebration. They brighten the night sky.

8. Today's American flag has 13 alternating red and white _____.

C. *This exercise uses vocabulary from the Declaration of Independence quoted in paragraph 10. Match each word in column 1 with its definition in column 2 by writing the correct numbers on the lines.*

1. self-evident   _____ rightful

2. secure   _____ obvious; easy to see

3. endowed   _____ given

4. instituted   _____ getting

5. deriving   _____ protect and keep

6. just   _____ created; established

III. Sharpening Reading Skills

A. Fun with Puns   *Puns* refer to using two different meanings of a word at the same time. Some puns are made with two words pronounced and spelled the same way. Other puns use words pronounced the same (or almost the same) but spelled differently.

Reread Ben Franklin's quote in paragraph 9.

Which word is used in two ways? _____.

B. Double and Single Quotation Marks   When authors want to repeat someone else's exact spoken or written words, they can do so in two different ways. In the reading, paragraph 1 uses double quotation marks, which look like this: "......." (They are always used in pairs.) However, paragraph 10, which contains a longer quotation, uses a different method. The quoted material is centered and single spaced.

1. *Scan this reading, find two more examples of quotations, and write the paragraph numbers.*

   paragraph _____   paragraph _____

2. *Look carefully at the quotation in paragraph 1. It contains a quotation inside a quotation. The quote within a quote has single quotation marks around it. Write the words that are inside the single quotation marks.*

   _____.

C. Quoting Poetry within a Paragraph   When authors want to quote a few lines of poetry within a paragraph, they use a diagonal line (/) to show where each line of poetry ends.

Scan the reading to find two examples of poetry quoted in this manner. Rewrite the beginning of "In Flanders Fields" (paragraph 8) as the poet wrote it.

_____

_____

IV. Understanding Idioms and Expressions

On each blank line, write the letter of the correct word or phrase to complete the sentence. The numbers in parentheses give the paragraphs in which the expressions are used.

1. In this paragraph, the meaning of *after all* (2) is _____.
   a. later
   b. considering the following information
   c. in addition

2. *On the other side of the coin* (2) means _____.
   a. in addition
   b. in contrast
   c. as a result

3. To *sum up* (10) means _____.
   a. to summarize
   b. to describe
   c. to explain in detail

4. When something *stands out* (12), it is _____.
   a. more noticeable than what is nearby
   b. vertical
   c. standing upright

5. When you *put your John Hancock* (12) on something, you are _____.
   a. expressing your patriotic feelings
   b. signing your name
   c. putting on a coat

6. The *endangered species* list (14) lists plants and animals that are _____.
   a. no longer living on Earth
   b. at risk of becoming extinct
   c. dangerous

7. The phrase *tourist attraction* (16) refers to a place that _____.
   a. native residents of a community visit regularly
   b. visitors to an area usually want to see
   c. is a popular place to bring children

8. When the flag is flown *at half mast* (20), it is _____.
   a. announcing a happy occasion
   b. halfway up the flagpole
   c. flying for only half the day

9. *Free speech* (20) refers to _____.
   a. speech that people can hear without paying for it
   b. the right to express an opinion publicly, whether it's popular or not
   c. the right to say anything you want about anyone

V. Taking Words Apart

Use an American English dictionary to find the following information.

1. All these words contain the word part *mem-*: *memorial, memory, remember, memorize,* and *commemorate.* What do you think *mem-* means? Write your answer.

   _____

2. Look up the word *grave* in a dictionary. Write down its most common meaning for each word form.

   Noun: _____

   Adjective: _____

3. Find two meanings of the word *veteran,* and write the definitions here.

   _____

   _____

VI. Practicing Sentence Patterns

It would be very dull if every sentence in a piece of writing began with the subject. One way to get more variety of sentence structure is to begin with an adverb. Here are two examples from the reading. The numbers in parentheses give the paragraphs in which the sentences appear.

<u>Unofficially,</u> the holiday has been extended beyond its military connection. . . . (4)

<u>Originally,</u> the holiday was called Armistice Day. (6)

1. Write a sentence about the number of stars on the first American flag.

   Originally, _____ .

2. Write a sentence about the number of states in the U.S. right after the Revolutionary War.

   Originally, _____ .

VII. Sharing Ideas

A. Issues

Debate these issues in small groups. Then choose one and write about it.

1. When we celebrate holidays honoring military victories and military heroes, are we teaching children that it's brave and noble to kill?

2. The U.S. has several territories, which are areas that belong to the U.S. but are not one of its 50 states. Should a territory and its residents be governed by people who live somewhere else? Can people and the land they live on "belong" to residents of another area?

3. What kind of behavior should be considered desecration of the flag? Is it desecration to wear the Stars and Stripes on one's jacket? On one's underwear? Should Americans be allowed to use paper plates with the stars and stripes on them? Where should one draw the line between decoration and desecration?

4. Love of country is commonly considered a virtue. Yet it sometimes leads to hatred of outsiders and to bloodshed. Would people be better off if nationalism were replaced by global feelings of love for all humanity?

B. On a Personal Note

Write about one of these topics.

1. Compare the extent of free speech in the U.S. and another country you've lived in or know about. Compare what can and cannot be said publicly in each country.

2. Draw and describe a flag you think would be appropriate and attractive for the city, state, or country you live in.

3. Some people consider fireworks beautiful and exciting. Others say they are too noisy and dangerous. Do you enjoy fireworks demonstrations? Do you think they're a good way to celebrate a patriotic occasion? Why or why not?

4. Throughout history, millions of people have died trying to keep a particular piece of land part of their country. Would you give your life for that purpose? Why or why not?

A Snapshot of More American Holidays

From February through mid-June, Americans celebrate several holidays that are bright threads in the fabric of the nation's culture. Some are for religious expression. Some are for the expression of devotion to loved ones. Still others are primarily for fun.

Religious Holidays

Easter. On Easter, American Christians, together with Christians around the world, celebrate the Resurrection (the coming to life again) of Jesus Christ, the founder of Christianity and, according to Christian beliefs, the Son of God. Easter is always on a Sunday, but the date varies from year to year. Symbols of rebirth, new life, and fertility are common Easter decorations. These include the Easter bunny and colored, elaborately decorated eggs. It's also traditional to wear new spring clothes on Easter, and many communities have an Easter parade. Easter has also become a very popular time for vacations, since many schools close for several days or more.

Passover. American Jews join Jews everywhere in celebrating this important holiday. It celebrates freedom and is based upon a story from the Old Testament of the Bible. In the story, Jews who were once slaves in Egypt were led to freedom by a great Jewish hero, Moses. Most Jews celebrate Passover for eight days, but for Reform Jews and Israeli Jews it's a seven-day holiday. The date of Passover is determined by the Jewish calendar, but it always begins between March 27 and April 24, and is often the same week as Easter. The holiday begins with a special feast called a *seder*, at which the story of the escape from Egypt is retold. During the holiday, observant Jews eat no bread or other products made with yeast. Instead, they eat flat bread called *matzos*.

Saint Patrick's Day. On March 17, Americans of Irish descent—who number about 37 million!—honor their patron saint, who brought Christianity to a pagan nation. The holiday is celebrated by church services, parades, banquets, and "the wearing of the green," a color in the flag of Ireland, a country commonly called *The Emerald Isle*.

Holidays to Express Love

Valentine's Day. On February 14, Americans send or give greeting cards called *valentines*. The holiday is primarily about romantic love, but many people also send valentines to their children and parents. In elementary school, children commonly exchange valentines with friends and teachers. Most valentines are decorated with a red heart. Many also show a picture of Cupid (the young son of the Roman goddess, Venus) with his bow and arrow. According to the myth, if Cupid's arrow hits a person in the heart, that person falls in love. This holiday originated in Europe in the 1400s, but today it is more popular in the United States than anywhere else. Traditional Valentine's Day gifts are flowers or a heart-shaped box of chocolate candy.

Mother's Day.   The purpose of this holiday is to honor one's mother and give her a day of rest. It is celebrated on the second Sunday in May. On this day, mothers and grandmothers receive greeting cards, gifts, and flowers. Also, moms may be served breakfast in bed and taken out for dinner to give them a day off from cooking.

Father's Day.   Father's Day customs are similar to those of Mother's Day. Dad gets cards, gifts, and a day of rest. This holiday is celebrated on the third Sunday in June.

Holidays Just for Fun

Groundhog Day.   According to legend, February 2 is the date that the groundhog (a small, furry animal) wakes up from hibernation (a long winter's sleep). People who live in colder parts of the United States eagerly await this moment because, tradition says, the groundhog is a weather forecaster. If he sticks his head out of his hole on a sunny day and sees his shadow, he'll be frightened and run back in to hibernate a little longer. That means six more weeks of winter weather. On the other hand, if he emerges on a cloudy day and stays out, there will be an early spring.

April Fools' Day.   When the French first adopted the Gregorian calendar in 1564, some people still used the old calendar and celebrated New Year's Day on April 1. These people were called *April fools.* Today on April 1, Americans celebrate this holiday by playing innocent tricks on family members, friends, coworkers, and classmates. This holiday is especially popular with kids, and the tricks and jokes are done in a fun-loving spirit.

Units of Measurement: U.S. and Metric

U.S. Units	U.S. to Metric Conversion	Metric to U.S. Conversion
Length and Distance		
12 in. = 1 ft.	1 in. = 2.54 cm.	1 cm. = .39 in.
3 ft. = 1 yd.	1 ft. = .3048 m.	1 m. = 39.37 in.
	1 yd. = .9144 m.	
5,280 ft. = 1 mi.	1 mi. = 1.609 km.	1 km. = .62 mi.
Area		
	1 sq. mi. = 2.59 sq. km.	1 sq. km. = .3844 sq. mi.
Weight		
16 oz. = 1 lb.	1 oz. = 28.35 gm.	1 gm. = .035 oz.
1 ton = 2,000 lbs.	1 lb. = .4536 km.	1 km. = 2.2 lbs.
	1 ton = .907 metric tons	1 metric ton = 1.057 tons
Volume		
1 pt. = 16 fl. oz.	1 fl. oz. = 29.573 ml.	1 ml. = .034 fl. oz.
1 qt. = 32 fl. oz.	1 qt. = .946 l.	1 l. = 33.814 fl. oz.
1 gal. = 4 qt.	1 gal. = 3.785 l.	1 l. = 1.0567 qt.

U.S. abbreviations		Metric abbreviations	
foot = ft.	pint = pt.	centimeter = cm.	liter = l.
gallon = gal.	pound = lb.	fluid ounce = fl. oz.	meter = m.
inch = in.	quart = qt.	gram = gm.	milliliter = ml.
mile = mi.	square mile = sq. mi.	kilogram = kg.	square kilometer = sq. km.
ounce = oz.	yard = yd.	kilometer = km.	

The United States, U.S. Territories, and Outlying Areas

The Northeast

New England

Connecticut (CT)
Maine (ME)
Massachusetts (MA)
New Hampshire (NH)
Rhode Island (RI)
Vermont (VT)

Middle Atlantic

New Jersey (NJ)
New York (NY)
Pennsylvania PA)

The Midwest

Illinois (IL)
Indiana (IN)
Iowa (IA)
Kansas (KS)
Michigan (MI)
Minnesota (MN)

Missouri (MO)
Nebraska (NE)
North Dakota (ND)
Ohio (OH)
South Dakota (SD)
Wisconsin (WI)

The South

Alabama (AL)
Arkansas (AR)
Delaware (DE)
District of Columbia (DC)
Florida (FL)
Georgia (GA)

Kentucky (KY)
Louisiana (LA)
Maryland (MD)
Mississippi (MS)
North Carolina (NC)
Oklahoma (OK)

South Carolina (SC)
Tennessee (TN)
Texas (TX)
Virginia (VA)
West Virginia (WV)

The West

Mountain

Arizona (AZ)
Colorado (CO)
Idaho (ID)
Montana (MT)
Nevada (NV)
New Mexico (NM)
Utah (UT)
Wyoming (WY)

Pacific

Alaska (AK)
California (CA)
Hawaii (HI)
Oregon (OR)
Washington (WA)

U.S. Territories and Outlying Areas

American Samoa
Baker, Howland, and Jarvis Islands
Guam
Johnston Atoll

Kingman Reef
Midway Islands
Navassa Islands
Northern Mariana Islands

Palmyra Atoll
Puerto Rico
U.S. Virgin Islands
Wake Island

The United States: Map with Time Zones

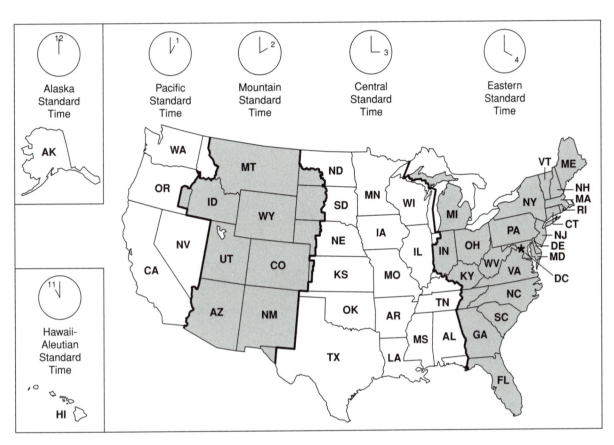

Appendix E

The Thirteen Original Colonies

Connecticut
Delaware
Georgia
Maryland
Massachusetts
New Hampshire
New Jersey

New York
North Carolina
Pennsylvania
Rhode Island
South Carolina
Virginia

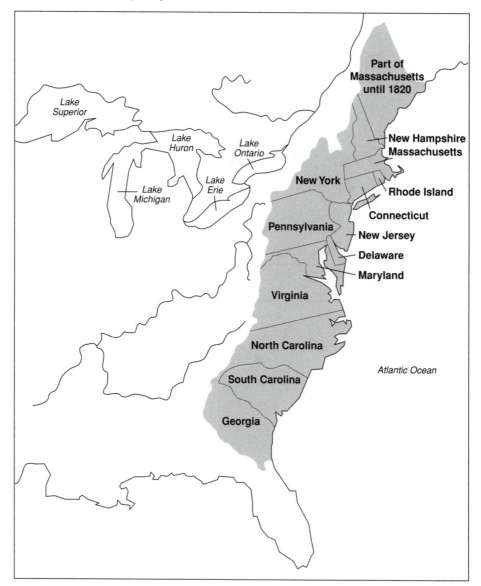

U.S. Free and Slave States and Territories, 1860

The Union (North)

California	Maine	New York
Connecticut	Maryland	Ohio
Delaware	Massachusetts	Oregon
Illinois	Michigan	Pennsylvania
Indiana	Minnesota	Rhode Island
Iowa	Missouri	Vermont
Kansas[1]	New Hampshire	West Virginia[2]
Kentucky	New Jersey	Wisconsin

The territories also fought on the side of the Union.

The Confederacy (South)

Alabama	Louisiana	Tennessee
Arkansas	Mississippi	Texas
Florida	North Carolina	Virginia
Georgia	South Carolina	

Although there were fifteen slave states, four of them—Delaware, Kentucky, Maryland, and Missouri—remained in the Union.

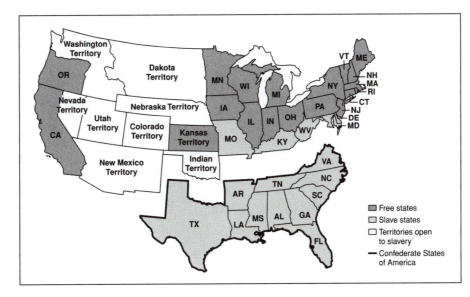

[1]Kansas became the thirty-fourth state in 1861.
[2]West Virginia broke off from Virginia and joined the Union in 1863 as the thirty-fifth state.

Notes

Notes

Notes